JOURNAL FOR THE STUDY OF THE OLD TESTAMENT
SUPPLEMENT SERIES

354

Sheffield Academic Press
A Continuum imprint

The Image, the Depths and the Surface

Multivalent Approaches to Biblical Study

Susan E. Gillingham

Journal for the Study of the Old Testament
Supplement Series 354

Copyright © 2002 Sheffield Academic Press
A Continuum imprint

Published by Sheffield Academic Press Ltd
The Tower Building, 11 York Road, London SE1 7NX
370 Lexington Avenue, New York NY 10017-6550

www.SheffieldAcademicPress.com
www.continuumbooks.com

British Library Cataloguing-in-Publication Data

A catalogue record for this book is available from the British Library

Typeset by Sheffield Academic Press
Printed on acid-free paper in Great Britain by Bookcraft Ltd, Midsomer Norton, Bath

ISBN 1-84127-297-3

To all those first-year theologians at Oxford
who over the past 15 years have studied these texts with me

אמרתי ימים ידברו ורב שנים ידיעו חכמה
אכן רוח־היא באנוש ונשמת שדי תבינם
Job 32.7-8

CONTENTS

Preface   ix
Abbreviations   x

Chapter 1
INTRODUCTION   1

Chapter 2
IN AND OUT OF THE GARDEN:
MULTIVALENT READINGS IN GENESIS 2–3   10
    Historical Readings of the Garden of Eden Story   13
    Literary Approaches to the Garden of Eden Story   31
    Some Final Observations   43

Chapter 3
IN AND OUT OF THE SHEEPFOLD:
MULTIVALENT READINGS IN PSALM 23   45
    A Psalm of David   45
    Historical Readings of Psalm 23 through the Shepherd Motif   46
    Literary Approaches to Psalm 23 through the Shepherd Motif   62
    Some Final Observations   77

Chapter 4
IN AND OUT OF THE LAWCOURTS:
MULTIVALENT READINGS IN AMOS   79
    Historical Readings of Amos 5.18-27: Where
        is 'Justice and Righteousness' to be Found?   82
    Some Final Observations   120

Chapter 5
CONCLUSION   122

Bibliography   128
Index of References   138
Index of Authors   145

PREFACE

My thanks are due in the first instance to Professor David Clines, who advised me to expand an article on Genesis 2–3 that I submitted for *JSOT* into a book. I therefore applied the same diachronic and synchronic ways of reading Genesis 2–3 to other well-known texts: research interests and teaching experience led me to choose Amos 5 and Psalm 23.

Professor Clines saw the manuscript through to its final stage, and I am most grateful for his decision to include it as a monograph in the *JSOT* Supplement Series. Professor Philip Davies took over the manuscript and he and his production team, Heidi Robbins and Sarah Norman, have been most helpful in every way.

I have been greatly helped by three graduate students at Worcester College, Francesca Stavrakopoulou, Sharon Moughtin and Helenann Francis, who in successive years as my research assistants have each contributed in different ways towards the completion of this book. They have all shown endless patience and diligence. My greatest debt is to my husband, Richard Smethurst, who though an economist has lived with historical and literary criticism of the Hebrew Bible longer than he cares to remember, and whose expert and critical eye has so often clarified both argument and expression.

Teaching and research work together in a dialectical relationship, and so it is appropriate that I dedicate this book to the many first-year under-graduates in the Theology Faculty at Oxford, who, since 1985, have shared with me their early insights into the texts of Genesis 1–11 and Amos (and indeed a good number of the Psalms).

Though this text has been shaped by the experience of teaching, and honed by careful editorial processes and helpful assistants, its mistakes and shortcomings are mine alone. In spite of them, I trust that this book will offer a clearer picture of those traditional and contemporary methods that can be used in reading the Hebrew Bible; perhaps it will also provide some practical guidelines for using them.

ABBREVIATIONS

AASOR	Annual of the American Schools of Oriental Research
AB	Anchor Bible
ABD	David Noel Freedman (ed.), *The Anchor Bible Dictionary* (New York: Doubleday, 1992)
AJSL	*American Journal of Semitic Languages and Literature*
ALBO	Analecta lovaniensia biblica et orientalia
ANET	James P. Pritchard (ed.), *Ancient Near Eastern Texts Relating to the Old Testament* (Princeton: Princeton University Press, 1950)
ATANT	Abhandlungen zur Theologie des Alten und Neuen Testaments
Bib	*Biblica*
BibInt	*Biblical Interpretation*
BibOr	Biblica et orientalia
BJRL	*Bulletin of the John Rylands University Library of Manchester*
BKAT	Biblischer Kommentar: Altes Testament
BN	*Biblische Notizen*
BT	*The Bible Translator*
BTB	*Biblical Theology Bulletin*
BZ	*Biblische Zeitschrift*
BZAW	Beihefte zur *ZAW*
CBQ	*Catholic Biblical Quarterly*
CJT	*Canadian Journal of Theology*
CRBS	*Currents in Research: Biblical Studies*
ExpTim	*Expository Times*
HAR	*Hebrew Annual Review*
HAT	Handbuch zum Alten Testament
HSM	Harvard Semitic Monographs
ICC	International Critical Commentary
Int	*Interpretation*
JBL	*Journal of Biblical Literature*
JBTh	*Journal of Biblical Theology*
JSNT	*Journal for the Study of the New Testament*
JSOT	*Journal for the Study of the Old Testament*
JSOTSup	*Journal for the Study of the Old Testament*, Supplement Series
JSS	*Journal of Semitic Studies*
JTS	*Journal of Theological Studies*

KAT	Kommentar zum Alten Testament
KEHAT	Kurzgefaßtes exegetisches Handbuch zum Alten Testament
KHAT	Kurzer Hand-Kommentar zum Alten Testament
OTG	Old Testament Guides
OTL	Old Testament Library
OTS	*Oudtestamentische Studiën*
PWCJS	*Proceedings of the World Congress of Jewish Studies*
RB	*Revue Biblique*
RevScRel	*Revue des sciences religieuses*
SBLSP	Society of Biblical Literature Seminar Papers
SJT	*Scottish Journal of Theology*
SR	*Studies in Religion/Sciences*
SVTP	Studia in Veteris Testamenti pseudepigrapha
TOTC	Tyndale Old Testament Commentaries
VT	*Vetus Testamentum*
WBC	Word Biblical Commentary
WW	*Word and World*
ZAW	*Zeitschrift für die alttestamentliche Wissenschaft*

Chapter 1

INTRODUCTION

It is widely acknowledged that from the middle of the nineteenth century onwards the concern of biblical studies to find in texts an original historical setting—and from this, one particular meaning—was a legacy from modernism. Historical-critical studies were primarily interested in finding the date, provenance and author(s) of a given text. Although this developed instead into a search for an individual compiler of early sources, or for the influence of the earliest community of faith upon the various forms of a given text, such a search for early origins yielded few clear-cut results. And even when scholars turned their attention instead to the final stages of the text, assessing either the influence of single editors and redactors, or of the later communities of faith, the results were hardly any more clear. But throughout the vicissitudes of its own history of scholarship, the historically orientated approach has consistently been used with an optimistic confidence that somehow the text would be able to reveal to the reader some clear signs of its ancient setting and earliest meaning. J. Barton describes the enterprise as follows:

> The concern was always to place texts in their historical context, and to argue that we misunderstand them if we take them to mean something they could not have meant for their first readers—indeed, most historical critics regarded this as obvious. The original meaning was the true meaning, and the main task of biblical scholars was to get back to this meaning, and to eliminate the false meanings that unhistorical readers thought they had found in the text.[1]

The rise of postmodernism has resulted in a reversal of this optimism. According to postmodernists, meaning is now what the reader finds in the text, rather than being something one can discover 'back then' or 'out there', and so it is impossible to discover anything clear and definite about

---

1. See John Barton, 'Historical-critical Approaches', in J. Barton (ed.), *Biblical Interpretation* (Cambridge: Cambridge University Press, 1998), pp. 9-20; here, p. 11.

ancient contexts and purported meanings given to texts by the biblical authors. Postmodernism has refuted most clearly the modernist assumption that there existed outside the text and outside the readers some grand 'metanarrative'—some unified system of thought under which the culturally-influenced myths and stories of the Bible held together. From the perspective of modern society, postmodernists would claim that any grand narratives that once legitimized the past and provided hope for the present have lost their power. Presuming all history to be in a constant state of flux, their understanding is that the old narratives have simply to be replaced by newer ones.[2] As a consequence, a text can produce as many interpretations as there are readers. Because biblical texts are so embedded within the complex developing history of Israelite religion, any presumption that we can probe such mysteries and isolate the setting of the text within this process is totally misguided. Furthermore, given the greater complex social and cultural influences on biblical readers today, the idea that one can read a text in any objective way and elucidate from it one clear meaning is deemed by postmodernists to be nonsensical.[3]

There is much to be learnt from this view: biblical texts do seem to be indeterminate in an objective sense. Biblical studies in the nineteenth and early twentieth century suffered a good deal from those who tried to control texts in the name of that supposedly objective exercise called 'historical criticism': there is something in this type of scholarship which we ought to oppose. However, the attempt to 'control' the text and find in it one particular meaning is nothing new: those who have preached and taught in faith communities from earliest times up to the present day are always susceptible to this sort of eisegesis, and postmodernism has

2.   See S.J. Grenz, 'Postmodernism as the End of the "Metanarrative"' in *idem*, *A Primer on Postmodernism* (Grand Rapids, MI: Eerdmans, 1996), pp. 44-46.

3.   One needs to be careful in assuming too much monolithic thinking in postmodernism when it comes to reading historically; postmodernism itself speaks with many voices. If one works from a more structuralist understanding of society as propounded by de Saussure—that different communities are bound together by linguistic and cultural conventions—this would allow for a more optimistic view of understanding other cultures, if only because they are different from ours. But if one reads from a more post-structural and deconstructionist view such as that of Derrida, each culture would be seen as a separate entity, so that all we have is the text, without any determinable origin or any previous societal identity. Whichever view, the overall consensus is that historically-orientated readers of texts, far from being objective, are full of hidden assumptions about what cultural influences can be ascertained from reading a text which belongs to a setting other than their own.

undoubtedly challenged both the church and the academy to give up on such an exercise. Postmodernism has shown us that there is a very different way of studying the Hebrew Bible—an approach which does not presume it knows the answers before it even asks the questions, and an approach which does not see knowledge as some detached truth, devoid of personality, but rather one in which the personal and relational play a major part.

Creative and enterprising as it may be, however, with its interest in subjective reading of texts, and hence in multivalency and open-ended questions, postmodernism on its own does not and cannot possess all the answers. Postmodernism itself can be irritatingly dogmatic about the way we should read biblical texts, simply replacing a set of historically orientated rules of reading with more literary-orientated forms of control. And although postmodernists claim more overtly to possess an integrity when it comes to reading the text—based upon their open acknowledgment that reading is a subjective enterprise—that claim results in an extremely sceptical view of the purpose of any historical study of the Bible (which is, after all, an ancient text), as well as a most cynical view about the search for meaning. Furthermore, literary study as defined by postmodernists— the dialogue between the text and reader, without any eye to historical-critical questions—is not the new development it often claims to be, but is a close relation of pre-critical studies ('pre' in this case meaning before the rise of modernism and the enlightenment) in a new guise. Hence it could be argued that 'postmodernism' is itself a term lacking some integrity—an odd paradox, given that its proponents accuse 'modernists' of a similar deficiency. Conversely, in defence of the historical-critical study of the Hebrew Bible, this method is not without its own literary concerns, nor is it devoid of any contemporary interests: the label 'literary criticism' was given in its earlier days precisely because it was seen to be this—a literary study of an ancient text from a modern point of view.

It would seem to be inappropriate to force an unbridgeable divide between historical-critical study of the Hebrew Bible on the one hand, and literary-critical study on the other. What is needed—and what has influenced the writing of this book—is some sort of *via media* between the two worlds. L. Wilkinson summarizes such a position in advocating 'a way of understanding which avoids the confident certainty of modern epistemology [*itself the legacy of modernist assumptions*] as well as the despairing "play" of deconstructionist hermeneutics'.[4] Rather than advocating one

4. See L. Wilkinson, 'Hermeneutics and the Postmodern Reaction Against

method over and against another, this study seeks to ask questions from both perspectives, with the purpose of recovering the wide range of answers offered through each approach. It is close to many postmodern ways of thinking in its recognition that all reading is a subjective process, and in its underlying assumption that one's reading can be enriched when the many different voices in a biblical text are allowed full expression. But it is equally close to earlier modernist approaches in its interest in historical questions and in its attempt to produce from the answers not so much a cacophony of voices but, rather, a unified chorus of many parts; this may sometimes be discordant, at other times harmonious, but the whole is nevertheless enriched by its many parts. This book is in many ways the continuation of an earlier work which explored the same idea of looking at more traditional historically-orientated questions alongside the more recent literary-influenced ones.[5]

The main difficulty in an approach which seeks to listen to the many voices in the Hebrew Bible is how to select the best biblical texts for appropriate case studies. Such a selection must be comprehensive and thus include texts from different parts of the canon of the Hebrew Bible. Three examples have been chosen to this end. *Genesis 2–3*, as a narrative text from 'The Law', is a good example because it is familiar, and it forms a clear prose unit by way of its literary style and theological content. *Psalm 23*, as a text from 'The Writings', is equally familiar; it is also a self-contained unit, to be read more as poetry than prose, being a liturgical prayer rather than a story in form. *Amos 5*, another poetic text, is not as self-contained and perhaps not as familiar; but as a smaller part of a larger composition this text offers a good example of the difficulties of finding answers to historical and literary questions within 'The Prophets'.

It is important to clarify what is meant by asking 'more traditional historically-orientated questions' and 'more recent literary-influenced ones'. First, *historically orientated questions*: the underlying issue is to ask questions about the text in its earliest contexts.[6] A wide variety of historical questions could be asked—source-critical questions, form-critical and tradition-critical ones, and questions with a more redactional or canoni-

"Truth"', in E. Dyck (ed.), *The Act of Bible Reading* (Carlisle: Paternoster Press, 1997), pp. 114-47; here, p. 143.

5.   See S.E. Gillingham, *One Bible, Many Voices* (London: SPCK, 1998).

6.   Assuming there will be a number of different answers, the word 'contexts' is used deliberately because it is difficult to know with any certainty the dating of a given passage and so a number of different historical settings may be proposed: the view taken here is that, historically speaking, a text still has many voices.

cal concern. But clearly such a process, when applied to one text, could be interminable; for the purpose of this study, it is necessary to use the historical-critical approach with more focus. Hence the choice has been a *tradition-critical approach*: this means that a particular 'tradition' within the text is examined in the light of the possible 'tradents' (i.e. different socio-religious groups) who could have preserved and transmitted that tradition through several different historical settings.[7]

For example, in Gen. 2–3, one such 'tradition' is the 'tree of knowledge', where at least four different 'tradents' may be proposed. These could be the wise (if 'knowledge' is to be seen as discernment or understanding), or the prophets (if knowledge is to be seen as sexual knowledge, with the prophets warning against its implicit dangers), or the court (if knowledge is seen more in relational terms, in this case pertaining to an intimate relationship between God and the king), or more popular and familial circles (if knowledge is to be seen as the acquisition of skills in terms of surviving on the land). Each tradent suggests a different date, a different provenance, and a different 'author' for the Garden of Eden story; this illustrates well how, even within historical criticism, different tradition-critical questions give rise to very different answers.

To take a different example, in Ps. 23 one dominant 'tradition' is 'God the Shepherd'. The various 'tradents' who might have incorporated this into a psalm could have been court officials (if the shepherding imagery denotes God's special relationship with the king, copying the style of similar practices throughout the ancient Near East), or cultic prophets (if the shepherding imagery refers more to the experience of the entire community in exile, with God seen as the Shepherd of his homeless people), or even a high priest (if the psalm is late, so that the shepherding image concerns God's relationship with those Hasmonaean priests who saw themselves as substitute kings). Such different answers about the provenance, date and author for this familiar text, from as early as the monarchy to as late as the second century BCE, raise important questions about the so-called singular nature of the historical-critical approach.

In the case of Amos 5, a 'tradition' which stands out in this text is the teaching about 'justice and righteousness'. In this case, the 'tradents' could have been the prophet himself (the presumed audience in this case would

---

7. The tradition-critical method offers interesting comparisons with socio-scientific criticism, an approach which is more close to literary criticism, and thus offers a good example of the overlap between the two disciplines. See, for example, K.W. Whitelam, 'The Social World of the Bible', in Barton (ed.), *Biblical Interpretation,* pp. 35-49.

be the northern kingdom), the disciples of the prophet (in which case the audience would be those in the southern kingdom after the fall of the north), the Josianic redactors (again presuming a southern audience, but a century later, when the people needed to be warned of their imminent fate) or exilic compilers (in which case the audience was an exiled community in Babylon). The 'tradition' of 'justice and righteousness' would have had quite different meanings in the context of such different historical audiences; asking historically-orientated questions of the text again results in proposing a number of different historical answers. To search for an 'original text' or the 'earliest meaning' is just not possible.

The following chapters will develop this theme: it will become clear that when we question each of these texts in a historically-orientated way many different historically-orientated answers may be given. So—taking first the concerns of modernism—we have to ask whether it is possible to classify these historical answers in any order of importance. The problem is deciding what criteria to use in such a classification. If we work with what is *historically* most plausible, this assumes we know more than we do about the beginnings of text over and against its further reception and later interpretation. If we determine that the best historical reading is the one which offers the most insights *theologically*, this places too much value on one theological tradition over and against another: for if we were to answer this from the Jewish tradition, we would arrive at different conclusions from those given from the vantage point of the Christian tradition. It is impossible to give one clear value-judgment about the 'best' or 'most convincing' historical answers. The maxim remains: the whole is enriched by the many parts, and in this sense, a postmodern pluralist view is the most appropriate.

Tradition criticism is context-centred; the context of the text is the focus of attention, and the primary questions are those about the transmission of traditions in various possible historical settings. But this offers a limited view of the text. Thus when it comes to asking *questions of a more literary orientation*, the perspective must be that of the text as it stands today and its relationship with the reader. Questions about historical context are in this case unimportant. However, as with historical readings, a clear method is needed in order to apply this literary approach more rigorously; the method which has been adopted is *rhetorical criticism*. This is in part because rhetorical criticism (as defined and used here) is so clearly reader-centred: the reader of the text is the subject, asking questions of the text whose boundaries the reader can choose to determine as he or she likes. Within a literary framework as complex as the Hebrew Bible, the reader is able to propose many different boundaries for one particular text; the reader is free to contract the text into a small unit, or expand it into a larger literary work. In assigning such different boundaries to a selected text, the reader is then able to find many different answers to the same literary questions. Because the reader decides whether the portion of the text should be small or large (in some ways therefore pre-determining the variety of meanings within the text) the particular literary method is clearly rhetorical. This contrasts clearly with the previous tradition-critical mode of reading, which as we have noted, is more centred on the historical context of the text.[8]

In asking rhetorical-critical questions of Gen. 2–3, the reader needs to focus on one key idea in the text: that of 'knowledge' is again a good one to use, not least because it affords an easier comparison with the tradition-critical method which uses the same motif. The taking of knowledge reads quite differently if the Garden of Eden story is taken as a self-contained unit than if the motif is read alongside the more poetic account of creation in Gen. 1.[9] The same two chapters offer different theological insights again if they are read within the wider cycle of stories and genealogies collected together as Gen. 1–11. And again, if Gen. 2–3 are read within the literary context of Genesis as a whole, the theological emphasis changes yet again as one sees these particular stories in their more primordial light. This way of enlarging the boundaries of a text can go on and on—by reading Gen. 2–3 within the Torah as a whole, then within the Hebrew Bible as a whole. The most obvious change occurs when the Garden of Eden story is read within the Old and New Testaments as a complete collection, when a wider range of historical, literary and theological criteria is used, and so different questions result in quite different answers

8.   Rhetorical criticism also reflects the close overlap between historical and critical studies. In the way we are using it here, with regard to the imposing boundaries upon a given text, it is quite close to canonical criticism, which is seen by many (for example, B.S. Childs) to belong to historical criticism rather than to literary criticism; see, for example, E. Dyck, 'Canon as Context for Interpretation', in *idem, The Act of Bible Reading*, pp. 33-64. The difference is that canonical criticism *starts* with the historical setting of the text within the literary setting of the Old and New Testaments taken together, whilst the rhetorical-critical approach (as applied here) *finishes* with the Old and New Testaments as a literary context.

9.   For example, how does the motif of the 'image of God' given to mankind (see Gen. 1.26) relate to the motif of the partaking of 'knowledge' in Gen. 2–3?

concerning what 'knowledge' is about and what has happened as a result
of our having it.[10]

In a similar way it is possible to read Ps. 23 as a self-contained unit, and
to ask questions of a literary nature about the particular motifs within the
particular psalm. (To keep up a consistent comparison, the 'shepherd'
motif has again been used.) But if one turns outwards to include Pss. 22
and 24 within this overall unit, the questions about the meaning of the
motif 'shepherd' take on a different light. And they would look different
again if one asked the same question of the same motif within the context
of Pss. 15–24 (with its interesting chiasmus focusing on Ps. 19), or within
the first book of the Psalter, Pss. 3–42, or within the Psalter as a whole, or
within the Writings as a whole, or within the Hebrew Bible as a whole. In
each case, the Shepherd Motif is seen within an ever greater and more
complex literary whole. Then—as with Gen. 2–3—when one turns to look
at Ps. 23 and its concern with God as Shepherd within the Old and New
Testaments together, the Psalm takes on a completely different dimension
altogether, when seen through the lens of Christ as Good Shepherd who
'lays down his life for the sheep'.[11]

Similarly for Amos 5: it is possible to understand the motif 'justice and
righteousness' in an entirely different way when reading Amos 5 as a unit
on its own, when the main concern seems to be directed towards the
behaviour of the people, than when, for example, reading the chapter in
the context of Amos 3–6, when it seems to be more about the forthcoming
judgment of God. There is a further development if we read 'justice and
righteousness' as found in Amos 5 within the context of the entire prophetic book; another change in interpreting the term is found when it is
seen within the literary context of the scroll of the twelve prophets; yet
another is apparent within the Prophets as a whole, and again another
when the text is read within the Hebrew Bible as a whole. What of the
meaning of 'justice and righteousness' when seen within the literary
context of the New and Old Testaments together? It should not be surprising that the term then takes on another entirely different slant when it

10. For example, a reading of Gen. 2–3 from a New Testament horizon introduces
a new range of questions about 'original sin' (a term which is hard to find within Gen.
2–3 on its own) and so opens up a further range of answers as to how this state of
affairs might be redeemed.

11. Again we may note the overlap between the practice of reading in historical and
literary approaches; this interpretation is as much concerned with the reception history
of the text as about its ever-expanding literary framework.

becomes clear that God in Christ is doing for the community of faith what they are incapable of doing themselves. Meanings change whenever the boundaries of the text change; and when the boundaries include the New Testament as well, the shift of meaning is very great indeed.

It would not be going too far to argue that, within these concentric literary readings of Gen. 2–3, Ps. 23 and Amos 5, the final interpretation—the New Testament reading—in many ways overturns (a better word in a literary context would be 'deconstructs', although it has too many other connotations) the other earlier readings. Just as with historical-critical readings, this raises the issue of evaluating one reading (the Christian reading) over and against the others: is this the one reading which can 'take over' and control the interpretation of the text? Again this answer should be in the negative; to evaluate the absolute worth of one interpretation over and against another would be to revert to a modernist position with its assumption that there is one ultimate meaning within the text. This, as we shall see in each of the case studies, is impossible to defend, for the text is made up of many equally valid interpretations.

These so-called tradition-critical and rhetorical-critical approaches lend themselves to an analogy of looking at an image reflected in the water. The title of this book (*The Image, the Depths and the Surface: Multivalent Approaches to Biblical Study*) is intended to indicate this. The 'image' is the tradition (in historical readings) or the *Leitmotiv* (using a more literary approach). The 'depths' are the various tradents from different historical and social settings who refract the image at different levels below the surface. The 'surface' is a way of looking at the image as it is reflected in ever-widening ripples; the wider the horizon, the more the image changes. The fact that this raises fundamental questions about whether we can actually know anything definitive about the image other than our perception of its different refractions under the surface and our perception of its different reflections above the surface is another reason for choosing this analogy.[12]

---

12. The term has been influenced by a phrase used by G. Bachelard, *The Poetics of Space: The Classic Look at How we Experience Intimate Places* (trans M. Jolas; Boston: Beacon Press, 1994 [1969]): 'but the image has touched the depths before it stirs the surface…' (p. xiii).

Chapter Two

IN AND OUT OF THE GARDEN:
MULTIVALENT READINGS IN GENESIS 2–3

^{2.4b}In the day that the LORD God made the earth and the heavens, ⁵when no plant of the field was yet in the earth and no herb of the field had yet sprung up—for the LORD God had not caused it to rain upon the earth, and there was no man to till the ground; ⁶but a mist went up from the earth and watered the whole face of the ground—⁷then the LORD God formed man of dust from the ground, and breathed into his nostrils the breath of life; and man became a living being. ⁸And the LORD God planted a garden in Eden, in the east; and there he put the man whom he had formed. ⁹And out of the ground the LORD God made to grow every tree that is pleasant to the sight and good for food, the tree of life also in the midst of the garden, and the tree of the knowledge of good and evil.

¹⁰A river flowed out of Eden to water the garden, and there it divided and became four rivers. ¹¹The name of the first is Pishon; it is the one which flows around the whole land of Havilah, where there is gold; ¹²and the gold of that land is good; bdellium and onyx stone are there. ¹³The name of the second river is Gihon; it is the one which flows around the whole land of Cush. ¹⁴And the name of the third river is Tigris, which flows east of Assyria. And the fourth river is the Euphrates.

¹⁵The LORD God took the man and put him in the garden of Eden to till it and keep it. ¹⁶And the LORD God commanded the man, saying, 'You may freely eat of every tree of the garden; ¹⁷but of the tree of the knowledge of good and evil you shall not eat, for in the day that you eat of it you shall die.'

¹⁸Then the LORD God said, 'It is not good that the man should be alone; I will make him a helper fit for him.' ¹⁹So out of the ground the LORD God formed every beast of the field and every bird of the air, and brought them to the man to see what he would call them; and whatever the man called every living creature, that was its name. ²⁰The man gave names to all cattle, and to the birds of the air, and to every beast of the field; but for the man there was not found a helper fit for him. ²¹So the LORD God caused a deep sleep to fall upon the man, and while he slept took one of his ribs and closed up its place with flesh; ²²and the rib which the LORD God had taken from the man he made into a woman and brought her to the man. ²³Then the man said,

'This at last is bone of my bones
and flesh of my flesh;
she shall be called Woman,
because she was taken out of Man.'
[24]Therefore a man leaves his father and his mother and cleaves to his wife,
and they become one flesh. [25]And the man and his wife were both naked,
and were not ashamed.
[3.1]Now the serpent was more subtle than any other wild creature that the
LORD God had made. He said to the woman, 'Did God say, "You shall not
eat of any tree of the garden"?' [2]And the woman said to the serpent, 'We
may eat of the fruit of the trees of the garden; [3]but God said, "You shall not
eat of the fruit of the tree which is in the midst of the garden, neither shall
you touch it, lest you die".' [4]But the serpent said to the woman, 'You will
not die. [5]For God knows that when you eat of it your eyes will be opened,
and you will be like God, knowing good and evil.' [6]So when the woman
saw that the tree was good for food, and that it was a delight to the eyes,
and that the tree was to be desired to make one wise, she took of its fruit
and ate; and she also gave some to her husband, and he ate. [7]Then the eyes
of both were opened, and they knew that they were naked; and they sewed
fig leaves together and made themselves aprons.

[8]And they heard the sound of the LORD God walking in the garden in the
cool of the day, and the man and his wife hid themselves from the presence
of the LORD God among the trees of the garden. [9]But the LORD God called
to the man, and said to him, 'Where are you?' [10]And he said, 'I heard the
sound of thee in the garden, and I was afraid, because I was naked; and I
hid myself.' [11]He said, 'Who told you that you were naked? Have you eaten
of the tree of which I commanded you not to eat?' [12]The man said, 'The
woman whom thou gavest to be with me, she gave me fruit of the tree, and I
ate.' [13]Then the LORD God said to the woman, 'What is this that you have
done?' The woman said, 'The serpent beguiled me, and I ate.' [14]The LORD
God said to the serpent,
'Because you have done this,
cursed are you above all cattle,
and above all wild animals;
upon your belly you shall go,
and dust you shall eat
all the days of your life.
[15]I will put enmity between you and the woman,
and between your seed and her seed;
he shall bruise your head,
and you shall bruise his heel.'
[16]To the woman he said,
'I will greatly multiply your pain in childbearing;
in pain you shall bring forth children,
yet your desire shall be for your husband,

and he shall rule over you.'
[17]And to Adam he said,
'Because you have listened to the voice of your wife,
and have eaten of the tree
of which I commanded you,
"You shall not eat of it",
cursed is the ground because of you;
in toil you shall eat of it all the days of your life;
[18]thorns and thistles it shall bring forth to you;
and you shall eat the plants of the field.
[19]In the sweat of your face
you shall eat bread
till you return to the ground,
for out of it you were taken;
you are dust,
and to dust you shall return.'
[20]The man called his wife's name Eve, because she was the mother of all living. [21]And the LORD God made for Adam and for his wife garments of skins, and clothed them.
[22]Then the LORD God said, 'Behold, the man has become like one of us, knowing good and evil; and now, lest he put forth his hand and take also of the tree of life, and eat, and live for ever'—[23]therefore the LORD God sent him forth from the garden of Eden, to till the ground from which he was taken. [24]He drove out the man; and at the east of the garden of Eden he placed the cherubim, and a flaming sword which turned every way, to guard the way to the tree of life.

Few would deny that Gen. 1–11 is a foundational text when it comes to articulating stories about the origins and early history of the world; only two centuries ago these chapters were still mined for what divine wisdom they might impart about disciplines as diverse as astronomy, horticulture, biology, botany, geometry, mathematics, zoology, the spread of ancient civilization and origins of human language.[1] And even today, a similar fascination with the accounts of the 'beginnings' of the cosmos is found in discussions as various as scientific, literary, social scientific and feminist; the only difference is that whereas previously these texts were seen as revealing divine wisdom about a prescribed order, they are now understood more often as human attempts at self-understanding.[2] From within these

---

1.   See J. Bennett and S. Mandelbrote (eds.), *The Garden, the Ark, the Tower, the Temple: Biblical Metaphors of Knowledge in Early-Modern Europe* (Oxford: Museum of the History of Science and Bodleian Library, 1998).
2.   For a discussion of recent contemporary approaches, see, for example, J. Rogerson, *Genesis 1–11* (OTG, 1; Sheffield: JSOT Press, 1991), pp. 50-52; also

chapters, the most frequently used is undoubtedly the Garden of Eden story in Gen. 2–3; perhaps because, as P. Morris points out, our primary relationships—man and woman, humanity and deity, mankind and nature —have been defined by the Jewish and Christian interpretations of this text.[3]

A story which offers such a rich reception history is of interest to anyone concerned with multivalent ways of reading biblical texts. To illustrate this further, and to make a particular hermeneutical point as a result, this chapter will focus on one significant motif which occurs several times in Gen. 2–3—that of the acquisition of דעת or 'knowledge' (or perhaps more specifically הדעת טוב ורע, 'the knowledge of good and evil')—and will read the relevant portions by using first the historical and then the literary methods of interpretation.[4] The reason for doing this is not only to illustrate how many very different readings might be proposed within Gen. 2– 3, but also to show the unreasonableness of commentators when they select one supposedly 'right' reading (a feature commonly found with regard to the Garden of Eden story) and then propose that it has a monopoly over any others.

Historical Readings of the Garden of Eden Story[5]

The Acquisition of Knowledge as Sexual Knowledge
Genesis 4.1, following the expulsion from the garden, reads 'and the man *knew* (ידע) Eve'. The result of the independent status of man and woman

J. Rogerson, 'Genesis 1–11', *CRBS* 5 (1997), pp. 67-90, which discusses modern scientific approaches, psychological interpretations, and feminist readings of the text. See also T. Stordalen, 'Man, Soil, Garden: Basic Plot in Genesis 2–3 Reconsidered', *JSOT* 53 (1992), pp. 3-26, which ranges over religio-historical, social, pyschoanalytical, feminist, structuralist and semiotic approaches (pp. 3-6).

3. See P. Morris, 'A Walk in the Garden: Images of Eden', in P. Morris and D. Sawyer (eds.), *A Walk in the Garden: Biblical, Iconographical and Literary Images of Eden* (JSOTSup, 136; Sheffield: Sheffield Academic Press, 1992), pp. 21-38. The reference above is from p. 21. For a discussion of the significance of this particular text in popular culture, see pp. 33-34 n. 7; and in philosophical debate, see pp. 35-36 n. 11.

4. Within Gen. 2–3, the most relevant units are 2.8-9 (the planting of the tree of life and the tree of knowledge of good and evil), 2.15-17 (the command by God to Adam not to eat of the tree of knowledge, lest he die), 3.1-13 (Eve's taking and eating of the 'fruit of the tree', and its consequences) and 3.22-24 (the protection by God of the tree of life by the expulsion of the couple from the garden).

5. It could be argued that, given its speculative nature, the historical-critical

is their intimate knowledge of one another (noting before that they were naked and not ashamed [2.25] but apparently innocent) and this knowledge complements God's previous intimate knowledge of them. The writer does not commend this, for the expulsion from the garden is part of God's *curse* on the couple; sexual activity may thus be seen as part of the experience of punishment for disobedience. This has an echo in Gen. 6.1-4, where the scene is transferred from the earthly garden to a heavenly realm: the 'daughters of men' (בנות האדם) and the 'sons of God' (בני האלהים) engage in sexual relations (v. 2) which go beyond the intentions of God (v. 3). Sexual knowledge is certainly not affirmed in either of these stories.

In Gen. 2.9, the tree of knowledge serves as a fertility symbol; the fact that the serpent, an image of sexual fertility, hides in the tree and speaks from the tree heightens this symbolism.[6] Its close proximity to the tree of life (also a popular symbol of fertility in the figurative art of Syro-Palestine[7]) further illustrates this is the case. The fact that the woman takes of the fruit is another pointer in this direction.[8] God forbids the couple to eat the fruit of the tree of knowledge (2.17); not only knowledge, but especially 'knowledge of good and evil' has sexual connotations.[9] The serpent,

method is no longer particularly useful. But our contention is that, once having recognized its limitations, we have an ideal tool to use to unearth a wide range of meanings within a text. On its strengths and weaknesses in relation to Genesis, see Rogerson, 'Genesis 1–11', *CRBS* 5 (1997), pp. 67-90 (73-76); also H.N. Wallace, 'Some Trends in the Study of Genesis 2.4b-3.24', in *idem, The Eden Narrative* (HSM, 32; Atlanta, GA: Scholars Press, 1985), pp. 1-28; and G. Wenham, *Genesis 1–15* (WBC, 1; Waco, Texas: Word Books, 1987), pp. 42-44.

6.   Cf. K.R. Joines, *Serpent Symbolism in the Old Testament* (Hadenfield, NJ; Hadenfield House, 1974); also J.A. Soggin, 'The Fall of Man in the Third Chapter of Genesis', in *idem, Old Testament and Oriental Studies* (BibOr, 29; Rome: Pontifical Biblical Institute, 1975), pp. 88-111.

7.   On references to the cosmological tree, rooted in the underworld, breaking through the centre of the earth for the healing of the nations, with branches extending to the heavens, see E.O. James, *The Tree of Life* (Leiden: E.J. Brill, 1966). Desire for its fruit was often expressed through fertility rites; on its use in Assyrian and Canaanite iconography, see Wallace, *The Eden Narrative*, pp. 111-15; on the tree as a symbol of an Asherah (noting Isa. 17.8 and 27.9), see L.M. Bechtel, 'Genesis 2.4b–3.24: A Myth about Human Maturation', *JSOT* 67 (1995), pp. 3-26, here, p. 11.

8.   Noting that mainly female figurines, depicting fertility cults, have been found as artefacts of popular religion in Syro-Palestine.

9.   The phrase implies sexual knowledge in Deut. 1.39 and Isa. 7.13-15, where *children* are seen as not yet ready for knowledge of good and evil. See J. Coppens, *La connaissance du bien et du mal et le péché du paradis* (ALBO, II/3; Gembloux:

the tree and the woman are all symbols of temptation which demonstrate that the writer views sexuality in a negative sense; it is noteworthy that the serpent (3.14-19), the medium of bringing about such knowledge, is the first recipient of the curses given by God. This negative view of sexuality may well be on account of the pagan fertility practices of the writer's day which, through forms of cultic prostitution, sought to gain a closer knowledge of the deity and to control divine activity in the world. As far as the writer of Gen. 2–3 is concerned, this sort of sexual knowledge is taboo for a Yahwistic faith.[10] The writer's God is an asexual deity, and his activity in the world cannot be controlled by human intervention: he alone is the giver of life and fertility. The earth is a waterless waste until God provides the life-giving rains (2.5-6); man is but dust of the ground until God provides the life-giving breath (2.7); and in the garden planted by God, 'every tree that is pleasant to the sight and good for food' (2.9) is given life by God's creative goodness. He alone is the source and giver of all that nature bestows. The tree of knowledge (and with it, the tree of life) is thus a test for obedience and a sign of dependency on God alone; by taking the fruit the couple signal their choice to use their own innate power to procreate for themselves.[11]

Some historical setting is surely required to explain this defence of God alone as the source of all life, and the prohibition of illicit sexual relations which displease the God of Israel; and for this at least three postulated origins are plausible.

J. Duculot, 1948), p. 13. R. Gordis uses an illustration from Qumran in 'The Knowledge of Good and Evil in the Old Testament and the Qumran Scrolls', *JBL* 76 (1957), pp. 123-38, where 1QSa 1.9-11 speaks of the appropriate age for sexual relations in terms of 'knowledge of good and evil'.

10. For examples of this view, see B. Reicke, 'The Knowledge Hidden in the Tree of Paradise', *JSS* 1 (1956), pp. 193-201; N.C. Habel, 'Discovering Literary Sources', in *idem, Literary Criticism of the Old Testament* (Guides to Biblical Scholarship; Philadelphia: Fortress Press, 1971), pp. 18-42, especially p. 26; T.E. Boomershine, 'The Structure of Narrative Rhetoric in Gen. 2–3', *Semeia* 18 (1980), pp. 113-29, especially p. 128; S. Dragga, 'Genesis 2–3: A Story of Liberation', *JSOT* 55 (1992), pp. 3-13; and on Gen. 2–3 as an aetiology on the origins of sexual desire, cf. G. Ward, 'A Postmodern Version of Paradise', *JSOT* 65 (1995), pp. 3-12, particularly p. 12.

11. Although this interpretation fits well in Gen. 2–3, it does not fit so well in Gen. 1, where we read of the command by God in 1.28: 'Be fruitful and multiply'. In Gen. 1, procreativity and independent governance of the world are part of the divine will, but in Gen. 2–3 both of these are deemed worthy of punishment.

From Judah, in the Tenth Century, after the Reign of Solomon. This view has much in common with the theories of scholars such as von Rad that the writer of this story ('J') was one of the earliest storytellers, from just after the so-called cultural 'awakening' which began with the reign of King Solomon.[12] The writer's critical view of human nature, and his implied polemic against fertility practices involving other deities, suggest he was writing at the time of the demise and separation of the kingdoms just after Solomon. In this way, the story is a criticism of King Solomon's aggrandisement and a comment on the consequences of his mixed marriages, for these compromised his faith through the adapting of the syncretistic fertility practices of surrounding cultures (see 1 Kgs 9.24; 11.1-8). Written in the southern kingdom and for the court of Rehoboam, this text serves as a warning to the southern king to avoid the same fall from grace as his father; the king is a steward to God alone, and all forms of fertility practices and syncretistic worship of other gods are taboo.

From the Northern Kingdom, from around the Ninth Century, by those Upholding Deuteronomic Ideals. It is clear that throughout the book of Deuteronomy there is an intense dislike for the fertility practices of Canaan (see 4.15-31; 7.1-5, 13.12-18, 16.21-22, 30.17-18) and that the later Deuteronomistic writers, following Deuteronomic ideals, attribute the disintegration of the northern kingdom to King Jeroboam I's fertility cults at Bethel and Dan (see 1 Kgs 12.25-33; 15.34; 16.31; 22.52; 2 Kgs 3.3; 11.29; 13.2; 14.24; 15.9, 24, 28; 2 Kgs 17.7-41). Thus another possible historical setting for a polemic against fertility practices and illicit sexual knowledge would be in prophetic circles in the northern kingdom. Adam and Eve in their independence and disobedience become analogous to Ahab and Jezebel, and the writer is thus close to the ninth-century prophetic reform movement, inspired by Elijah and Elisha, which waged war against Jezebel and the prophets of Baal.[13] One might

---

12. See G. von Rad, *The Problem of the Hexateuch and Other Essays* (trans. E.W. Trueman Dicken; Edinburgh: Oliver & Boyd, 1966), pp. 63-78, who proposes J represents a universal and humanistic worldview from the time of Solomon. See also H.W. Wolff, 'The Kerygma of the Yahwist', in W. Brueggemann and H.W. Wolff (eds.), *The Vitality of Old Testament Traditions* (Atlanta: John Knox, 1975), pp. 41-66; and W.H. Schmidt, 'Ein Theologe in salomonischer Zeit? Plädoyer für den Jahwisten', *BZ* 25 (1981), pp. 82-102.

13. A ninth-century date, northern orientation and prophetic concern is advocated by J. Wellhausen, although attributed more to the E material rather than to J; J/E

even propose that 'J' is part of an early Deuteronomic reform movement which identified sexual promiscuity with religious ritual and forbade all such compromise for Yahwistic faith. Certainly this teaching is part of the message of the northern prophet Hosea[14] whose message is close to Deuteronomic ideals. In Gen. 2, it is clear that blessing and fertility are the gift of God alone; this, and the description of the curse upon the land as a punishment for the defiance by the couple in the garden, fit well with the theme of blessing and curse upon the land in the Deuteronomistic writings.[15]

From the Time of the Exile, in the Sixth Century, against the Idolatrous Practices of the Exiles. There have been several recent attempts to date J as late as the exile.[16] This is not so much because of an assumed link between J and the Deuteronomistic writers, as due to the supposition that J is a later correction of the priestly writers, supplementing the idealistic and

combined together could be said nevertheless to include such influences. Cf. J. Well-hausen, *Prolegomena to the History of Ancient Israel* (Edinburgh: Adam and Charles Black, 1885), reprinted with Preface by W. Robertson Smith (Gloucester, MA: Peter Smith, 1973), pp. 297-318.

14. Given that Hosea uses the unusual expression 'knowledge of God' (Hebrew דעת אלוהים) three times (4.1, 6; 6.6), this could well be a similar comparison of illicit sexual knowledge through cultic prostitution with appropriate knowledge of God through worship of him alone.

15. Cf. H.H. Schmid, *Der Sogenannte Jahwist: Beobachtungen und Fragen zur Pentateuchforschung* (Zürich: Theologischer Verlag, 1976); R. Rendtorff, 'The Yahwist as Theologian? The Dilemma of Pentateuchal Criticism', *JSOT 3* (1977), pp. 1-10; H. Vorländer, *Die Entstehungszeit des jehowistischen Geschichtswerkes* (Frankfurt: Peter Lang, 1978); and M. Rose, *Deuteronomist und Jahwist* (ATANT, 67; Zürich: Theologischer Verlag, 1981). For a critical appraisal of this association of J with D, see J. Blenkinsopp, 'P and J in Genesis 1.1–11.26: An Alternative Hypothesis', in A.B. Beck *et al.* (eds.), *Fortunate the Eyes that See: Essays in Honor of D.N. Freedman* (Grand Rapids, MI: Eerdmans, 1995), pp. 1-15.

16. See F.V. Winnett, 'Re-examining the Foundations', *JBL* 84 (1965), pp. 1-19; N.E. Wagner, 'Pentateuchal Criticism: No Clear Future', *CJT* 13 (1967), pp. 225-32; J. Van Seters, 'Confessional Reformulation in the Exilic Period', *VT* 22 (1972), pp. 448-59; E. Blum, *Studien zur Komposition des Pentateuch* (BZAW, 189; Berlin: W. de Gruyter, 1990); and Blenkinsopp, 'P and J in Genesis 1.1–11.26'. See the larger surveys in, for example, E.W. Nicholson, 'The Pentateuch in Recent Research: A Time for Caution', in J.A. Emerton (ed.), *SVTP Congress Volume XLIII, Leuven 1989* (Leiden: E.J. Brill, 1991), pp. 10-21, who argues strongly against J as exilic; and R. Rendtorff, 'Directions in Pentateuchal Studies', *CRBS* 5 (1997), pp. 43-65.

simplistic depiction of the beauty and order in the world in the light of the horror of the exile. The expulsion from Eden is thus the expulsion from the land of Judah into exile; the cause of this—according to the prophets' explanation of the exile—is in large measure the people's religious syncretism and their fertility practices. Illustrations of this interpretation are found in the description of the atrocities in the Temple, for example in 2 Kgs 23.4-14; in spite of Josiah's supposed reforms, the same religious practices continued into the time of the exile, as in Ezek. 8.7-15. In both case the deities are not only Canaanite but also Babylonian—both being well-known fertility cults which have turned the heart of the people from their God and their God from them. Ezekiel's particularly strong use of sexual imagery to describe the disobedience of the people of Jerusalem (see Ezek. 16.6-14 and 23.5-21) gives further support to this explanation of the cause of the exile; It is therefore quite reasonable to place 'J' alongside the voices of Ezekiel and the Deuteronomistic historians in exile: the acquisition of forbidden sexual knowledge from other deities has resulted in the expulsion from the land that was first given to them.[17]

In spite of their variant readings, all three settings could be read as directed at the ministers of the cult—priests and prophets alike—whose concern it was to safeguard true worship of the Lord God, whether in tenth-century Judah, the northern kingdom in the ninth century, or among the exiles. Yet can all these variations be right if we are discussing the *original* religio-historical context and purpose of the Garden of Eden story? Clearly they cannot; but together they help us value both the limitations and potential of historical-critical analysis, on account of its reconstructive, speculative and imaginative nature.

The Acquisition of Knowledge as the Intimate Communion between God and the King

If fertility practices involving other deities were forbidden fruit, then the role of the king was to prevent such idolatry. This could be achieved by a

---

17. See J. Blenkinsopp, *The Pentateuch* (London: SCM Press, 1992), pp. 63-67, who notes several correspondences also with *Gilgamesh* in the themes of fertility and knowledge. See also Blenkinsopp, 'P and J in Genesis 1.1–11.26', who, dating J in post-exilic times and hence later than P, notes: 'The sense that the author is attempting to come to terms with an experience of spiritual and moral failure suggests familiarity with later prophecy, especially Jeremiah and Ezekiel…' (p. 15). It may be that Song of Songs, with its explicit sexual imagery—and its setting in a garden—is intended as a correction of the more critical view set out in Gen. 2–3; see J. Magonet, 'The Themes of Genesis 2–3', in Morris and Sawyer (eds.), *A Walk in the Garden*, pp. 39-46, especially p. 42.

reign of justice and righteousness (Ps. 72.1-2, 4). This would (ironically) bring about fertility to the land (Ps. 72.3, 6)—but this would be the result of the blessing of Israel's God. Both in Israel and throughout the ancient Near East, a reign of justice and righteousness was achieved through the gift of 'wisdom', bestowed by the patron deity of a particular king.[18] The analogy has often been made between Adam, the ideal figure close to God in the garden, and the king in his royal court.[19] Adam, a kingly model, was given the choice of using wisdom aright, but he abused his freedom and this led to his demise; let Davidic kings take heed and beware.

The example of Adam as a prototype king has several correspondences with the passage about the prince of Tyre, 'in Eden, the garden of God', in Ezek. 28.13. With wisdom and understanding (28.3-4) the prince considered himself 'as wise as a god' (vv. 2, 6, 9); but instead of recognizing his wisdom to be a gift from God, he took it as a right, and in his hubris he was duly reduced to size. This passage in Ezek. 28 shows how Eden was understood as a type of palace garden; indeed, the reference to it being the mountain of God (Ezek. 28.16) suggests instead a temple attached to the palace where God and the king had intimate fellowship together.[20] For example, Gen. 2–3 could be read to suppose that Adam, who in his paradise garden was close to the presence of God like the ideal Davidic king, represented the harmony of the divine order in the royal court and in the Temple (Gen. 2.15, 19). The description of the four rivers in Eden (2.10-

---

18. A biblical example of this is Solomon's gift of wisdom at the sanctuary of Gibeon in 1 Kgs 3.1-28.

19. See, for example, G. Widengren, *The King and the Tree of Life in Ancient Near Eastern Religion* (Uppsala: Lundequistska bokhandeln, 1951); also I. Engnell, '"Knowledge" and "Life" in the Creation-Story', *VTS* 3 (1955), pp. 103-119; also M. Hutter, 'Adam als Gärtner und König (Gen. 2, 8.15)', *BZ* 30 (1986), pp. 258-62. H-P Müller sees the royal prototype not only in Gen. 2–3 but also in Gen. 1 and Ps. 8, through the imagery of world-rule and the subjugation of all creation to the 'adam', or 'the son of man', who is a royal figure; cf. H.-P. Müller, 'Schöpfung, Zivilisation und Befreiung', in M.D. Carroll, D.J.A. Clines and P.R. Davies (eds.), *The Bible in Human Society: Essays in Honour of John Rogerson* (JSOTSup, 200; Sheffield: JSOT Press, 1995), pp. 355-65.

20. For further insights on Ezek. 28, cf. H.G. May, 'The King in the Garden of Eden: A Study of Ezekiel 28.12-19', in B.W. Anderson and W. Harrelson (eds.), *Israel's Prophetic Heritage: Essays in Honor of James Muilenburg* (London: SCM Press, 1962), pp. 166-76. On the correspondences between the garden of God and the garden of Eden in other ancient Near Eastern literature (whereby the idea of a Temple is implied) see Wallace, *The Eden Narrative*, pp. 70-83.

14), the cherubim (3.24) and the intimacy between Adam and God (2.18-20), all would suggest the presence of God in the Jerusalem Temple.[21] But both life and knowledge are gifts which God offers to the king; the tree of life could thus be seen a symbol of the everlasting covenant made between God and king, ratified by the building of the Temple (2 Sam. 7.13-16). It is a covenant for life (Ps. 89.27-37), but its worth is dependent upon the obedience of the king to God. The tree of knowledge could be seen as the gift of divine wisdom imparted to king Solomon at Gibeon (see 1 Kgs 3.3-9). These are all gifts of God; the king cannot presume them by right.

Thus, according to this interpretation, 'knowledge' refers to the gift of wise government imparted by God to the king. What sort of political situation, and what sort of historical setting, would have brought about a story telling the demise of the king, which resulted in his expulsion from the presence of God and the end of an intimacy between God and king in court and royal Temple? Again, three scenarios may be suggested.

From Judah, after the Reign of Solomon. The background for such a setting is similar to that described on p. 16 previously: the setting is the division of the kingdom, and the writer is showing how the influence of foreign women, represented by the figure of Eve, brought about king Solomon's demise and the loss of his ability to use aright the gift of wisdom.[22]

21. The 'mountain of God' in Ezek. 28 would of course be seen in Israelite religion as Mount Zion, or the Jerusalem Temple (see Pss. 46.4 [EV] and 48.1-2 [EV]). The Jebusite (Canaanite) background for this sort of mythology cannot be missed; see, for example, the references to El Elyon (Ps. 46.4) and the 'far north' (Ps. 48.2). The reference to the four life-giving rivers in Ezekiel's vision for the new Temple in Ezek. 47.1-2 has similar mythological motifs and links back to the Garden of Eden in Gen. 2.10-14. On the identification of Eden with the Jerusalem Temple, see Wenham, *Genesis 1–15*, pp. 64-66, 90, and also *idem*, 'Sanctuary Symbolism in the Garden of Eden Story', *PWCJS* 9 (1986), pp. 19-25. See also M. Barker, *The Older Testament* (London: SPCK, 1987), pp. 127, 233-45; Wallace, *The Eden Narrative*, pp. 70-83; and T. Stordalen, *Echoes of Eden: Genesis 2–3 and Symbolism of the Eden Garden in Biblical Hebrew Literature* (Leuven: Peeters, 2000), pp. 111-36.

22. Cf. G.H. Wittenberg, *King Solomon and the Theologians* (Pietermaritzburg: University of Natal Press, 1988), who argues that 'J' is anti-Solomonic propaganda. See also H. Bloom, *The Book of J* (London: Faber and Faber, 1991), pp. 144-45, who sees instead that this account has a more negative eye to Rehoboam, and was written by a woman lamenting the estrangement as a consequence of post-Solomonic culture (pp. 149-54): 'For J's contemporaries, in what I take to be the final years of Solomon and the early reign of his inadequate son, Rehoboam, it may have seemed less a straightforward fable of human origins than a sophisticated parable of the decline of

This places the writer of Gen. 2–3 close theologically to the writer of 1 Kgs 3-12, who sees Solomon as the 'wise fool'—the king who was given wisdom but who, like the prince of Tyre, did not know how to use it properly and allowed it to serve his own aggrandisement rather than the glory of God.[23] The Temple imagery in the Eden story serves as further polemic against king Solomon; the Temple was built to reflect God's name and God's glory, and prayer for true worship is offered (1 Kgs 8.15-21), but the king has concern only for his own name and his own glory (1 Kgs 10–11). The tree of knowledge, in this reading, becomes again the symbol of false worship; the gift of wisdom, once celebrated as intrinsically good, is now the cause of his corruption.

In Judah, after the Fall of the North but Before the Exile. This would set the polemic against the king in the same context as the Deuteronomic reform movement. The law of the king in Deut. 17.14-20 makes it clear that the royal figure is not to seek military might, nor wealth, nor foreign marriages, when these serve his own ends rather than the glory of God (17.14-17); the importance of the law of God (17.18-20) is the means whereby true wisdom, resulting in the fear of the Lord, is to be found.[24] Following the same criticism of the institution of the monarchy, the writer of Gen. 2–3 gives an explanation for the ongoing deterioration of the Davidic dynasty. This is due to the loss of an ideal—the Davidic kings (each an Adamic figure) have acted in disobedience by failing to keep the laws of God. This was even more the case with the kings of the north; the pollution of the Bethel sanctuary by Jeroboam was a key reason for the abandonment of the north by God (2 Kgs 17.21-23), for this was an act of violation which ended with the invasion of the Assyrians and the dispersion of the people.

Hence in Gen. 2–3, the writer is concerned to prevent the same demise in the south by the same abuse of another more strategic cultic sanctuary, Jerusalem. Thus the taking of the tree of knowledge in the garden is analogous to the pollution of the Temple, and the expulsion from the

David's kingdom from imperial grandeur to division and turbulence' (pp. 153-54). Yahweh is depicted as an unpredictable tease, Adam (as the new Judean king) as spoilt and chidlike; the lament is on the loss of the wisdom of Solomon.

23. Cf. K. Parker, 'Repetition as a Structuring Device in 1 Kings 1–11', *JSOT* 42 (1988), pp. 19-27.

24. Noting the important link between the fear of the Lord and wisdom by means of keeping the law in wisdom literature—e.g. Prov. 2.5, 6; 3.1-2, 5-7.

presence of God in the garden is akin to the detachment of the presence of God from the Temple. In this way the story of Adam and the garden, a story about the king and the Temple, has an apologetic intention; it is written both as an explanation for the ongoing demise of the southern kingdom and as a warning to prevent the southern kingdom succumbing to the fate of the north. This reading thus sets the writer in the southern kingdom and makes his concerns more akin to those of Isaiah, Jeremiah and the Deuteronomists.[25]

Some Time between the Exile and the Early Restoration Period. According to this reading, the writer not only explains the exile in terms of the expulsion from the garden, as was discussed previously, but explains more particularly why neither the monarchy nor the Temple has been restored. The writer places the blame for the expulsion from Judah not on the people in general, but more particularly on the corruption of the Davidic dynasty (the disobedience of Adam) and its abuse of Temple worship (the corruption of the intimacy with God in the garden). In Gen. 4.13-16, Cain, the son of Adam, is condemned to a life of wandering outside the land, 'east of Eden'; this could be applied to the life of the king in exile in Babylon, excluded from the 'Eden' (Judah) which his father knew. This is yet another way of using the Garden of Eden story as a parable, and corresponds with the use of parables to explain the people's fate, by prophets such as Ezekiel (see chs. 16, 17, 23). The sense of the absence of God and the questions about theodicy would thus place the writer in the exilic period, and would again date him later than P, for he is bringing the reality of the suffering and hardship of exile into the more idealized world of beauty and order which P has already depicted.

Thus again we may note at least three possible settings for the Garden of Eden story. The main difference between these interpretations and the three proposed earlier is that the assumed audience is different: whereas previously this was more likely to be cultic personnel concerned with proper worship in the sanctuary, in this case it is more likely to be officials within the royal court. How can we be sure of this? Again, we cannot. We are again left with a number of options in proposing an *original* audience as well as an original purpose. Hence again we may note both the possibilities and the limitations of the historical approach.

---

25. See n. 15 for reference to the identification of J with D.

The Acquisition of Knowledge as an Independent Wisdom, Opposed to God
This interpretation rests on the assumption that, from the time of the
monarchy, there existed in Israel a pursuit of 'wisdom' which was seen by
many, not least those with prophetic concerns, as an activity which was
devoid of trust in Yahweh alone.[26] It was an activity opposed to God, for it
sought to stand in place of God by seeking sovereign omniscience over the
affairs of the world. Certainly this issue is found in Isaiah of Jerusalem;
the prophet chides those who counsel the king yet who abuse their gift of
insight and wisdom for their own political interests (see Isa. 28.14-18;
29.13-14, 15-16, 22-24); and, outside Judah, Isaiah also mocks Assyria's
'proud boasting' about its own might and wisdom (see Isa. 10.12, 13—an
echo of the same boasting of the King of Tyre in Ezek. 27–28).[27]

The key point in this interpretation is that 'knowledge' concerns not so
much those who act in part as the conscience of the leaders, but those who
offer political counsel in national and international affairs—the so-called
'wise counsellors' referred to in Isaiah, who seek some personal gain from
their advice. This pursuit of knowledge could be described as a narcissistic
activity; there is no doubt that there is an echo of this in Gen. 2–3. For
example, the serpent—associated with wisdom and cunning in the ancient
Near East[28]—tempts Eve by stating that the eating of the tree will make
the couple 'like God, knowing good and evil' (Gen. 3.5); the fruit is seen
as 'a delight to the eyes' and the tree is described as 'to be desired to make
one wise' (Gen. 3.6).[29] This story has a resonance in the later story of Gen.

---

26. In this sense wisdom (חכמה) is to be seen as an all-inclusive term, covering
crafts and skills (see Exod. 28.3; 31.3, 6), military prowess (Isa. 10.13) and shrewd
thinking (2 Sam. 14.20, concerning the wise woman of Tekoa), as well as forms of
mantic activity (dreams and visions involving secret knowledge). This is not neces-
sarily the same as that wisdom which rests in 'the fear of Yahweh' (Prov. 1.7; Job
28.28; Ps. 111.10).

27. On this view of wisdom in Isaiah, cf. H.G.M. Williamson, 'Isaiah and the
Wise', in J. Day, R.P. Gordon and H.G.M. Williamson (eds.), *Wisdom in Ancient
Israel* (Cambridge: Cambridge University Press, 1995), pp. 133-41; J. Barton, *Isaiah
1-39* (OTG; Sheffield: Sheffield Academic Press, 1995), pp. 45-63; E.W. Heaton, *The
School Tradition of the Old Testament* (Oxford: Oxford University Press, 1994), pp.
93-96; J. Whedbee, *Isaiah and Wisdom* (Nashville: Abingdon Press, 1971); and
W. McKane, *Prophets and Wise Men* (London: SCM Press, 1965).

28. See Wallace, *The Eden Narrative*, pp. 160-61.

29. The play on words is interesting here. The serpent is *'ārûm* (ערום; see 3.1)—
shrewd and cunning, and proud of it; and the woman, on eating the fruit, unexpectedly
becomes *'êrôm* (עירם; see 3.7)—naked, and ashamed of it, and far from possessing the

6.1-4, which is also about a type of self-aggrandisement, this time in the realm of semi-divine beings. Here we find many associations with other stories about semi-divine beings who attempt to gain heavenly secrets but are denied access to them because they are in danger of using them to serve their own self-image.[30] Further on, in Gen. 11.1-9, the building of the tower of Babel illustrates the same motif: here 'the sons of men' (בני האדם) rather than 'the sons of God' (בני האלהים) as in Gen. 6.2 desire to build a tower 'with its top to the heavens' and hence 'make a name for ourselves' (Gen. 11.4). This idea of the 'going up' and so becoming like the gods is met by God who 'comes down' and, by the confusion of speech, fragments such attempts at human pride and *hubris*. A recurrent theme throughout these early chapters of Genesis is the danger of trying to become like God; humanity's place is on earth, constrained by earthly things, and their work on earth is to praise God and to uphold his otherness. Hence attempts to gain access to the heavenly realm and stand in the place of God—evident especially in Gen. 2–3 and Gen. 11—are punished by God.

so-called wisdom promised by the serpent. On this theme, see L. Alonso-Schökel, 'Sapiental and Covenant Themes in Genesis 2–3', in J.L. Crenshaw (ed.), *Studies in Ancient Israelite Wisdom* (New York: Ktav, 1976), pp. 456-68; B.I. Reicke, 'The Knowledge Hidden', pp. 193-201; H.S. Stern, 'The Knowledge of Good and Evil', *VT* 8 (1958), pp. 405-18; B. Vawter, *On Genesis: A New Reading* (Garden City, NY: Doubleday, 1977), pp. 76-78; E. Pagels, *Adam, Eve and the Serpent* (New York: Random House, 1987); C.M. Carmichael, 'The Paradise Myth: Interpreting without Jewish and Christian Spectacles', in Morris and Sawyer (eds.), *A Walk in the Garden*, pp. 47-63; and B.J. Stratton, *Out of Eden: Reading, Rhetoric, and Ideology in Genesis 2–3* (JSOTSup, 208; Sheffield: Sheffield Academic Press, 1995), pp. 223-50; A. Lacocque, 'Cracks in the Wall', in A. Lacocque and P. Riceour (eds.), *Thinking Biblically: Exegetical and Hermeneutical Studies* (trans. D. Pellauer; Chicago: University of Chicago Press, 1998), pp. 3-29. Furthermore, in 'The Myth of Adapa' (*ANET*, p. 100), we read that the god Ea gives Adapa wisdom '…but eternal life he had not given him'. This has interesting associations with the wisdom theme of the Genesis story; cf. W.F. Albright, 'The Goddess of Life and Wisdom', *AJSL* 36 (1919), pp. 258-94.

30. For example, the myth about Asael, which describes the fall of Semihozah and the birth of giants in *1 En.* 6–11, has several correspondences with Gen. 6.1-4 in its depiction of the attempts of angelic beings to become god-like. Especially relevant is *1 En.* 7, which takes up the story of the daughters of men and sons of God, but here the semi-divine beings teach the women arts, magic, astrology and the like—thus creating an alternative mantic form of knowledge which is independent of God.

Genesis 2–3 thus belongs to that collection of stories which portrays how humans fail to submit to the greater wisdom of God, and how such arrogance and self-sufficiency deserve punishment. The motif of the tree of knowledge of good and evil is an important means of instruction in this respect; it shows the importance of freedom of choice alongside the prohibition not to partake of independent knowledge, and it makes clear that the choice has to be to honour God rather than to seek self-aggrandisement, whether privately or publicly. The story serves as a parable to those who abuse the gift of knowledge and warns them of the consequences that follow from such actions.

When, we might ask, would such teaching be most relevant? Three possible dates might be proposed.

From the Solomonic Court, or Just After its Demise. This interpretation assumes this is a polemic against the abuse of knowledge by those who served as wise counsellors to the king. King Solomon typifies this state of affairs, for he undoubtedly misuses God's gift of wisdom (1 Kgs 11.1-13); his demise serves as a warning for future kings who use God's gift of governance for their own ends. This view assumes that the author of Gen. 2–3 is an early 'story-writer', with a fairly negative view of human nature, preoccupied with the theme of *hubris* as exhibited by Solomon and his royal court; his concern is to expose those in Judah who had gained from the economic and political expansion from Solomon's time onwards.[31]

From the Jerusalem Court, after the Time of the Fall of the North. This reading assumes that the contrast between human knowledge and God-given wisdom was a very real issue at the time of the threat of Assyrian invasion in the eighth century; the evidence for this is found in the

31. See G. von Rad, *Old Testament Theology*, I (trans. D.M.G. Stalker; 2 vols.; London: SCM Press, 1975), pp. 139-40; also E.W. Heaton, *Solomon's New Men: The Emergence of Ancient Israel as a National State* (London: Thames & Hudson, 1974); also G.E. Mendenhall, 'The Shady Side of Wisdom: The Date and Purpose of Genesis 3', in H.N. Bream, R.D. Heim and C.A. Moore (eds.), *A Light unto my Path: Old Testament Studies in Honor of Jacob M. Myers* (Philadelphia: Temple University, 1974), pp. 319-34; also Wallace, *The Eden Narrative*, p. 186; also Habel, 'Discovering Literary Sources', pp. 18-20; and, in a more cautious vein, P. Southwell, 'Genesis is a "Wisdom" Story?', *Texte und Untersuchungen* 126 (1982), pp. 467-69. On a variety of options, of which the Solomonic setting is one, see also H.N. Wallace, 'Tree of Knowledge and Tree of Life', in D.N. Freedman (ed.), *Anchor Bible Dictionary*, VI (6 vols.; New York: Doubleday Press, 1992), pp. 656-60.

preaching of Isaiah. Like Amos before him, Isaiah uses wisdom sayings in order to parody the vanity of the wise courtiers who sought to give advice which was politically expedient and which bought them out of trouble. By contrast, real trust in Yahweh meant avoiding costly political alliances and allowing history to run its course so that Yahweh could order the events.[32] In this way, the writer of Gen. 2–3 is using the tree of knowledge as a symbol of the abuse of political counsel in international affairs; true wisdom consists of utter trust in Yahweh rather than taking autonomous action based upon one's own insight. The writer thus teaches those aspiring to be wise about the consequences of disobeying the voice of God (Gen. 2.16-17); they must not be misled by false wisdom, even when it is represented by the voice of a serpent who is 'more subtle than any other wild creature that God had made' (Gen. 3.1, 4-5). Those who follow counterfeit wisdom risk forfeiting status and privilege (in the motif of the exclusion from the garden, in Gen. 3.14-19, 22-24).[33]

From the Time of the Exile, in the Sixth Century. If the abuse of wisdom results in alienation from God and exclusion from the land, then there may be some hints of the experience of the exile in this story. Certainly this view accords with the more pessimistic understanding prevalent in the exile about the appropriate use of God-given gifts. Instead of affirming cosmic harmony and the essential goodness of God and humankind (a theme evident in some wisdom poetry and also Gen. 1)[34] in Gen. 2–3 we note only toil, pain, family conflict and fear of mortality. This scepticism is indeed a theme developed in later wisdom literature; Proverbs, Job and Ecclesiastes each observe in different ways the futility of human knowledge and affirm that true wisdom is a gift only from God. That this was a theme which developed through the loss of everything in exile, continuing

32. For wisdom as parody in Amos, see 3.1-7; 5.19-20; and 6.12. For Isaiah, see 10.15; 28.9-10. Isaiah's message both to Ahaz and to Hezikiah is to trust in God to bring about a resolution without acting upon the advice of their so-called wise counsel.

33. See W.M. Clark, 'A Legal Background to the Yahwist's Use of "Good and Evil" in Genesis 2–3', *JBL* 88 (1969), pp. 266-78. On the theme of the writer's opposition to the power and control of the affairs of the nation by the advisers in the royal court, see Barker, *The Older Testament*, pp. 279-82.

34. Cf. H.-J. Hermisson, 'Observations on the Creation Theology in Wisdom', in J. Gammie (ed.), *Israelite Wisdom: Theological and Literary Essays in Honor of Samuel Terrien* (Missoula, MT: Scholars Press, 1978), pp. 43-57; also Blenkinsopp, 'P and J in Genesis 1.1–11.26', pp. 14-15.

amongst those who returned when their hopes for a new beginning were not fulfilled, is highly likely.[35]

Which of these readings is the right one? It is impossible to say. Each proposal is interesting, but each involves a certain amount of theological reconstruction, again reflecting the contingent nature of historically-orientated readings.

The Acquisition of Knowledge as an Explanation of the Suffering and Hardship of the 'People of the Land'

The purported audiences for the previous three interpretations of 'knowledge' were associated with representatives of power (the leaders of worship, members of the royal court, and wise counsellors). Whichever interpretation is preferred, the assumption is that the overall intention of the writer was to reform the religious and political leaders of the day. But there is another way of reading the story, which assumes that the recipients were not so much adherents of official state religion as participants in popular folk religion. Instead of seeing the story as a cleverly crafted parable, rich with layers of meaning, but essentially iconoclastic in its indictment of the various ruling classes, it is possible to see it as a complex collection of aetiologies about the hardships of ordinary everyday life, encouraging the ordinary lay person to understand why things are the way they are. Essentially their concern is explanatory; for example, explaining why all agricultural activity is a toil and curse (Gen. 3.17-19a), why there is family conflict (Gen. 3.15, 16b), why there is pain at birth (Gen. 3.16a) and why there is fear of nothingness at death (Gen. 3.19b).

In short, this reading assumes that, far from being detached from popular culture by being part of the royal court and intellectual élite, their audience is familiar with the ordinary problems which beset everyday life; the writer is very much part of popular culture and folk religion, and writes quite simply for everyone and anyone.[36] As well as providing some explanation for existential questions, the writer is also offering some theological apologetic as well; the underlying question is: why could an appar-

35. On the undermining of human wisdom in Gen. 2–3 and the proposal for a post-exilic redactional date, see D. Carr, 'The Politics of Textual Subversion: A Diachronic Perspective on the Garden of Eden Story', *JBL* 112 (1993), pp. 577-95.

36. Cf. H. Gunkel, *The Legends of Genesis* (Chicago: Open Court, 1901), whose introduction argues that the purpose of these stories is aetiological; also C. Westermann, *Genesis 1–11* (Darmstadt: Wissenschaftliche Buchgesellschaft, 1976; trans. J. Scullion; London: SPCK, 1984), pp. 53, 195, 590-92.

ently all-powerful, all-loving, all-knowing God allow such alienation between himself and his creatures, and between his creatures and the world he had made for them? Such an approach again suggests a variety of settings.

From Solomonic Times. This would presume some fifty years' experience of the monarchy, after a period of settlement in the land. The experience of hardship, the toiling on the land and the laborious upkeep of family life would have been particularly hard from the settlement time onwards. According to Carol Meyers, who offers an important social-scientific analysis of the place of women during the beginning of urbanization in the early days of the monarchy, Gen. 2–3 could be read as a complete aetiology concerning the difficulties of agricultural life.[37] From such a setting, woman's desire for knowledge—which is here understood in terms of human skill and practical wisdom for living[38]—is part of her need to be in control of her own life and her own environment. Thus the serpent's persuading her to find such skill is closer to the reality of her own needs than the naive optimism implied in the prohibitions laid down by God. Although the ultimate perspective of the writer is more likely to be male,[39] the fact that the woman is at the centre of the story in the garden, and the description of the consequences which first and foremost affect the woman—that knowledge of good and evil was ultimately about

37. Cf. C. Meyers, *Discovering Eve: Ancient Israelite Women in Context* (Oxford: Oxford University Press, 1988), pp. 51-56, 142-49, 180-81; also A. Gardner, 'Genesis 2.4b-3: A Mythological Paradigm of Sexuality or of the Religious History of Pre-exilic Israel?', *SJT* 43 (1990), pp. 1-18. There are several variations on this theme. See, for example, A. Laffey, *Wives, Harlots and Concubines: The Old Testament in Feminist Perspective* (London: SPCK, 1988); D.F. Sawyer, 'Resurrecting Eve? Feminist Critique of the Garden of Eden', in Morris and Sawyer (eds.), *A Walk in the Garden*, pp. 273-89; S. Niditch, 'Genesis', in C.A. Newsom and S.H. Ringe (eds.), *The Women's Bible Commentary* (London: SPCK, 1992), pp. 10-25; A.J. Bledstein, 'Are Women Cursed in Genesis 3.16?', in A. Brenner (ed.), *A Feminist Companion to Genesis* (Sheffield: Sheffield Academic Press, 1993), pp. 142-45. On the account serving as an aetiology for the conflicts between the sexes, see P. Trible, 'A Love Story gone Awry', in *idem, God and the Rhetoric of Sexuality* (Overtures in Biblical Theology, 2; Philadelphia: Fortress Press, 1978), pp. 72-143, especially pp. 73, 120, 128.

38. See n. 26 on the different uses of wisdom within the biblical literature.

39. This is *contra* Bloom, *The Book of J*, pp. 23-44, who understands the writer to be a Solomonic princess; yet the hierarchy of the sexes and the description of the woman's temptation—viewed negatively—seem to have a particular male bias.

knowing conflict and pain between husband and wife, parent and child—has a particular aetiological relevance for the women toiling on the land (a land which bore 'thorns and thistles' [3.18] instead of 'pleasant plants and trees' [2.9]).[40]

Throughout the Time of the Divided Kingdoms. The inception of the monarchy, followed so quickly by the rift between south and north, inevitably left a social divide between the rich and the poor. If the Solomonic period was a time of initial hardship for women in the rural settlements in the hill country, at least the reign was a brief time of peace; the time following it was particularly hard for women when the men went on innumerable military exploits to defend the boundaries of the kingdoms, and the women were left not only to raise their families but also to till the land. Particularly in the rural mountain areas west of the Jordan, where it is clear that the largest proportion of settlements were founded, the soils were poor, water was scarce and the topography was irregular, making 'dry farming' the norm; the men would build water cisterns, both for defence and for subsistence purposes, and the women's role would be to help till the land and provide more children for basic labour. Hence when military crises created a break-up of family hierarchies within these settlement areas, the burden fell increasingly upon the women to provide, both in terms of security and of survival.

So the expulsion from the Garden of Eden reads like a parable; it serves to explain why women and men face a mutual conflict in their quest for survival.[41] It also serves to explain theologically why life is so costly: this was not God's intention, but rather the result of making wrong choices which appeared to be a quick and easy route to self-fulfilment.[42] Further-

---

40. Noting here the number of times the word אָכַל (eat) occurs in these two chapters (Gen. 2.16, 17; 3.1, 2, 3, 5, 6, 11, 12, 13, 14, 17, 18, 19, 22)—a motif which is particularly striking in that its only other occurrence in Gen. 1–11 is in Gen. 9.4, regarding Noah. This may also be compared with the more optimistic assumption in Gen. 1 that the world is full of naural resources; the struggle for food presents no problem for the writer.

41. See Meyers, *Discovering Eve*, pp. 56, 93, 105, 108 and 146. Affirming this reading from a Third World viewpoint today, see also M. Oduyoye, *The Sons of God and the Daughters of Men: An Afro-Asiatic Interpretation of Genesis 1–11* (Maryknoll, NY: Orbis Books, 1984).

42. On this account a few scholars have read into this story a commentary on a peasants' revolt from the time of Solomon onwards. See, for example, J.M. Kennedy, 'Peasants in Revolt: Political Allegory in Genesis 2–3', *JSOT* 47 (1990), pp. 3-14,

more, the paradise days of Solomon were over; and (to use a phrase from an proverb quoted in exile) the fathers—and mothers—had tasted the fruits, but the children's teeth were set on edge. In this way, by placing the blame on Solomonic times, and by interpreting the story of the taking of the fruit of knowledge in a negative way, the writer weaves a web of aetiological stories to explain why things are as bad as they are.

From the Land of Palestine, in Exilic Times. This presumes that the story of explanation of conflict and suffering comes from a period of disintegration in society. Rather like the previous reading, it seeks to place the blame for the present state of affairs upon the shoulders of the previous generation. It is as if the web of aetiologies now reads like a lament on the land, and that the focus of attention is upon the impoverished group left behind as 'the people of the land'.[43] These are those who, separated from the ruling classes who have been taken to Babylon in exile, have been left in the land, and see themselves as the main victims of the loss of blessing; however, this was not their doing, but was a result of the foolishness and disobedience of an earlier generation (this is of course similar to the view expressed by the Deuteronomistic historian regarding Manasseh, for example in 2 Kgs 23.26-27).

The writer thus encourages the people of the land to see, in hindsight, that the bid for independence and self-rule without reference to God as the giver and the king was doomed for failure. This is a theodicy which seeks to justify the ways of God to those suffering the loss of livelihood as a result of exile. Being a more realistic and pessimistic theological reflection on the sin and suffering in the world compared with the idealistic and optimistic account in Gen. 1, this interpretation accords well with the theology of the prophets and Deuteronomists, for example, during the earlier period of exile.

Thus at least three settings may be proposed for the interpretation of 'knowledge' in this way, even when it is assumed the audience is very

especially pp. 8-10, who sees Yahweh as a symbol of royal authority against whom the couple rebel.

43. The phrase 'people of the land' (עמי הארץ) occurs 73 times in the Old Testament, with a variety of meanings. In earlier parts of 2 Kings, before the first deportation, it could suggest a wealthy class of landowners; but it seems clear that the term changed as a result of the exile, when its plural use signified a group opposed to the returning exiles (Ezra 9.1; 10.2, 11; Neh. 10.20-31). See E.W. Nicholson, 'The Meaning of the Expression 'am ha'arez in the Old Testament', *JSS* 10 (1965), pp. 59-66.

different from those in our previous proposals—in this case no longer the powerful élite, but the ordinary people of the land. It seems clear again that Gen. 2–3 is a text which defies precise contextualization. Consequentially historical criticism, when it is applied to a text like Gen. 2–3, cannot be seen as a more objective mode of reading—as a type of 'alternative' to literary criticism. The variety of interpretations illustrate well its subjective and imaginative nature—thus making it little different from literary-critical readings in this respect.

Literary Approaches to the Garden of Eden Story

Literary criticism, unlike historical criticism, is more open about its bias and inevitable subjectivity; the reader, rather than any hypothetical ancient setting, gives the text its meaning, and much of this depends on the theological agenda which is brought to the text rather than purportedly arises out of it. Given the nature of the Garden of Eden story, it should not be surprising that several literary interpretations have been applied to these chapters as well.[44]

Furthermore, depending upon where the reader decides the text begins and ends, entirely different modes of readings become evident. Five 'boundaries' for reading Gen. 2–3 will be proposed below, and in each case a very different way of interpreting the motif of the acquisition of knowledge is possible.

Knowledge as a Symbol of Mortality or of Human Maturity? Looking at Genesis 2–3 as a Self-contained Unit
There is no doubt that Gen. 2.4b–3.24 works well as a self-contained literary unit.[45] Yet, even if this is a unity, two very different interpretations of the meaning of 'knowledge' may be proposed, depending upon whether one sees this concept being used positively or negatively within the whole.

The negative reading has a good deal in common with the first three historical approaches outlined earlier. In this case, however, the motif of

---

44. See Stordalen, 'Man, Soil, Garden', pp. 5-6 nn. 1 and 2, which provides a lengthy list of such approaches, noting especially the seminal influence of D. Jobling in this respect. P.J. Achtemeier (ed.), *Society of Biblical Literature 1978 Seminar Papers*, I (Missoula, MT: University of Montana, 1978) also has a number of papers on Gen. 2–3; see, for example, D. Jobling, 'A Structural Analysis of Genesis 2.4b–3.24', pp. 61-69.

45. See J.T. Walsh, 'Genesis 2.4b–3.24: A Synchronic Approach', *JBL* 94 (1977), pp. 161-77; also Achtemeier, *Society of Biblical Literature 1978 Seminar Papers*.

the two trees—of knowledge, and of life—is not seen as two separate traditions (for of course the question of 'tradition' never arises) but rather as one *Leitmotif* in the story overall. They are both trees 'in the midst of the garden' (2.9) and are connected in the woman's dialogue with the serpent (3.3). By taking together the intricate relationship between the desire for knowledge and the desire for immortality, the story may be read as a myth concerning human mortality. The offer of the fruit of 'knowledge of good and evil' is thus a trick, for its effect is rather only this-worldly knowledge. To choose the knowledge of good and evil paradoxically leads to a more acute sense of our finitude: the more we know, the more we know we do not know. This point is made in the references to the 'dust of the earth' from which all come and to which all go, as in 2.7 and 3.19. But the conversation between the man and God (see 2.15-16) and the conversation between woman and the serpent (3.1-5) indicate that there is a choice between the acquisition of knowledge of good and evil which leads to death, and dependency on God which leads to life. In this way, a paradox is to be found in the story: the tree of knowledge actually becomes the tree of death.[46]

There is a problem with such a reading: given that humans are already made from clay and dust, and thus are by nature mortal, it is difficult to see how any fruit of any tree can make any difference to their physical state. This is perhaps why later Jewish writers (e.g. *2 En.* 30; *Gen. R.* 8) have to speak of Adam as an *angel* before his creation in the garden, already immortal (*4 Ezra* 3.7; *2 Bar.* 17.3) before his time on earth. J. Barr deals with this issue, proposing that is not so much the threat of death that is the issue, as the manner of dying, through eking out a living on the land.[47] But whichever way one reads this, the story is about accepting mortality, and about achieving life through dying, rather than circumventing death altogether. This reading understands the tree of knowledge in a negative sense, seeing that it is about our understanding of our own mortality.[48]

Another interpretation of the text is to read it not so much by way of a negative warning—about a choice as to which form of knowledge we desire—but as a positive challenge. Rather than seeing the story as a myth

46. See J. Barr, *The Garden of Eden and the Hope of Immortality* (London: SCM Press, 1992), pp. 5-11, 72-73.

47. Barr, *The Garden of Eden*, pp. 9 and 91.

48. Note how different this choice between life and death is from the theme of the choice of wisdom, human and divine, as outlined in the third of the historical approaches (pp. 23-27) earlier.

about human mortality, this is to see it as an explanation for a coming of age—a statement about human 'maturation'. This presumes that 'knowledge of good and evil' is essential for our gain of independence, autonomy and freedom. Indeed, if in Eden there was no birth, no death and no work, it could be argued that neither was there any real life. P. Trible asks whether the Garden could ever be seen as Paradise, as it is a place of fulfilment only within limits, a place of distinctions and hierarchies, a place of temptation with the form of a serpent lurking within it.[49] Furthermore, in the so-called perfect world in the garden, both God and the serpent lied: God warned that the eating of the fruit of the tree of knowledge would make them die (2.9, 17) yet it did not; and the serpent promised that the knowledge would make them like God (3.5), which it did not. This being the case, to leave the garden was essential for human maturation. The story is thus a celebration of life, rather than a warning about death: the expulsion from the garden marks the high point of the story, for it is when man and woman come into their own. Thus Eve who first took the fruit is the heroine of the story—the 'mother of the living' (3.20) for she alone had the initial courage to act for herself and to persuade Adam to do the same. The fact that a number of feminist scholars have put forward variations of this reading of the story is notable.[50]

49. See Trible, 'A Love Story Gone Awry', p. 74.
50. See S. Niditch, 'Genesis 1–11: Five Themes', in *idem, Chaos to Cosmos: Studies in Biblical Patterns of Creation* (Chico, CA: Scholars Press, 1985), pp. 11-24, who contrasts Eve's curiosity and search for knowledge with Adam's passivity and lack of robustness; M. Hayter, *The New Eve in Christ* (London: SPCK, 1987), especially pp. 95-98; S.S. Lanser, '(Feminist) Criticism in the Garden: Inferring Genesis 2–3', in H.C. White (ed.), *Speech Act Theory and Biblical Criticism* (Semeia, 14; Decatur, GA: Scholars Press, 1988), pp. 67-84; E. van Wolde, *A Semiotic Analysis of Genesis 2–3: A Semiotic Theory and Method of Analysis Applied to the Story of the Garden of Eden* (Studia Semitica Neerlandica; Assen: Van Gorcum, 1989), especially pp. 217-19; also *idem*, 'Facing the Earth: Primeval History in a New Perspective', in P.R. Davies and D.J.A. Clines (eds.), *The World of Genesis: Persons, Places, Perspectives* (JSOTSup, 257; Sheffield: Sheffield Academic Press, 1998), pp. 22-47, especially pp. 28-37; Dragga, 'Genesis 2–3', pp. 3-13; Sawyer, 'Resurrecting Eve?', pp. 273-89; also S. Dowell and L. Hurcombe, *Dispossessed Daughters of Eve* (Philadelphia: Fortress Press, 1978; London: SCM Press, 1992), especially pp. 24-28; L.M. Bechtel, 'Rethinking the Interpretation of Genesis 2.4b–3.24', in A. Brenner (ed.), *A Feminist Companion to Genesis* (Sheffield: Sheffield Academic Press, 1993), pp. 77-117; Stratton, *Out of Eden*, pp. 85-108. This view has also support from male scholars as well. See D.G.R. Beattie, 'What is Genesis 2–3 About?', *ExpTim* 92 (1980), pp. 8-10; D. Jobling, 'The Myth Semantics of Genesis 2.4b–3.24', *Semeia* 18 (1980), pp. 41-49; J. Baker,

Whether one reads the motif of knowledge positively, in terms of possession of life, or negatively, in terms of the transience of life, both readings have one feature in common: they link together the motifs of knowledge and life, and so assume knowledge and life to be mutually complementary. Whichever interpretation one follows depends on whether one sees that the couple passed the tree test, or whether they failed it. Furthermore, whichever view one takes, both readings take the text as a whole unit, complete in itself: these readings do not need to refer to Gen. 1, for example, to back up their case. But what happens to the text when we include Gen. 1 as well? The reading changes, as will be seen below.

Looking at Genesis 1–3 as a Unity Overall: Knowledge as a Choice between Cosmic Harmony and Human Discord?
The historical-critical reading of Gen. 1–3 has always placed a good deal of emphasis on the contrast between Gen. 2–3 and Gen. 1. The key difference which interests us here concerns the different views of cosmic harmony and knowledge of God: Gen. 1 offers a more theocentric view, which depicts order in the natural order and humankind living in harmony with God, and Gen. 2–3 reflects a more anthropocentric view, which sees the world as full of pain, disorder, a state caused by the abuse of God's gifts of knowledge and life.[51]

'The Myth of Man's "Fall"—A Reappraisal', *ExpTim* 92 (1981), pp. 235-37; R.H. Allaway, 'Fall or Fall-Short?', *ExpTim* 97 (1986), pp. 108-110; Barr, *The Garden of Eden*, pp. 91-92; Magonet, 'The Themes of Genesis 2–3', pp. 29-33; D.J.A. Clines, *What Does Eve Do to Help? and Other Readerly Questions to the Old Testament* (JSOTSup, 94; Sheffield: JSOT Press, 1990); T. Fretheim, 'Is Genesis 3 a Fall Story?', *WW* 14 (1994), pp. 144-53; K.I. Parker, 'Mirror, Mirror on the Wall, Must We Leave Eden, Once and for All? A Lacanian Pleasure Trip through the Garden', *JSOT* 83 (1999), pp. 19-29; also P. Alexander, 'The Fall into Knowledge: The Garden of Eden/ Paradise in Gnostic Literature', in Morris and Sawyer (eds.), *A Walk in the Garden*, pp. 91-104, especially pp. 91-92, 99-100 on Nag Hammadi, where the taking of the fruit breaks the knowledge of the evil archons and so dispels the evil forces; also S. Gelander, *The Good Creator: Literature and Theology in Genesis 1–11* (Atlanta: Scholars Press, 1997), especially pp. 32-33.
    51. See pp. 23-27. See also P. Davies, 'Making It: Creation and Contradiction in Genesis', in M.D. Carroll, D.J.A. Clines and P.R. Davies (eds.), *The Bible in Human Society: Essays in Honour of John Rogerson* (JSOTSup, 200; Sheffield: JSOT Press, 1995), pp. 249-56, who argues that by reading Gen. 1–3 as a whole, Gen. 2–3 serves to *undermine* Gen. 1 (pp. 252-54). See also M.G. Brett, 'Genesis 1–11. Creation and Dominance', in *idem, Genesis: Procreation and the Politics of Identity* (Old Testament Readings; London: Routledge, 2000), pp. 24-48, especially pp. 24-35.

A literary reading is still able to compare and contrast the two descriptions of divine order and human chaos in Gen. 1 and 2–3 respectively, but the issue of sources, and origins and purpose of those sources, is as irrelevant as was the issue of the traditions of the two trees in the previous discussion. The focal point is the complementary binary themes between the two parts of the same account, creating a sense of diversity within the unity of the whole.

It is clear that a unity of purpose is to be found within these three chapters. For example, there is the continuous belief that the world was created for good by one God (see the refrain 'God saw that it was good' in Gen. 1.10, 12, 18, 20, 25, and the description of the paradise garden in Gen. 2.4b-9); furthermore, there is a consensus that humans have the capacity to live at one in true knowledge of God (see the description of the image of God given to man and woman in Gen. 1.27, and the description of the breath of God making Adam a living being in Gen. 2.7); and there is the shared view that humankind may achieve this knowledge and live at one with God by obeying particular 'ordinances' laid down by the Creator God. In Gen. 1 this is through the command to man to 'have dominion' over the created order, as in Gen. 1.28-30, and in Gen. 2–3 this is through the command not to eat of the tree in the midst of the garden, as in 2.15-16.

The difference is that in Gen. 1 there is no emphasis on the human choice: the first couple are depicted as cooperating with the beauty and goodness in the world by the ordering of their lives (see Gen. 1.27, 28). By contrast, Gen. 2–3 focuses on the importance of that freedom of choice—and the acquisition of knowledge is of course an essential step towards acquiring that freedom. As a result of this, there is always the possibility of a deep divide between mankind and God, should humans use their freedom to suit themselves rather than to please God. Hence a different world-view as well as a unity of purpose is to be found in Gen. 1–3 as a whole. In Gen. 1, the key motif is the blessing of God (see 1.22, 28): there is perfect cooperation between the ways of God and the ways of man in the right ordering of the world. In Gen. 2–3, by contrast, the key motif appears to be the curse of God (see 2.14, 17): the couple and the natural order are ultimately placed in opposition to God.[52]

---

52. These two pictures of God, humanity and the world are also found together in several other texts outside Genesis. For example, in Job, the hymnic form offers several insights about the harmony and order in the world (the hymn in Job 28 and the divine speeches in 38–41) whilst the lament forms, uttered by Job, reveal the gulf between the Creator and his creation, and stress instead the chaos and conflict in the

It might be argued that Gen. 1–3, as a unity, presents in miniature the contrasting views about the Creator and his creation which we find worked out on a larger canvas elsewhere in the Hebrew Bible. This reading has much in common with the historical reading concerning divine and human wisdom which was addressed earlier.[53] It is as if there are two ways of knowing the world, two forms of wisdom—God-given and human-made —and Gen. 1–3 seeks to hold these together in tension but as part of the same whole.[54] But at this point the reading is quite different from the historical approach; the nature of these two paradigms is more complex, and not just a case of contrasting one with the other, for they belong together: the one represents the reality of the way things are, and the other, the ideal of how things should be.[55] Both views of the world are necessary, for without the hope of the ideal, the reality would lead to unbearable despair, and yet without the affirmation of reality, the hope of the ideal would be but impossibly abstract. In this way the two forms of knowledge —that of intimate communion with God, as in Gen. 1, and that of a freedom of choice which sets us apart from God, as in Gen. 2–3, are necessary parts of the same story.[56]

world. Another example is found in the Psalter: the hymns reflect the presence of God upholding the order of creation (as in Pss. 8, 19, 33 and 104), whilst the laments reveal more the absence of God and the conflict between faith and experience (see Pss. 38, 44, 88).

53. See 'The Acquisition of Knowledge as an Independent Wisdom, Opposed to God' on pp. 23-27 above.

54. On the theme of the interrelationship between these two sorts of wisdom in Gen. 1–3, see pp. 20-21 previously; also Niditch, *Chaos to Cosmos*, pp. 1-7 and 11-24; Wallace, 'Tree of Knowledge and Tree of Life', pp. 656-60; on Gen. 2–3, see especially Reicke, 'The Knowledge Hidden', pp. 193-201, and Stern, 'The Knowledge of Good and Evil', p. 418; on Gen. 1, see M. Bauks and G. Baumann, 'Im Anfang war…? Gen. 1, 1ff und Prov. 8,22-31 im Vergleich', *BN* 71 (1994), pp. 24-52.

55. For further reflections on these observations, see J.F.A. Sawyer, 'The Image of God, the Wisdom of Serpents and the Knowledge of Good and Evil', in Morris and Sawyer (eds.), *A Walk in the Garden*, pp. 64-73; also E. van Wolde, *Words Become Worlds: Semantic Studies of Genesis 1–11* (Leiden: E.J. Brill, 1994), and *idem*, *Stories of the Beginning: Genesis 1–11 and Other Creation Stories* (trans. J. Bowden; London: SCM Press, 1995), pp. 71-73.

56. See R. Williams, *The Wound of Knowledge* (London: Darton, Longman & Todd, 1979). Another illustration is expressed in an as yet unpublished poem, entitled 'Sophie's Song', by Francis Young: Sophie is pure undefiled wisdom, whose song brings creation to birth, living harmoniously with her Creator. Yet all the while a

Knowledge as an Apologetic Motif for Yahweh's Justice: Looking at Genesis 1–11 Overall

The two themes found in Gen. 1–3 are developed further in Gen. 1–11 as a whole. As was noted earlier, the theme of *hubris* occurs in at least two other places beyond Gen. 2–3, in the intermarriage of the sons of God with the daughters of men in Gen. 6.1-4, and in the building of the tower of Babel in Gen. 11.1-9.[57] Yet the theme of the order and harmony in the world is represented by the carefully constructed genealogies of Gen. 5, 10 and 11, and by the references to the heroes of faith such as Enoch (Gen. 5.21-24) and Noah (Gen. 6.9) who 'walked with God'.

So by focusing on the theme of knowledge as it occurs in Gen. 1–11, yet another interpretation of the story may be found: in this case, the motif of knowledge serves more to justify the character of God than it does to explain the human predicament. Genesis 1–11 overall may be seen as a theodicy, whereby the motif of 'knowledge' highlights the difference between the ways of God and the ways of man: the serpent, the tree and its fruit (in Gen. 2–3) are all necessary symbols of divine and human freedom within the story as a whole.

The problem of monotheism is that it needs a scapegoat. In a polytheistic world-view there would be no need for such aberrations, for evil and suffering in the world can be explained by the clash between different deities. But in a monotheistic faith there is a need for some other counter-forces to stand in the place of the other gods, whilst still allowing humans their freedom of choice. In Gen. 2–3, therefore, the counter-forces are the serpent and the tree of knowledge. In Gen. 4 it is 'sin crouching at the door' (4.7); and in Gen. 6, it is the beauty of the daughters of men (6.2). In

---

shadow-image, 'pseudo-Sophie', calls Sophie's people into a self-induced abyss. The choice is to follow the seduction of the dark double, or the call of Sophie herself:

> For Sophie's tinkling roar within the soul
> Images the rationality
> That underlies the wild order of things,
> The grand design of life that's Sophie's work...
> Sophie is God clad in the world and the Word.
> Through lustless passion, through sharing the pain of the earth
> The soul may consummate its unity
> With all the beauty, goodness and truth of God.
> For us and in us and with us Sophie is God...

57. See pp. 24-25 above; also P.D. Miller, *Genesis 1–11: Studies in Structure and Theme* (JSOTSup, 8; Sheffield: JSOT Press, 1978).

each case, the temptation to use the freedom of choice—for good and for evil—is depicted as arising outside the human will, and then acting upon it.

In Gen. 3, the serpent undoubtedly plays this role. The 'tempter' is not in the first instance God himself—for if it were, it would undermine the view that God is entirely good; nor is it entirely within—for this would undermine the view that God is just. A intermediate 'foil' is essential. The tree of knowledge is the first foil within the Garden of Eden story, and the serpent is the second.[58]

Hence the tree of knowledge is but one of a number of motifs running throughout Gen. 1–11 which form a necessary part of the apologetic to 'let God off the hook'. The fruit of the tree is offered by the serpent, then taken by the woman; this means that it is not exactly God's fault that the humans choose to sin, and so in this way neither his essential goodness nor his omnipotence is compromised. Without the tree of knowledge, and from this the emphasis on the freedom of choice, God would appear to be fundamentally at fault for the consequent cycles of human disobedience and divine punishment which run throughout chapters 1–11.

Knowledge as the Antithesis of the Law? Looking at the Pentateuch Overall

Several commentators have noted that, from Gen. 2–3 onwards, themes such as those of sin–punishment–mercy–restoration run throughout the entire Pentateuch.[59] The key theological point is that God's grace and provision in times of need is always greater than human shortcomings (for example, Gen. 3.21—the clothing of humans on leaving the garden; Gen. 4.15—the mark of Cain; Gen. 6.11-22; 7.1-5—the provision of the ark for Noah). But this is not only a feature of Gen. 1–11; although with a different emphasis, it is also evident in the rest of Genesis, where the goodness of God constantly outweighs the shortcomings of his people.[60]

---

58. The serpent and the tree together function in Gen. 2–3 rather like 'the Satan' in Job 1–2, and 'the devil' in the temptations of Christ in, for example, Lk. 4.1-13.

59. See D.J.A. Clines, *The Theme of the Pentateuch* (JSOTSup, 10; Sheffield: JSOT Press, 1978), pp. 61-79; N. Whybray, *The Making of the Pentateuch* (JSOTSup, 53; Sheffield: JSOT Press, 1987), pp. 221-42; also Rogerson, *Genesis 1–11*, pp. 26-30.

60. The important contrast between Gen. 1–11 and the rest of the Pentateuch is that the first chapters focus on God's mercy for all people, and Gen. 12–25 focus on God's mercy, through Abraham, for the people he has chosen as his own. Although the emphasis on recipients differs, the theme of human weakness/divine mercy runs through both parts.

The revelation of the law to Moses on Mount Sinai provides a climax to this sequence: it is the final culmination of the covenants referred to in the Pentateuch as a whole—first with Noah and all humanity (Gen. 9.12-17), then with Abraham and God's chosen people (Gen. 17.4-8), and finally with Moses himself (Exod. 6.5-9). In the giving of the law, the God of covenantal mercy makes a definitive demand for obedience, whereby the independence and disobedience exhibited first by the couple in the garden is now both constrained and redirected by God. Without the tree of knowledge, the law as 'a hedge' on human obedience would not be required: humans would have lived in obedience to God by intuition (though not by freedom of choice) so that any external restraint would be superfluous. Thus the taking of the fruit of knowledge from the tree of good and evil becomes a symbol of the disobedience of all humanity, whilst the giving of the law on Sinai becomes the symbol and the hallmark of the obedience of God's particular people. Without the curse resulting from eating the fruit of the tree of knowledge, there would be no blessing resulting from the gift of the law, which is in fact God's gracious provision for human need. The tree of knowledge is the negative image, and the tablets of stone for the law represent the positive one.[61]

This comparison is alluded to in at least two psalms. Psalm 19 contrasts the right use of knowledge as expressed in the law with the wrong use of knowledge as an expression of folly: 'the commandment of the Lord is pure, *enlightening the eyes...more to be desired* are they than fine gold' (Pss. 19.8, 10) being almost certainly an echo of the language in the garden in Gen. 3.5-6.[62] Similarly, Ps. 1 speaks of one whose delight is in the law of the Lord, and who sees himself as a tree planted by the waters

61. Perhaps one of the best examples of this is to be found in *Genesis Rabbah*, a fourth/fifth century CE rabbinic commentary on the book of Genesis. This has correspondences with the earlier book of Jubilees, in its comparison of God's creation of the world with God's 'new creation' represented by the Torah. This may be seen as the Jewish parallel to the antithesis of Christ and the law, particularly in the New Testament (see below) and—more relevantly here—between Christ and Adam.

62. Cf. D.J.A. Clines, 'The Tree of Knowledge and the Law of Yahweh', *VT* 24 (1974), pp. 8-14; also P.R. Davies, 'Women, Men, Gods, Sex and Power: The Birth of a Biblical Myth', in Brenner (ed.), *A Feminist Companion to Genesis*, pp. 194-201, especially p. 200. See also *The Authorised Daily Prayer Book* (London: United Synagogue, 3rd edn, 1990), p. 374: 'This is the Torah which Moses set before the children of Israel...she is a Tree of Life to those who grasp her'—i.e. in contrast to the tree of knowledge which brought Adam and his descendents to sin: see P. Morris, 'Exiled from Eden: Jewish Interpretations of Genesis', in Morris and Sawyer (eds.), *A Walk in the Garden*, pp. 117-66, especially p. 118.

(vv. 2-3). But more explicitly, it is a theme developed in later rabbinic literature: *Gen. R.* 24.7 speaks of Adam being given six commandments, yet failing to keep any of them, whilst Moses was given 613 commandments which Israel still keeps: the Torah thus saves Adam's descendants from Adam's fate. *Gen. R.* 24.5 explicitly compares Adam with Moses. *Gen. R.* 19.7 speaks of Adam's sin resulting in God's glory distancing itself from earth and so moving up to the seventh heaven through six further stages (Cain, Enoch, the Flood, Babel, Sodom, and the sojourn in Egypt), which was then brought back to earth in six later stages (Abraham, Isaac, Jacob, Levi, Kahath, Amran) culminating in Moses and the Law. Thus Adam is the antitype to Moses, and the giving of the law on Sinai brings back the knowledge and life which was lost by the eating of the fruit in Eden.[63]

Knowledge as the Antithesis to the Work of God in Christ? Reading Genesis within the Christian Bible as a Whole

This way of reading assumes that we are no longer interpreting the Hebrew Bible as the Scripture of the Jewish people, but rather we are reading the Old Testament, the Scripture of the Christian Church. Thus this canonical reading of the biblical texts presumes an even wider theological context than before.

One type of antithesis in New Testament theology is between Christ and the law: Christ is the act of God's grace in relation to the effects of the failure of God's people to keep the Law.[64] This is a very different approach from that discussed previously which saw the Law as the act of God's grace in relation to the effects of the first couple taking the fruit of the tree of knowledge.

---

63. See the discussion in Morris, 'Exiled from Eden', pp. 121-30, who goes on (pp. 136, 146) to note how the contrast is also made in *Zohar* 1.26b, where the first giving of the commandments (Exod. 19–24) is compared with the tree of life, and the second giving of them (Exod. 32–34) is seen as the tree of knowledge. It is also found in *Zohar* 2.162b and 3.113a, where the Torah is described as an antidote to Adam's sin. Similarly in *A Guide to the Perplexed* 1.2, Maimonides compares Adam and our lower nature with the Torah and our higher nature.

64. See Rom. 5.12-14 (on Adam and Moses); 5.15-17 (on Adam and Christ); 5.18-21 (on Christ and the Law); also Gal. 3.23-24, which refers to the law as 'our custodian' until Christ came (ὥστε ὁ νόμος παιδαγωγὸς ἡμῶν γέγονεν εἰς Χριστόν, ἵνα ἐκ πίστεως δικαιωθῶμεν). Regarding the Pauline use of the Genesis texts, see F. Watson, 'Strategies of Recovery and Resistance: Hermeneutical Reflections on Genesis 1–3 and its Pauline Reception', *JSNT* 45 (1992), pp. 79-103.

Hence the motif of knowledge now becomes an important theological device on an even larger canvas. If the giving of the law on Sinai is the antithesis to the taking of the fruit of the tree of knowledge, then, within a much larger literary framework, the offer of forgiveness through the obedient suffering of Christ is an even greater antithesis to the taking of the fruit and its consequential loss of intimacy with God. Paul is one of the first Christian theologians to grasp the full implications of this insight in his Adam/Christ typology: 'For as in Adam all die, so in Christ shall all be made alive' (1 Cor. 15.22) and 'Yet death reigned from Adam to Moses, even over those whose sins were not like the transgression of Adam, who was a type of the one who was to come. But the free gift is not like the trespass' (Rom. 5.14-15).[65]

The previous antithesis between the tree of knowledge (a negative sign illustrating the cost of disobedience) and the tablets of the Law (a positive sign illustrating God's grace in responding to the effects of that disobedience) is now replaced by a different antithesis: Christ, who replaces the Law (for the Torah, like the tree of knowledge, ultimately failed to bring the people back to their God) is also the one who redeems the negative effects of the tree of knowledge. This typology has been frequently used in Christian spirituality, which plays on an antithesis between the two gardens—the garden of Eden as a symbol of disobedience and resulting alienation from God, and the garden of Gethsemane as a symbol of obedience and the resultant restoration to God—as well as the antithesis between the two trees—the one tree of knowledge which symbolized self-fulfilment and ultimate alienation from God, and the other tree of the cross which symbolized self-giving and ultimate restoration to God.[66]

65. Paul may have used this Adam/Christ typology as it was an expression of his own experience of death and life on the Damascus road: see D.F. Sawyer, 'The New Adam in the Theology of St Paul', in Morris and Sawyer (eds.), *A Walk in the Garden*, pp. 105-116; also C.K. Barrett, *From First Adam to Last: A Study in Pauline Theology* (London: SPCK, 1962). For Paul, Adam normally represents universal (Gentile) sinfulness, whilst Moses represents particular (Jewish) sinfulness.

66. For example, see J.H. Newman, 'Praise to the Holiest in the Height', Hymn 185 in *Hymns Ancient and Modern Revised* (London: William Clowes and Sons Ltd, n.d.), pp. 246-47, which speaks of Christ as the 'second Adam' 'who to the fight and rescue came':

> O wisest love! that flesh and blood, which did in Adam fail,
> Should strive afresh against the foe, should strive and should prevail…
> And in the garden secretly, and on the cross on high,
> Should teach his brethren, and inspire to suffer and to die.

From the above examples, it can be seen that it is possible to 'absolutize' this antithesis so that—continuing the typology—Christ's work on the cross restores *for once and for all* the results of the eating of the fruit of the tree of knowledge which had resulted in a fall away from God *for once and for all*. It is at this point—and *only* at this point—that we have a Christian doctrine of original sin (the result of the 'first couple' eating of the tree of knowledge) and of restoration to grace (the result of Christ, the embodiment of humanity, negating the effect of that original sin). The tree of knowledge thus becomes a symbol of original sin and a cosmic fall from grace; the cross of Christ, by contrast, becomes a symbol of the cosmic restoration of all humanity from that first disobedient act and hence fall from grace.[67]

This is a curious theology, for it enfolds the Genesis story from a Christian perspective (noting that the story of Adam and Eve eating from the tree of knowledge occurs nowhere else in the entire Hebrew Bible) and so fails to do justice to the different levels of meaning in the story itself. For the story of the Garden of Eden, in itself, hardly reads as a comment on the cosmic fall of entire humanity; this is another theological agenda brought to the text, created by using other texts from outside it. Instead of reading the story of the taking of the fruit of knowledge as an aetiology about human freedom and human disobedience, the story becomes part of a systematic theology: re-reading the text, the humanity which Adam and Eve represent is seen as 'falling short' of God, and the whole story is theologized in such a way that humans are put in an impossibly negative light, which, according to New Testament teaching, only the work of God in Christ could atone for. Of course this is a legitimate reading, in the sense that all readings are. But it is only one reading among many, in spite of the fact that in Christian theology it has become the primary interpretation of the story.

---

67. In early Christian iconography the cross was depicted as the tree of life; for example, in the San Clemente Basilica, Rome, the cross has branches and leaves (probably of the vine) spreading from it, with water at its base—like the cosmological tree, it brings about the healing of the nations. In this way the tree of death (the tree of knowledge) has become, theologically speaking, the tree of life (the cross of Christ). See J. O'Reilly, 'The Trees of Eden in Medieval Iconography', in Morris and Sawyer (eds.), *A Walk in the Garden*, pp. 167-204, especially p. 171; also G.A. Anderson, *The Genesis of Perfection: Adam and Eve in Jewish and Christian Interpretation* (Louisville, KY: Westminster/John Knox Press, 2001).

Some Final Observations

In conclusion, we may note that the specifically defined historical or literary framework radically affects the theological emphasis of a given text. On the positive side, both approaches undoubtedly provide a rich resource for multivalent interpretations. But there is also a clear problem here. Theological readings—whether provided from a historical approach or from a literary persuasion—are as much dependent on the theology of the interpreter as they are on any fixed quality inherent in a text: the theology of the text is very largely dependent upon what the interpreter chooses to find there.

So is there any way in which we might counter such inevitable subjectivity? One helpful way forward is undoubtedly to start with a proposed theological motif, and from there to discover if it is apparent in all the approaches to the text. With regard to Gen. 2–3, the theme of 'knowledge' does in fact work very well in this respect. For whatever types of question one might ask of the text, it becomes clear that one recurring theme is the *interplay between divine and human knowledge.* One may interpret human knowledge negatively, and divine knowledge positively, or indeed the reverse; but nevertheless, this interplay on the theme of knowledge is a constant throughout.[68]

If one can discover one theological theme which is common to most, if not all, levels and circles of interpretation, other less frequent and obvious themes are less significant than they may first appear. For example, one such theme in Gen. 2–3 which is *not* constant in every reading is the idea of a 'fall from grace', although this has been held as the key theological theme in later Jewish and early Christian tradition.[69] Hence our approach can serve to exercise some control on those who isolate one reading and see it as primary: to see 'original sin' as the most fundamental hermeneutical key is quite clearly not appropriate, a point which has been made by several scholars already.[70]

68. Cf. Baker, 'The Myth of Man's "Fall"', p. 236.

69. If anyone fell from grace, it was not Adam and Eve, but Cain. Adam and Eve exercised a freedom of choice, but they never acted upon the evil possibilities inherent in that choice, whilst Cain's murder of his brother Abel did. The parallelism between Cain and Christ—the murderer and the victim—might be seen to work somewhat better than that between Adam and Christ.

70. Cf. Vawter, *On Genesis: A New Reading*, especially pp. 89-90; D. Patte, *Genesis 2 and 3: Kaleidoscopic Structural Readings* (Semeia, 18; Chico, CA: Scholars Press, 1980); Allaway, 'Fall or Fall-Short?', pp. 108-110; Barr, *The Garden of Eden*, pp. 1-20; R. Roberts, 'Sin, Saga and Gender: The Fall and Original Sin in Modern Theology',

Hence a multivalent approach to reading helps us to have some perspective on what a text may be about, for it helps us to decide its theological family likeness, within all diverse relations. By finding readings which are less familiar it enables us to see in a broader context those readings in our own tradition which have become most familiar; but it also enables us to know just how much those unfamiliar readings match with the familiar ones, and so to judge them for what they are. So as far as the Garden of Eden story is concerned, attempts to see as normative just one reading—that of a cosmic fall from grace, redeemed by the cross of Christ —is undoubtedly an approach that should be viewed with a good deal of caution.

in Morris and Sawyer (eds.), *A Walk in the Garden*, pp. 244-60; and Stratton, *Out of Eden*, pp. 203 and 254-57, on the multivalent reception history of the text.

Chapter 3

IN AND OUT OF THE SHEEPFOLD:
MULTIVALENT READINGS IN PSALM 23

A Psalm of David

[1]The LORD is my shepherd, I shall not want;
[2]he makes me lie down in green pastures.
He leads me beside still waters;
[3]he restores my soul.
He leads me in paths of righteousness
for his name's sake.
[4]Even though I walk through the valley of the shadow of death,
I fear no evil;
for thou art with me;
thy rod and thy staff,
they comfort me.
[5]Thou preparest a table before me
in the presence of my enemies;
thou anointest my head with oil,
my cup overflows.
[6]Surely goodness and mercy shall follow me
all the days of my life;
and I shall dwell in the house of the LORD
for ever.

Genesis 2–3 is a foundational prose text about primary relationships, human and divine; and Ps. 23 is renowned for similar reasons. Its deeply personal nature, affirming that in both life and death we are sustained by the protective presence of God, has made it widely used. Familiar texts are usually the richest in meaning: different questions asked of well-worn clichés can provide an array of different answers, as was seen when examining the motif of 'knowledge' in Gen. 2–3.

Like the story of the Garden of Eden, Ps. 23 is undoubtedly open to a wide variety of meanings. In Gen. 2–3 it is due in part to the enigmatic nature of the story, with its use of myths, folklore and aetiologies; these mask the intentions and identity of the author(s), making the actual cultural setting most unclear. In Ps. 23 it is partly because of the ambiguous nature of the poetry, set in the context of liturgy and prayer, with all the attendant difficulties of establishing with any certainty the author(s) of the psalm and hence its socio-religious setting. Furthermore, as we saw in the previous chapter, interpretations are also very much affected by assumptions made about the boundaries of a given text. And so readings can change according to whether we take Ps. 23 as a unit on its own, or within the context of Pss. 22 and 24, or within Book 1 of the Psalms, or within the Psalter as a whole: this is little different from the shifts in meaning of Gen. 2–3, depending upon whether the story is taken on its own, or within the context of Gen. 1–3, or within Gen. 1–11, or with the book of Genesis as a whole.

In spite of the number of possible interpretations, many commentators have focused on one dominant reading of Ps. 23, whether this is biographical (assuming Davidic authorship), cult-functional (assuming it to have some ancient sacral use), didactic, or simply spiritual. Such over-categorization goes against the grain of the text, where poetic ambiguity requires a more multi-faceted and open-ended approach. Jörg Sandberger, for example, arguing against monolithic interpretations of Ps. 23, observes that no amount of tortuous exegetical work can bring the dead poet to life; we will never know what the composer of Ps. 23 really intended, and on this account the text should be opened up to a wide variety of interpretations.[1]

In order to appreciate fully the wide range of readings which arise from a study of this psalm, the same approach as for Gen. 2–3 will be used, concentrating on one particular motif. And as in Gen. 2–3 this was the acquisition of knowledge, here it will be the image of God as Shepherd. By asking different historical and literary questions of the purpose of this motif, the multivalency of the text is brought to life.

Historical Readings of Psalm 23 through the Shepherd Motif

The overall theme of the psalm concerns God's guidance and protection. An important question is whether the theme comprises one image (God as

---

1.   Cf. J.V. Sandberger, 'Hermeneutische Aspekte der Psalmeninterpretation dargestellt an Psalm 23', in K. Seybold and E. Zenger (eds.), *Neue Wege der Psalmenforschung* (Herder Biblische Studien, 1; Freiburg: Herder, 1994), pp. 317-44. See, for example, p. 327: 'Kein exegetisches Folterwerkung bringt den toten Dichter zum Reden. Er sagt nun einmal nicht... Er verschweigt... Erstaunlich bleibt, wie wenig Exegeten die Vieldeutigkeit des Textes wahrhaben wollen.'

Shepherd) or two (God as Shepherd and Host) or even three (God as Shepherd, Guide and Host). Yet 'God as Shepherd' would appear to be the dominant theme of the psalm: it is explicit in the descriptions of green pastures and still waters in vv. 1-2, it is implied in the picture of God the Shepherd-Guide who protects his flock when in danger in vv. 3-4, and it is evident in the picture of the Shepherd-Host who brings his flock safely home in vv. 5-6.[2]

It is the shepherding image which above all has encouraged a *royal* interpretation of the psalm. One reason is the tradition of David as a shepherd boy, which in turn could have influenced the pastoral imagery for God as Shepherd as well.[3] Another reason is that the king in the ancient Near East was often known as the 'shepherd' who guided and protected his people, a model of the deity who guided and protected the king and so was also known as the Shepherd of the people.[4] Given the

2. See B.W. Anderson, *Out of the Depths: The Psalms Speak for us Today* (Philadelphia: Westminster Press, 1983), p. 2. Whilst recognizing the transition from animal to human figurative speech from verses 5 onwards, Y. Mazor similarly shows how the two images are complementary aspects of the character of God in his protection as Shepherd and in his generosity as Host. See 'Psalm 23: The Lord is my Shepherd—Or is he my Host?', *ZAW* 100.3 (1988), pp. 416-20. The rod and the staff in vv. 3-4 thus act as a bridge between these two sets of images: they are both literal (the club being used to ward off wild animals, the rod like a crook seeking out the wandering sheep) and metaphorical (symbols of God's protection in leading his people to safety). See E. Power, 'The Shepherd's Two Rods in Modern Palestine and Some Passages of the Old Testament', *Bib* 9 (1928), pp. 434-42; also R.W. Corney, '"Rod and Staff" (Psalm 23.4): a Double Image?', in S.L. Cook and S.C. Winter (eds.), *On the Way to Nineveh* (Atlanta: Scholars Press, 1999), pp. 28-41.

3. See Ps. 78, where in vv. 52-53 God is depicted as the shepherd of his flock (in the context of the Exodus tradition), and in vv. 70-72 described as 'the shepherd of Jacob his people' (in the context of the Zion tradition).

4. Such descriptions given to *kings* are found as far back as the third millennium, when Enmerkar, king of Uruk, is called a shepherd after his defeat of Aratta: see S.N. Kraemer, *From the Tablets of Sumer* (Colorado: Indian Hills, 1959), p. 26. An example from the second millennium is Hammurabi, who is named a shepherd, called by Enlil: see *ANET*, p. 164. And in the first millennium, Assyrian kings were described as shepherds: the title served for Shalmaneser I, Tiglath-pileser I, Sargon II and Sennacherib. By the time of the exile we may note how Cyrus is called a shepherd (Isa. 44.28). The naming of the *deity* as a shepherd is also found as early as Sumerian times, where Enlil is called the faithful shepherd: cf. *ANET*, p. 337. In second millennium Egypt, the god Osiris is often depicted with a crook and called a shepherd. And in Babylon by the first millennium, Marduk receives the same title: cf. *ANET*, pp. 69, 71, 72; furthermore, a

royal associations of the Shepherd motif, we shall first interpret the psalm as if the motif belongs to the life-experience of king David, whilst the next reading will interpret Ps. 23 as if it were composed for regular coronation rituals of Davidic kings.

God as Shepherd for King David: A Biographical-Historical Reading
In an article discussing Ps. 23 as a 'song of passage', Jack Lundbom makes an interesting case for the Davidic authorship of the psalm, and much of it is linked to the fundamental motif of God addressed as Shepherd.[5] David, once shepherd and protector of his flock, is now driven into the desert as vulnerable and as unprotected as one of his sheep, and so God becomes to David in his need a Shepherd figure. Lundbom sees the life-setting for Ps. 23 narrated in 2 Sam. 15-19, when David is forced to leave Jerusalem after Absalom has proclaimed himself king. According to Lundbom, the encounter with Ziba and the provision of bread and summer fruit, followed by the cursing by Shimei, marks the beginning of David's affirmation of trust in God—'I shall not want' (Ps. 23.1). David's arrival at the fords of Jordan, where rest and refreshment restore his morale, is to be read as the context of Ps. 23.1-2 'in green pastures' and 'beside still waters'. Although protected by Yahweh, Absolom's pursuit of David—through the rocks and hills where there are shadows for enemies to hide—is, for Lundbom, the context for the reference to paths of deliverance (where צדק is read as 'deliverance' rather than 'righteousness') and to the valleys of 'death-shadow' (Ps. 23.3-4). The provision of food for a wearied David by Shobi the Ammonite at Mahanaim (2 Sam. 17.27-29) is the reference to God's preparing a feast for him in spite of the presence of his enemies (Ps. 23.5a); as the honoured guest, David's head is anointed with oil and the wine so that the cup overflows (Ps. 23.5b). It is this experience of God's provision in a time of danger in the wilderness which gives David the confidence to believe that one day he will return to the land and city which God had promised his people, where he will dwell secure (Ps. 23.6).[6]

Babylonian hymn depicts the Sun-God Shamesh as the shepherd of the lower world and guardian of the people of the world above (*ANET*, pp. 387-88).

5.   See J. Lundbom, 'Psalm 23: Song of Passage', *Int* 40 (1986), pp. 5-16.

6.   It is interesting to see how Lundbom places this psalm alongside Ps. 3, which bears the superscription as the occasion when David fled Absalom. Lundbom sees Ps. 3 (a lament) as a Davidic composition, marking David's passage into exile, while Ps. 23 (a psalm of confidence) is seen as a song of passage at the point of David's return from exile. See Lundbom, 'Psalm 23: Song of Passage', p. 14.

> Psalm 23 is then best understood as a song of passage. Broadly speaking, it recounts David's passage out of Jerusalem, into the wilderness, and back to Jerusalem again. There are other passages too which II Samuel 15–19 makes explicit. A mountain crossing, two crossings of the Jordan, two important meals, and one passage at least through a valley of death-shadow (II Sam. 18.6-8).[7]

Lundbom's reading is significant because it is unusual nowadays to find scholars taking so seriously the Davidic authorship of a psalm and finding the narrative within the historiographical texts as evidence for its setting. But Lundbom has simply brought up to date the views of scholars some 120 years earlier: F. Delitzsch, for example, comments on Ps. 23 in a very similar way: 'If David is the author, and there is no reason for doubting it, then this Psalm belongs to the time of the rebellion under Absalom, and this supposition is confirmed on every hand.'[8]

David's experience seeking refuge in the wilderness is compared to his earlier shepherding days in the wilderness; just as he protected his sheep, so now God as Shepherd protects him. A problem in this interpretation is its circular nature: by starting with the hypothesis of Davidic authorship, and by finding a narrative text to support it, the hypothesis is simply reiterated rather than proven.

The most obvious reason for assuming Davidic authorship is the superscription, 'A Psalm of David'. By reading the heading literally (where the

---

7. See Lundbom, 'Psalm 23: Song of Passage', p. 15.

8. Cf. F. Delitzsch, *Biblical Commentary on the Psalms* (trans. F. Bolton; Grand Rapids, MI: Eerdmans, 1952), I, pp. 402-407 (the German edition dates from 1868); here, p. 403. A similar view, using a different setting from Samuel, is found in Eduard König's *Die Psalmen eingeleitet, übersetzt und erklärt* (KAT, 3; Gütersloh: C. Bertelsmann, 1927), pp. 177-79: 'Der Dichter dieses Psalms kann David gewesen sein, der...nach seiner Verstoßung aus Jahwes Land [1 S 26,19] möglicherweise viel Sehnsucht nach der Rückkehr zu Jahwes Haus spüren mußte, mochte damit nun das Kultuszelt [vgl. 1 S 21,1ff] oder das Land des Jahwevolkes als die bevorzugte Erscheinungsstätte Jahwes gemeint sein.' See too A.R. Johnson, 'Psalm 23 and the Household of Faith', in J.R. Durham and J.R. Porter (eds.), *Proclamation and Presence* (London: SCM Press, 1970), pp. 255-71, who takes a similar position: by reading the references to the 'house of the Lord' as a metaphor, describing a longing for the cultic sanctuary, rather than a literal description of the Temple (in which case the reference is anachronistic for it could only date from Solomon's time onwards) and by reading the rest of the psalm in a similar spiritual/cultic vein, he concludes: 'As for the original author, it must remain uncertain whether or not this psalm was composed by David...' (p. 271); earlier Johnson also noted the correspondence between the psalmist and the situation with David when he fled from Absalom (p. 261).

prefix ל means 'of' David, rather than 'to' or 'in honour of' David, as it would be read in the ascription למנצח 'to the choirmaster') the psalm is a seen as a personal autobiographical prayer of king David himself.[9] This has been upheld most consistently in conservative Jewish and Christian traditions, and it is the result of theological assumptions brought to the text about the *Messianic* associations of such a psalm, both Jewish and Christian. If the psalm can be understood as by David, the first anointed king uniting Israel, this then provides a continuum whereby it can also pertain to a second David, the Messiah *par excellence*: the shepherding imagery is part of the bridge between the historical (God as Shepherd who protects the human king) and the eschatological (the Messiah as Shepherd of God's people).[10]

The Davidic interpretation is very much the tradition which lies behind the *Midrash* on the Psalms: v. 2 is read as an allusion to David when he fled from Saul (not from Absalom), and v. 4 is seen as referring to David's seeking protection in the wilderness of Judah from Saul, whilst v. 5 is a reference to the enemies of king David in the guise of Doeg the Edomite and Ahithopel.[11] The *Midrash* adds another layer of meaning after this stage: 'David the messiah' gives way to a belief in a 'coming Messiah of the house of David', by way of giving the psalm a communal interpretation. Israel will receive God's protection in a similar way in the age to come, in the presence of the Messiah 'who will be anointed with the oil of anointing'.[12] A. Cohen offers a similar reading: God who is the Shepherd-King of David is the same God who will lead his flock, the people of Israel, to everlasting bliss.[13] The primary historical reading has thus taken

---

9. See, for example, H.-J. Kraus, *Psalms 1-59: A Commentary* (trans. H.C. Oswald; Minneapolis: Augsburg, 1988), pp. 22-23; also P.C. Craigie, *Psalms 1–50* (Waco, TX: Word Books, 1983), pp. 33-35.

10. See, for example, 2 Esd. 2.34, where the shepherding imagery is applied to a coming figure: 'Await your shepherd: he will give you everlasting rest, because he who will come at the end of the age is close at hand.' See also *Pss. Sol.* 17.21-46, where the coming figure is of royal lineage and again the Shepherd Motif is used; the prayer begins with military imagery ('Raise up for them their king, the son of David…and give him strength, that he may shatter unrighteous rulers') and ends (vv. 67-72) with a prayer for protection using the shepherd imagery ('Who then can prevail against him…shepherding the flock of the Lord faithfully and righteously?').

11. Cf. W.G. Braude, *Midrash on the Psalms* (New Haven: Yale University Press, 1959), pp. 327-35. The references to vv. 2, 4 and 5 are from pp. 332-33.

12. Cf. Braude, *Midrash on the Psalms*, pp. 334-35.

13. See A. Cohen, תהלים: *The Psalms* (The Soncino Books of the Bible; New

on a secondary, more spiritualized and future-orientated approach. But what this approach has in common with the previous ones is the *historical* orientation: the psalm is of David the shepherd boy, now shepherded by God, whose exemplary faith allows others of the flock of God to identify with his experience and make it theirs.

God as Shepherd for the Davidic Dynasty: A Cult-Historical Reading
A few commentators have also read the psalm in a personal and autobiographical way, yet have chosen to date it not from the time of David, but in the reigns of later Davidic kings. They see the overall mood of confidence in God the Shepherd as referring to more peaceful and prosperous times, at some period between kings Solomon and Jehoshaphat.[14] In this way the Shepherd Motif is not so much particularly tied to David, but more generally is an indication of the royal connotations behind the term, and the ascription of God as Shepherd is simply a way of the king addressing God as his King and protector of his people.

For most commentators who take a royal interpretation, however, the reason for maintaining such a setting (yet detaching it from David himself) is a cultic one, and the ascription of God as Shepherd is very much part of it. For example, A. Merrill, identifying Ps. 23 with the Jerusalem cult tradition in pre-exilic times, asserts that 'The proclamation of Yahweh as רֹעִי is part of the cultic tradition of Jerusalem... In Ps. lxxx 2 he is the רֹעֵה of Israel: ...enthroned upon the cherubim. The Shepherd is the king of Israel, his people. As the Shepherd-King he brings life to his own; life symbolised by the grass and the water.'[15]

The paths of righteousness (v. 3) signify the cultic procession (with the ark) going up to Jerusalem, where the name of God (v. 3) is known. The rod and staff—originally referring to the imagery from the pastoral scene with the shepherd and flock—are now to be seen as royal symbols of

York: Soncino Press, 1992). On Davidic authorship: 'It was composed during one of David's most difficult periods—while on the run from Saul and his men, alone in a desolate forest (1 Sam. xxii)' (p. 67). And on a future interpretation: 'It [the psalm] is dedicated to those who forsake all their worldly comforts and thank God for whatever they have. Their sole aim is to merit special bliss in the world to come' (p. 67).

14. See, for example, C.A. Briggs, *A Critical and Exegetical Commentary on the Book of Psalms* (Edinburgh: T. & T. Clark, 1906), I, pp. 207-12; here, p. 208.

15. See A.L. Merrill, 'Psalm XXIII and the Jerusalem Tradition', *VT* 15 (1965), pp. 354-60; here, pp. 357-58. The quotation continues in noting that the waters (מְנֻחוֹת) are those of the spring Gihon by the temple of Jerusalem as in 1 Kgs. 1.32-37, Ps. 132.8, 14 and 95.11; see also Ps. 46.3.

majesty and power (as in Ezek. 37.16, like the two rods of the Shepherd-King—although noting that there neither of the two terms מִשְׁעַנְתֶּךָ ('your staff') and שִׁבְטְךָ ('your rod') in Ps. 23.4 is used in Ezekiel). From this Merrill infers that the speaker is the king in the Temple during a coronation ritual, speaking after some procession around the city during which he would dramatise some experience of conflict with his enemies (v. 4).[16] This also makes sense of the cultic banquet and the anointing with oil in v. 5, and the final climax of the psalm which speaks of the king finding refuge in the Temple all the rest of the days of his life (Ps. 2.6 might be another example of this, given its associations with a coronation ritual, in its affirmation that the king is set on Zion, God's holy hill).

Merrill finds another confirmation of this cultic interpretation in the placing of Ps. 23 between two other psalms which he sees as cultic actions relating to the enthronement of the king. Psalm 22 is part of the king's ritual suffering prior to his coronation, and Ps. 24 is part of a procession with the ark following the ceremony. In terms of setting the composition of the psalm within a historical period, this could mean any time in the 350 year period of history of the Davidic dynasty in Judah—i.e. from the time of the divided monarchy (c. 950 BCE) up to the exile (c. 597 BCE).

Merrill is one of the few commentators who explicitly places Ps. 23 in relation to a specific royal coronation ritual, where all the imagery is read liturgically to denote various cultic rituals in the Temple. But he is not alone in placing such an emphasis on a cult-functional interpretation for a so-called 'royal psalm'. Many scholars (for example, S. Mowinckel) are more cautious with respect to Ps. 23[17] but find less of a problem with this interpretation elsewhere.[18] And other Scandinavian scholars such as Widengren

---

16. Merrill, 'Psalm XXIII', p. 359.

17. See S. Mowinckel, *The Psalms in Israel's Worship* (trans. D.R. Ap-Thomas; 2 vols.; Oxford: Basil Blackwell, 2nd edn, 1982): 'One would like to able to say something about the occasion for this pearl among the psalms; but perhaps, what gives it a priceless value to all ages may be the very fact that it stands there as a pure expression of confidence in God, unhindered by all special historical circumstances…' (II, p. 41). This has to be a most unusual observation for one so committed to cultic reconstruction as is Mowinckel.

18. See Mowinckel, *The Psalms in Israel's Worship*, I, pp. 61-70, on the place of royal psalms in the cult. See also Kraus, *Psalms 1-59*, pp. 303-309, on Ps. 23: 'If we follow MT in 6b, the singer of the psalm ought to be someone involved in the cultus, someone who in "the house of Yahweh" has experienced extraordinary blessings' (pp. 305-306). This is also one who participates in a sacrificial meal in full view of his

and Bentzen are close to Merrill's position, with respect not only to Ps. 23, but also to Pss. 22 and 24.[19] J.H. Eaton, A.R. Johnson and S.J.L. Croft are examples of other non-Scandinavian commentators who take a similar view.[20]

With respect to the first interpretation, reading the motif of God as Shepherd personally as part of the life of David as king, it was argued that this is a circular argument, beginning with a hypothesis and then bringing in other biblical material which simply served to confirm the prejudice. The same criticism could be made of this second interpretation: it could be one legitimate reading, but we have to be honest about our starting-point in believing this to be the case. As A.G. Hunter observes: 'Sadly, the assumption of cultic origins within pre-exilic Jerusalem has become the starting-point rather than the conclusion of most Psalms' study, and the specifying of cultic genre merely a confirmation of that presupposition.'[21]

God as Shepherd for the Exilic Community: A Communal-Historical Reading
If the narrative texts of Samuel provided information for the setting of the psalm in the life of David, poetic texts—from the psalms and from the prophets—have provided confirmation that the psalm was composed and used not in pre-exilic times, but in the time of the exile and after it; in this

enemies; the most likely figure is thus the king; hence the Jerusalem royal cult is highly likely (p. 306).

19. See G. Widengren, *Hebrew and Accadian Psalms of Lamentations as Religious Documents* (Stockholm: Aktiebolaget Thule, 1937); and A. Bentzen, *Messias-Moses redivivus-Menschensohn* (ATANT, 17; Zürich: Zwingli Verlag, 1948), both quoted in Merrill, 'Psalm XXIII', p. 360.

20. See J.H. Eaton, *Psalms* (Torch Bible; London: SCM Press, 1967), pp. 76-79, who, whilst being cautious about the specifics of coronation rituals, notes that the psalm would have been recited 'by the royal head and representative of the community'. Johnson, in 'Psalm 23 and the Household of Faith', looks at the possibility of Davidic authorship but sees the preservation and use of the psalm within the cultic setting of later Davidic kings, when the reference to the 'House of Yahweh' is no longer figurative but literal (pp. 269-70). S.J.L. Croft, in *The Identity of the Individual in the Book of Psalms* (JSOTSup, 44; Sheffield: JSOT Press, 1987), sees in the psalm 'evidence of royal style' in the special relationship between Yahweh and the psalmist, the hints at some victory over enemies, and the anointing with oil. 'Both a ritual and a general historical usage would be possible' (p. 130).

21. See A.G. Hunter, *Psalms* (Old Testament Readings; London: Routledge, 1999), p. 180.

reading this is not so much a composition by or for the king as a composition by a representative of the community as a whole. Again the Shepherd motif provides an important piece of evidence.

Four scholars deserve mention in connection with this idea.[22] David Freedman is particularly interesting because of the way he builds his theory from the motif of the 'Divine Shepherd' in the first part of the psalm. '(Thus) the expression *yahweh rō 'ī* "Yahweh is my shepherd"…is unique in the Bible, although the figure of God as shepherd of his people is well-known, especially in relation to the Exodus, and to the Restoration from Exile.'[23]

Freedman uses Ps. 78.52:

> Then he led forth his people like sheep,
> and guided them in the wilderness like a flock.
> (ויסע כצאן עמו וינהגם כעדר במדבר)

as a good example of the same shepherding imagery referring to the Exodus tradition, where God as Shepherd leads his people out of Egypt 'like sheep' (כעדר) and 'like a flock' (כצאן).[24] Other relevant exilic prophetic texts are Ezek. 34.11-16, 25-31, where God is described as the shepherd seeking his sheep out (of exile) and finding them new pasture (restoration to the land). Isaiah 40.11 ('he will feed his flock like a shepherd, he will gather the lambs in his arms') is another example. From this, other phrases in Ps. 23 are seen to echo phrases elsewhere associated with the Exodus: 'Thou preparest a table before me' (v. 5) echoes the setting of

22. See P. Milne, 'Psalm 23: Echoes of the Exodus', *SR* 4 (1974–75), pp. 237-47; D.N. Freedman, 'The Twenty-Third Psalm', in C.I. Orlin (ed.), *Michigan Oriental Studies in Honor of George C. Cameron* (Michigan: Ann Arbor, 1976), pp. 139-66; and M.L. Barré and J.S. Kselman, 'New Exodus, Covenant and Restoration in Psalm 23', in C.L. Meyers and M. O'Connor (eds.), *The Word of the Lord Shall Go Forth: Essays in Honor of David Noel Freedman in Celebration of his Sixtieth Birthday* (AASOR Special Volume Series, 1; Winona Lake, IN: Eisenbrauns, 1983), pp. 97-127. The idea is also found in a less developed form in two commentaries in French: see R. Tournay and R. Schwab, *Les Psaumes* (La Sainte Bible; Paris: Cerf, 1955), pp. 136 and 200-203.

23. See Freedman, 'The Twenty-Third Psalm', p. 140. The key psalmic texts—where God is called Shepherd of the entire people—would be Pss. 80.2, 95.7 and 100.3 Where this relates specifically to the Exodus theme, Pss. 77.20, 78.52-73, 95.7-11 and 100 are all important.

24. It is noteworthy that in Ps. 78.20-29 earlier the reference to God's provision for his people in the wilderness also takes up the other theme in Ps. 23, God as Host.

the table in the wilderness (see also Ps. 78.19). The phrase 'beside still waters' (v. 2: עַל־מֵי מְנֻחוֹת) is an exact opposite of the phrase 'by the waters of strife' (עַל־מֵי מְרִיבָה) as in the descriptions of the rebellion in the wilderness in Pss. 81.7; 106.32 and Num. 20.13, where the people are forbidden to enter God's rest (Ps. 95.10-11). The reference to God guiding (Ps. 23.2-3) (using the verb נחל) is also found in Exod. 15.13, part of the Exodus tradition. Part of the more rare phrase 'valley of deep shadow' (Ps. 23.4: בְּגֵיא צַלְמָוֶת is found in Jer. 2.6 (בְּאֶרֶץ צִיָּה וְצַלְמָוֶת) in the same context of God leading his people out of Egypt 'in a land of drought and deep darkness'.

With these and other examples, Freedman argues that Ps. 23 has marked resemblances to the vocabulary and ideas of the exilic period: the psalm was composed, he argues, during the exile as a means of assuring the people (as second Isaiah does) that there would soon be a period of a new Exodus, a time of 'miraculous deliverance and a safe march through the verdant plains to the permanent abode of Yahweh... The Psalm may well have been used in connection with one or another of the great feasts which celebrates the Exodus (Passover) and the march through the wilderness (Tabernacles)'.[25]

Milne and Barré/Kselman make a similar point, although neither work links the psalm to any specific cultic occasion. Milne, like Freedman, finds the shepherding imagery a most compelling argument for a play on the Exodus traditions, using examples not only from Ezekiel and Isaiah, but from the post-exilic prophets as well: Isa. 63.11 describes the shepherd bringing his flock up out of the sea, and throughout Zech. 10 Yahweh assumes the role of shepherd, bringing the people home, in a new Exodus. Like Freedman, both Milne and Barré/Kselman see other motifs and vocabulary in Ps. 23 that also echo the Exodus (for example, his leading, again using נחל, the promise of rest, the refreshment by the waters, the table in the wilderness, and the experience of deep darkness). The close affinities with two key Exodus texts, Exod. 15 and Ps. 78, point further in this direction.

> Exile in Babylon would provide the need for such a psalm of con-
> fidence...liberation is hoped for, expected confidently from Yahweh, but
> not yet achieved... In summary, then, Psalm 23 may be a song in which the

25. Freedman, 'The Twenty-Third Psalm', pp. 165-66. In his view, the explicit connections of the vocabulary with Exodus traditions mean that the psalm must have been composed deliberately for this purpose, rather than having been an earlier Davidic composition and later used and adapted to this end.

community in exile in Babylon reflected upon the original exodus experience, the liberation from Egyptian bondage, the wilderness wanderings, and the entrance into the land, and found therein a source of hope for its own redemption.[26]

For these commentators, the psalmist is a representative of the exilic community—one with a prophetic and liturgical awareness, gifted at taking up the traditions of the past and applying them with new force to his audience, the community in exile. This is quite different from the psalm being a personal composition of king David, or the creation of a cultic official writing a coronation psalm during the Davidic dynasty. But could the psalm serve all these purposes at one and the same time? Before we answer this question, we need to set it in the still wider discussion of two other entirely different readings, again based upon a particular historical interpretation of the shepherding theme.

God as Shepherd for the Community of Restoration: A Personal-Historical Reading

Freedman's initial observation about the expression *yahweh rō 'î* ('Yahweh is my Shepherd') is that it is unique in the Bible. He then turns to the more corporate designations of God as Shepherd, for example in Ps. 77 ('Thou didst lead thy people like a flock' [v. 20]), Ps. 78 ('Then he led forth his people like sheep, and guided them in the wilderness like a flock' [v. 52]) and Ps. 100 ('We are his people and the sheep of his pasture' [v. 3]) and in the prophets (Ezek. 34 and Isa. 40) without asking whether any more should be made of the uniqueness of this expression as it occurs in Ps. 23. Several other scholars have however taken this up, noting the psalm is about *yahweh rō 'î*: 'Yahweh...*my* shepherd', with an individual rather than communal tenor. The reference to 'you are with me' (כי־אתה עמדי) in the heart of the psalm (v. 4a) reinforces this interpretation. Given other more personal and pious expressions in the psalm, they propose that this can only indicate a post-exilic setting, when individual piety as expressed in the Temple cult was more widely practised.[27]

There have been several variations of this interpretation. Some have taken the emphasis in v. 6 on dwelling in the house of the Lord for ever to

---

26. Milne, 'Psalm 23', p. 246.

27. See, for example, A.A. Anderson, *The New Century Bible Commentary, Psalms 1–72* (Grand Rapids: Eerdmans; London: Marshall, Morgan and Scott, 1972), pp. 195-200 (on Ps. 23) who notes that the theology in this psalm—its interest in 'righteousness' and in pilgrimage to the Temple—suggests a post-exilic setting (p. 208).

imply that the writer is a cultic official, probably a Levite, living in the Temple precinct—one who expresses his quiet confidence in the protection of Yahweh in both a deeply personal and a broader representative way (in that he composed for others to use as well). In this way the reading of God as Shepherd is both personal ('*my* Shepherd') and corporate ('Yahweh' is the one who is the Shepherd). Eduard Dhorme sees the tension between the personal and the corporate resolved by identifying the poet as a Levite; so too does E. Hirsch; and H.-J. Kraus has considered it.[28]

Another possibility is to place more emphasis on the *individual* piety expressed so clearly throughout in the psalm, and less emphasis on what might be termed 'Temple piety' found only at the end of the psalm (v. 6). In this interpretation, the psalm is a pilgrimage psalm; it is a composition to be used by pilgrims making their way to Jerusalem for one of the three annual festivals. In this sense, its piety and theology are close to the Songs of Ascents in Pss. 120–134. E. Vogt takes this view, seeing this as a thanksgiving psalm offered by a visitor to the Temple fairly soon after experiencing some grave danger or trouble.[29] The pilgrim has just offered some sacrifice of thanksgiving and now awaits some sacrificial banquet. According to Vogt, the psalm forms a pair with Ps. 27, whose longing for being in the Temple is expressed in very similar ways (compare 27.4 שבתי בבית־יהוה כל־ימי חיי 'that I may dwell in the house of the Lord all the days of my life' with 23.6b ושבתי בבית־יהוה לארך ימים 'and I shall dwell in the house of the Lord for ever'): Ps. 27 speaks of the offering of

---

28. See E. Dhorme, *La Bible, L'Ancien Testament*, II (2 vols.; Paris: Gallimard, 1959), p. 936: 'Il s'agit d'un jeune Lévite, qui va trouver la paix au service de Iahvé dans le Temple. Son avenir est assuré.' See also E. Hirsch, 'Predigtmeditation zu Psalm 23', *Die Spur* 17 (1977), pp. 145-49: 'Der Psalm ist das zur feierlichen Einführung eines Leviten in seinen Tempeldienst gehörende liturgische Stück. In den ersten Versen, welche von Jahwe in der dritten Person reden, singt der Levitenchor …Dann tritt die Einzelstimme des in seinen Temelpdienst Tretenden auf, welche in Gebetsanrede Gott persönlich preist, seine Wohltaten aufzählt und mit dem Gelöbnis schließt, froh and gern sein Leben lang im Tempeldienst zu bleiben' (p. 145 [quoted in Sandberger, 'Hermeneutische Aspekte', pp. 327-28]). Kraus, whilst preferring a pre-exilic setting, sees that the cultic allusions could instead suggest a Levite: 'Verse 6b could originally have been a Levitical confession… He who has experienced Yahweh's ישועה would forever like to stay in the area of salvation, in the sanctuary' (*Psalms 1–59*, p. 309).

29. See E. Vogt, 'The "Place in Life" of Ps. 23', *Bib* 34 (1953), pp. 195-211, especially pp. 198-203.

sacrifice as a future intention, and so chronologically precedes Ps. 23.[30] The shepherding imagery is explained by comparing the Temple to

> a rich pasture, with a resting-place provided with a water-pool, and the psalmist is like to a lamb [*sic*] that the LORD feeds and waters there… This is also the meaning of *rō ʿī*. We can translate *yahweh rō ʿī* either as 'The LORD is my shepherd', or in a more literal sense, 'The LORD tends, feeds me.'[31]

Other commentators who take the same 'pilgrim' view but offer a slightly different liturgical reconstruction from the psalm, include W. Beyerlin, who proposes the psalmist is undergoing some form of trial in the Temple in order to prove his innocence: Ps. 23, like several other psalms, is spoken as an accompaniment to some sort of ritual trial to persuade Yahweh to intervene and proclaim his innocence and offer judgment in his favour.[32] K. Seybold takes up the same idea: the psalmist comes to God's Temple to seek acquittal from some kind of false charge, and the Temple thus acts like a divine court of law.[33] A variation of this, staying with the pilgrim theme, is to see the psalm offered by one exiled from the land but participating in a festal communal meal in a local sanctuary.[34] In each case the shepherd image is thus seen as a metaphor for God's protection of the psalmist.

Several other variations on this theme are to be found. W. Brueggemann, for example, believes that the quiet confidence expressed by the psalmist is a result of some oracle of salvation received by the pilgrim at the Temple, although Brueggemann is more cautious about interpreting the language of the psalm as rubrics for individual cultic rituals.[35] M. Smith offers a slightly different reading: he recognizes its linguistic

---

30. Vogt, 'The "Place in Life" of Ps 23', pp. 210-11.

31. Vogt, 'The "Place in Life" of Ps 23', p. 204.

32. See W. Beyerlin, *Werden und Wesen des 107. Psalms* (BZAW, 153; Berlin: W. de Gruyter, 1979), concerning Pss. 3, 4, 5, 7, 11, 17, 23, 26, 27, 57 and 63.

33. See K. Seybold, *Die Psalmen* (HAT, 1/15; Tübingen: J.C.B. Mohr [Paul Siebeck], 1996), pp. 100-102.

34. W. Schottroff, 'Psalm 23. Zur Methode sozialgechichtlicher Bibelauslegung', in W. Schottroff and W. Stegemann (eds.), *Traditionen der Befreiung* (Münich: Kaiser Verlag, 1980), I, pp. 78-113: for Schottroff, the shepherding imagery is a clear indication of his thesis: 'Die Fürsorge des göttlichen Hirten bestärkt hier nicht die schon Starken und stützt hier nicht die gesellschaftlich Herrschenden, sondern wendet sich den Schwachen und Verfolgten zu' (p. 85).

35. See W. Brueggemann, *The Message of the Psalms* (Minneapolis: Augsburg, 1984), pp. 154-56.

links with Ps. 27, seeing that both are pilgrimage psalms expressing the joy of being in the Temple (rather like the longing expressed in Pss. 42–43, which also describes the presence of God that accompanies the pilgrims on their journey [Ps. 23.6; 43.3]); however, Smith also argues that the emphasis in Ps. 23 is more on the internal spiritual journey than it is on the external physical one, as in Pss. 27 and 42–43, an inward journey made clear by the tripartite structure in the psalm itself (vv. 1-3: the pastures and waters; v. 4: the valley of danger; vv. 5-6: the table and the house of God).[36]

Other scholars go one stage further and see this psalm as entirely 'cult-free'. Wellhausen's brief commentary on this psalm is unclear, but his emphases (and his understanding that the later psalmists were the inheritors of the independent piety of the pre-exilic prophets) seem to imply it.[37] H. Gunkel is more explicit: its individual spirit and its focus on personal piety both require an interpretation of the imagery, from God as Shepherd in v. 1 to the house of God in v. 6, in a spiritual, metaphorical, a-cultic and inward way. The psalm belongs to that number of 'cult-free' psalms which, according to Gunkel, represent 'personal piety' in the Psalter.[38] O. Eissfeldt develops this further still: by noting that the 'Arad-Ostracon of the Lachish letters (approximately sixth century) speaks of the individual being under God's protection in an inward and spiritual way, Eissfeldt sees that the reference to God as Shepherd in Ps. 23 is simply a poetic image, used in a metaphorical and cult-free way.[39] So too C. Westermann

36. See M.S. Smith, 'Setting and Rhetoric in Psalm 23', *JSOT* 41 (1988), pp. 61-66.

37. See J. Wellhausen, 'Notes on Psalm 23', in J. Haupt (ed.), *The Polychrome Bible* (trans. H.H. Furness; London: James Clark & Co, 1898), p. 174.

38. See H. Gunkel, *Die Psalmen übersetzt und erklärt* (Göttingen: GHAT, 1926), pp. 98-99: 'Diese Psalmisten haben ein ganz persönliches Verhältnis zu ,ihrem Gott' and dürfen Gedanken auf sich selber anwenden, welche die Propheten von dem ganzen Volke aussprechen. Das ist ein kleines Kennzeichen für einen großen, bedeutsamen Vorgang: der einzelne rückt in der Religion der Psalmen an die Stelle, die in der älteren Religion die Gemeinde innegehabt hat.' The motif of confidence which dominates the psalm is further evidence of the psalm's cult-free nature, according to Gunkel: psalms of confidence have broken away from the traditional forms of both lament and thanksgiving and are no longer genuine cultic forms presupposing a cultic setting.

39. See O. Eissfeldt, 'Bleiben im Hause Jahwes', in R. Altheim-Stehl and H.E. Stier (eds.), *Beiträge zur Alten Geschichte und deren Nachleben* (Festschrift F.I. Altheim; Berlin: W. de Gruyter, 1969), pp. 76-81.

sees the psalm as belonging to a 'setting-in-life', rather than 'setting-in-cult'.[40]

Finally, M. Buttenweiser links Ps. 23 more explicitly with a different biblical composer: the psalmist is the author of Job. For example, the shared expressions 'shadow of death' and 'they comfort me' suggest this is a psalm by one who, like the author of Job, has triumphed over suffering.[41] The imagery in the psalm evokes a quiet trust in God as Shepherd who is with the psalmist in the heights and depths of his faith (hence the expression 'dwell in the house of the Lord' really means 'live in the presence of God'). This shows that the psalmist is the spiritual heir of the prophets, with a piety which is quite detached from cultic ritual:

> Though nothing definite is known about the author, one thing is certain—it was not David. The religious inwardness revealed in the psalm was utterly foreign to him, who glorified in military victories as the fulfilment of his soul's desire.[42]

Nothing could be further removed from the assumptions of those who saw Ps. 23 as a composition by David the erstwhile shepherd-boy in the first section of our historical readings.

God as Shepherd for the Maccabean High Priests: A Messianic–Historical Reading

Some commentators, taking the cultic setting at face value (for example, the reference to the house of the Lord in Ps. 23.6) and assuming that individual piety is a late development in Jewish religion, propose that the author of the psalm is in some authority and so is a leader of the cultic community. In this reading they opt for a much later post-exilic setting. This was the position taken by many commentators in the middle of the last century: the psalm was cultic, it was royal, but it was late. Its lateness also lent it some sense of yearning for a better future—a messianic reading

---

40. See C. Westermann, *Ausgewählte Psalmen* (Göttingen: Vandenhoeck & Ruprecht, 1984), pp. 95-98. The psalmist's concern for his 'daily bread' and his prayer for guidance for walking in the right path has little to do with the cult and everything to do with daily life.

41. See M. Buttenweiser, *The Psalms: Chronologically Arranged with a New Translation* (New York: KTAV, rev. edn, 1969 [1938]), pp. 552-54. Buttenweiser notes the first of the two phrases occurs ten times in Job (3.5; 10.21, 22; 12.22; 16.16; 24.17 [twice]; 28.3; 34.22; 38.17) and the second phrase, with its derivatives, also ten times (2.11; 6.10; 7.13; 15.11; 16.2; 21.2, 34; 29.25; 42.6, 11).

42. Buttenweiser, *The Psalms*, p. 552.

of the psalm, with the hope focused on the present leader, rather than a Messianic one, when the hopes would be focused on one yet to come.

The most likely setting, these commentators argued, was that of the Hasmonaean priesthood (with its claims to be part of the Davidic line) in the second century BCE. J. Olshausen, for example, sets the psalm within a narrative setting in the same way as did J. Lundbom and F. Deliztsch with regard to David's life history; but here the narrative framework is no longer the book of Samuel, but the book of Maccabees.[43] B. Duhm places the psalm in a similar Hasmonaean setting, although he understood the provenance to be from a different 'priest-king'.[44]

In a similar way, but using a different narrative context from Maccabees to highlight his thesis, M. Treves understands the psalmist could only be a Maccabaean high-priest. Taking the reference to the 'house of the Lord' literally, and noting that it could not possibly therefore pertain to David, Treves sees that the composer has a theology (not least, his understanding of God as Shepherd) which post-dates not only David but Ezekiel and the other exilic and post-exilic prophets who used the phrase in terms of *God* coming to his people (e.g. Jeremiah, Isaiah and Zechariah). According to Treves, the composer must have been a member of the Temple staff, one who dwelt in the Temple precincts, and who was aware of all the Messianic and eschatological expectations in calling God 'Shepherd'. He is the one who presides over the cultic feast, the one who has been anointed with oil, who knows he is an exemplary figure who must walk in the ways of 'righteousness' (and so keep the Torah): so he must be a leader of the community. He can only be, according to Treves, the high- priest himself. Yet (according to Treves) there is clear evidence in the psalm of party strife, and the psalmist is looking towards a time of peace and prosperity after years of apostasy and confusion: Treves' only option is to date Ps. 23 at the time of the high priest Jonathan, who after the death of his brother Judas in 160 BCE had endured eight years of exile whilst the Jews in Jerusalem were suffering

---

43. See J. Olshausen, *Die Psalmen erklärt* (KEHAT, 14; Leipzig, 1853), pp. 128-30. 'Welcher Art die zum Grunde liegede Situation wenigstens sein könne, zeigt z.B. 1 Macc. 13, 21f. 49f., wo wir die Feinde Israels, die syrische Besatzung der von Simon belagerten Burg zu Jerusalem, vom Hunger verzehrt sehn, während es den Belagerern, deren natürlicher Mittelpunct des Heiligthum war, an Nichts fehle' (p. 129).

44. See B. Duhm, *Die Psalmen* (KHAT, 14; Tübingen: J.C.B. Mohr, 2nd edn, 1922 [1899]), pp. 99-100. 'Sein Verfasser könnte wegen der großen inneren and äußeren Aehnlichkeit dieses Psalms mit 27 1-6 ein Mann wie der Hohepriester Simon II (Sir 50) oder Onias III gewesen sein' (p. 100).

intense persecution. Jonathan was anointed as high-priest at the Feast of Tabernacles in 152 BCE; Ps. 23 was therefore composed near this event, during a period of renewed hope for Temple and people.[45]

With this last reading, the historical approach has come full circle, with the first and last readings ascribing to the psalm a personal and autobiographical focus, whether on the first king David or the late priest-king Jonathan. By interpreting the phrase 'The Lord is my Shepherd' as having been spoken by the king, or a cultic representative, or the community in exile, or an individual, or the high priest, a wide variety of interpretations can be gleaned from just one psalm. Is one reading the right one? Probably not: no single answer can adequately interpret the psalm. As we noted in the course of the study of Gen. 2–3, historical readings are a subjective process, because they have to start with the theological motifs in a passage and from this intuit as best they can the religious and social context.

Literary Approaches to Psalm 23 through the Shepherd Motif

In the discussion of a literary assessment of Gen. 2–3, it was seen that the reader's theological agenda very much influenced the marking out of boundaries for that text—for example, within a specifically Jewish tradition it is important to set the text within the Torah as a whole, and within a Christian tradition, it is set as a kind of preface to the Gospels and the teaching of Jesus Christ. To set a text within the context of Torah or Gospel gives it very different boundaries; and such delineation is usually made on the basis of particular theological assumptions brought to the text rather than arising out of it. In the case of Ps. 23, the same issue is evident. If the psalm is read within the overall context of the Hebrew Bible, a different interpretation will be found compared with a reading which places the psalm within the context of Old Testament and New Testament together. And again such a delineation of the boundaries of the psalm will have been determined by theological criteria brought to text, rather than arising out of it. How this works out in detail is developed below.

Looking at Psalm 23 as a Self-contained Poetic Prayer: Confidence within Doubt

It has already been argued that the Shepherding motif gives the psalm a completeness, whereby three vows of confidence are brought together. The

45. See M. Treves, *The Dates of the Psalms: History and Poetry in Ancient Israel* (Gennaio: Giardini Editori e Stampatori in Pisa, 1988), pp. 32-34.

themes of God's provision of rest and refreshment in the normal course of life (vv. 1-2), and of God's protection in times of danger (vv. 3-4) are brought together at the end of the psalm (vv. 5-6) where the references to God's nourishment have an additional liturgical connotation.

We noted at the beginning of this chapter that the Shepherd motif is clearer in the first four verses than it is in the latter two, where the animal imagery of vv. 1-4 recedes and the human figures of speech (vv. 5-6) take over.[46] This does not mean that in order to maintain the Shepherd motif throughout we have to force the human figures of speech into a continuation of the animal imagery, by interpreting the oil (שֶׁמֶן) as healing oil, anointing the wounds of sheep,[47] and the cup (כוֹס) as a shallow trough from which the sheep may get water,[48] and amend the final phrase as 'I will remain in the hand of the Lord' (בְּיַד־יהוה) rather than 'I will dwell in the house of the Lord' (בְּבֵית־יהוה).[49] There is a clear transformation of the figures of speech in the latter part of the psalm from pastoral, rural imagery to more homely, familial imagery, from animal figures of speech in vv. 1-4 to human figuration in vv. 5-6, from the primary emphasis on Yahweh only as Shepherd to a secondary picture of Yahweh as Host. But overall, the motifs of rest, refreshment and protection thread a progressive theme throughout the psalm, whereby the last two verses draw together what has already been developed in the earlier part of the psalm.[50]

These observations are confirmed when we note several images which recur in the first two parts of the psalm and the third. The oil and overflowing cup in v. 5 echo the restful waters and the green grass in v. 2 (indeed, there may well be some intentional paronomasia between דִּשַּׁנְתָּ בַשֶּׁמֶן (the oil of anointing) in v. 5 and בִּנְאוֹת דֶּשֶׁא (the green grass) in v. 3. So too the reference to וְחֶסֶד 'mercy' in v. 6 echoes phonetically אֶחְסָר 'I shall [not]

---

46. See Mazor, 'Psalm 23: The Lord is my Shepherd', pp. 417-18.

47. See L. Köhler, 'Psalm 23', *ZAW* 68 (1956), pp. 227-34, who sees transhumance rites as the background to the whole psalm, interpreting the later two verses as references to the healing and protecting of sheep: see p. 232.

48. See J. Morgenstern, 'Psalm 23', *JBL* 65 (1946), pp. 13-24 (here, p. 18).

49. See the discussion in Merrill, 'Psalm XXIII', p. 356, referring to E. Power's reading (see footnotes 1–4). Power also argues for emending שֻׁלְחָן (table) to שֶׁלַח (spear, javelin) to read in v. 5 'thou preparest arms for my defence'. On a similar emendation of 'house of the Lord' to 'hand of the Lord', see also Köhler, 'Psalm 23', p. 232.

50. See Kraus, *Psalms 1–59*, pp. 304-305; also Craigie, *Psalms 1–50*, pp. 204-205; also Anderson, *Psalms 1–72*, p. 195.

lack)' in v. 2, as does וֹשַׁבְתִּי 'I shall dwell' in v. 6 with יְשׁוֹבֵב 'he restores' in v. 3.[51]

In terms of structure, in vv. 1-3 as in v. 6, Yahweh is addressed in the third person (vv. 4-5, crossing over the second and third parts, address God in the second person). The repetition of the name Yahweh in v. 1 and v. 6 (the only places where the name of God occurs) form an *inclusio* around the rest of the psalm; and the three key statements of confidence by the psalmist in vv. 1, 4 and 6 ('I lack nothing'; ' I fear no evil'; and 'I shall dwell in the house of the Lord') each come at the beginning of the three sections, from a unity of confession of faith. Furthermore, vv. 4a and 5b have correspondences: 'in the valley of the shadow of death' anticipates 'in the presence of my enemies'. And finally, vv. 4c and 6a have close parallels: 'your rod and your staff' corresponds to 'goodness and mercy'; in v. 4 הֵמָּה (reading this as 'surely', an interjection, along the lines of the Ugaritic hm, rather than the pronoun 'they'[52]) parallels אַךְ ('surely' in v. 6); and יְנַחֲמֻנִי (they will comfort me) parallels יִרְדְּפוּנִי ('they will follow me'). As R. Tappy has noted, the psalm has a kind of chiasmus:[53] vv. 1 and 6 form an expression of trust at the beginning and end of the psalm, matched by a similar expression of trust in the heart of the psalm (v. 4a), enclosed by a horizontal form of address (vv. 2-3) and a vertical form of address (vv. 4b-5).[54]

In this interpretation, Ps. 23 is undoubtedly a self-contained poetic unit. Against this intrinsic unity of structure and contents and language, one might argue that the rhythm of the psalm is odd, because there is no adherence to any one consistent pattern. This problem is exacerbated by the fact that most other psalms expressing confidence and trust do have a clear and steady rhythmic pattern: the lack of it in this psalm suggests that

51. See Smith, 'Setting and Rhetoric', p. 62, referring to Y. Bazak, 'Psalm 23—A Pattern Poem', *Dor le Dor* 11 (1982–1983), pp. 71-76. See also Freedman, 'The Twenty-Third Psalm', pp. 143 and 147, and Milne, 'Psalm 23', pp. 238-39.

52. See Milne, 'Psalm 23', p. 239, using an interesting example from Ps. 43.3: שְׁלַח־אוֹרְךָ וַאֲמִתְּךָ הֵמָּה יַנְחוּנִי : 'Surely (שְׁלַח : literally, 'send') your light and your truth shall surely (הֵמָּה) lead me!')

53. R. Tappy, 'Psalm 23: Symbolism and Structure', *CBQ* 57 (1995), pp. 255-80.

54. This assent to a unifying and self-contained structure is taken one stage further by J. Bazak, 'Numerical Devices in Biblical Poetry', *VT* 38 (1988), pp. 333-37, who argues that the expression 'for you are with me' in v. 4 is found exactly midway between 26 words after the first word and 26 words the end of the psalm, whilst the 'you' refers to the Tetragrammaton, whose numerical value is itself 26: according to Bazak, this indicates an intended coherence within the psalm as a whole.

the trust is expressed within a context of some uncertainty and hesitancy.[55] Furthermore, there is a similar lack of consistent parallelism in Ps. 23, again strange, as parallelism is a poetic feature characteristic of psalms of confidence. Only v. 2 has any real evidence of the binary ideas which suggest parallelism:

> He makes me lie down in green pastures
> He leads me beside still waters...

This lack of parallelism and clear consistent rhythm is thus unusual. It could suggest the psalmist's lack of concern to present a polished poetic whole, reflecting the more turbulent side of the psalm; the dark image of the 'valley of the shadow of death'—the valley of shades, a place of imminent danger and confrontation with enemies, both physical and imagined—in the middle of the psalm, picked up by 'the presence of my enemies' in the next verse, perhaps illustrate this further. Or it could simply be that the psalmist had little interest in this more phonetic aspect of Hebrew poetry, focusing instead on the sense of the psalm, and the balance of words and phrases in the psalm as a whole.

Stylistically, the psalm could be read as a unit on its own. Its message is of a searching soul, reaching out in some uncertainty for the provision and protection of God, and it points more to the reality of human need in the midst of danger and fear than to a life of uninterrupted communion with God.[56] The confidence which dominates the psalm at the beginning and the end is thus an expression of one who is looking to future fulfilment rather than contemplating any present realization of it.[57]

---

55. The usual rhythm for a psalm of confidence is a consistent beat (2.2, 3.3, 4.4) for each line. Ps. 23 does not have such consistency of sound: only vv. 1 and 4 are sustained in a 2.2 beat (2.2.2 in v. 4), the other verses being less regular: indeed, vv. 5-6 suggest more a 3.2 stress. Thus the psalm exhibits a tension between the sense, which is coherent and integrated in the psalm as a whole, and the sound, which through the lack of rhythm and lack of parallelism breaks some of the conventions of Hebrew poetry.

56. This point is affirmed by J. Magonet in 'Through Rabbinic Eyes: Psalm 23', in *idem, A Rabbi Reads the Psalms* (London: SCM Press, 1994), pp. 64-65.

57. This reading thus runs counter to the earlier historical readings which saw the psalm as composed in the life of king David, looking *back* on what God had done at a time of earlier need, or those readings which see the psalm as a type of thanksgiving offered by any individual pilgrim in the Temple, still looking *back* on what God had done to save the pilgrim in the past. This reading sees the psalm as orientated more to the *future* than to the past; and the confidence expressed is more about the nature of God than the nature of life.

Looking at Psalm 23 in the Context of Psalms 22 and 24: Moving Towards Increasing Trust in God

The connection between Pss. 22, 23 and 24 has already been noted with regard to Merrill's theory that Ps. 22 is a psalm of the ritual suffering of the king, prefacing Ps. 23, the coronation ceremony, and Ps. 24, the procession of the ark around the sanctuary following the ceremony itself.[58] These observations are based upon a historical reading, setting the psalms in the period of the monarchy in Judah. It is possible, however, to look at these three psalms from a more literary point of view, without asking any questions about their historical setting, and still to find important connections between them.

For example, the movement in Ps. 22 is from a cry of despair (vv. 1-21) to a vow of trust (vv. 22-31); Ps. 23 picks up the same theme of trust. Just as Ps. 22 starts with the suppliant isolated from the community of faith and from the presence of God, yet returned to both by the end of the psalm, so Ps. 23 begins personally ('The Lord is *my* shepherd') and ends with the suppliant anticipating a safe restoration in the community of faith ('the house of the Lord'). In this phrase, Ps. 23 anticipates Ps. 24: 'I shall dwell in the house of the Lord for ever' (23.6).[59] In this way Ps. 23 moves on from Ps. 22, and Ps. 24 in turn takes up the theme of hope in the presence of God in the Temple in Ps. 23. Furthermore, Pss. 22 and 24 both develop the themes of the coming generations testifying to the goodness and deliverance of the Lord: Ps. 22.30 states 'men shall tell of the Lord to the coming generation (לאדני לדור), and proclaim his deliverance to a people yet unborn', whilst Ps. 24.6 records 'Such is the generation (דור) of those who seek him'. It is as if Ps. 23, anticipating Ps. 24, represents the present generation of those who seek God whilst Ps. 22, leading into Ps. 23, anticipates that faith.

The imagery of water also links together the three psalms. The suppliant in Ps. 22 sees his strength 'dried up like a potsherd' (v. 14) for he has been 'poured out like water' and his tongue cleaves to his mouth in parched thirst; he is laid in the 'dust of death'. Overall, such imagery might be read literally, concerning a plague or fever (see also Ps. 32.4), but could refer

58. See Merrill, 'Psalm XXIII', p. 360.

59. It is interesting that in the only copy of Ps. 23 (albeit fragmentary, consisting of vv. 5-6) found in the Dead Sea Scrolls—not at Qumran but at Cave Naḥal Hever—the end of the psalm runs on without a break into Ps. 24.

more metaphorically to the experience of the absence of God. This complaint of the absence of God in Ps. 22, expressed through the imagery of thirst, compares with the affirmation of the presence of God in Ps. 23, expressed through the imagery of the still waters (v. 2) and the overflowing cup (v. 5). In its water imagery, Ps. 23 is thus the corollary of Ps. 22—faith expressed through hope and trust, as compared with faith expressed through despair and fear. Psalm 24.1-2, by contrast, develops the imagery of water in another way: this takes up an ancient cosmogeny of the salt and fresh waters with dry land suspended between the space: 'he has founded it [the earth] upon the seas, and established it upon the waters'. Only Yahweh's constant vigilance allows this equilibrium to be maintained:[60] thus what Yahweh provides in terms of refreshment for the individual, both in despair (Ps. 22) and in hopeful trust (Ps. 23), he is able to do on account of his sustaining power of the cosmos (Ps. 24).[61]

How is this reading of Ps. 23 affected by placing it between a personal psalm of lament and a public liturgy of entrance to the Temple? When comparing this with our earlier reading of the psalm on its own, which concluded that the expressions of confidence in God were being offered in the midst of the uncertainties of life, this reading enables us to see the psalm's expression of trust as part of a process, rather than an end in itself. The psalm leads towards an eventual answer, in that it develops more positively the lament of Ps. 22 and anticipates the liturgical acclamation of Ps. 24. Hence in this reading, the faith of the psalmist of Ps. 23 could be seen as more resolute.[62]

---

60. See Hunter, *Psalms*, p. 135.

61. For a deconstructionist reading of Ps. 24, see D.J.A. Clines, 'A World established on Water (Psalm 24): Reader-Response, Deconstruction and Bespoke Interpretation', in J.C. Exum and D.J.A. Clines (eds.), *The New Literary Criticism and the Hebrew Bible* (JSOTSup, 143; Sheffield: JSOT Press, 1993), pp. 79-90, who observes that a faith in a God who forms a world founded on seas and rivers is hardly a securely established faith. If we are to ascend to the hill of the Lord, we need first to know that our world is indeed founded on firm bedrock. In this reading the water imagery undermines the confidence in God's favour expressed in the rest of the psalm, and stands in contrast to Ps. 23 where water imagery confirms his favour.

62. For a similar understanding of the interrelationship of Pss. 22–24, see M. Millard, *Die Komposition des Psalters* (Tübingen: J.C.B. Mohr [Paul Siebeck], 1994), pp. 135-37, who sees the psalms united in a pilgrimage theme, reflecting some yearning for being able to worship God in Zion: for example, Pss. 22.26 hints at it, Ps. 23.6 develops it, and Ps. 24 is the full expression of it.

Looking at Psalm 23 in the Context of Psalms 15–24: Confidence in the Midst of Life's Crises

By taking the entrance liturgy of Ps. 24 ('Who shall ascend the hill of the Lord?'—v. 3) and setting it alongside a similar liturgy, Ps. 15 ('O Lord, who shall sojourn in thy tent? Who shall dwell on thy holy hill?'—v. 1) it is possible to propose a larger liturgical collection of psalms, from Pss. 15–24. Within this collection, an interesting chiasmus is to be found: the second psalm and the last psalm (16, 23) are of confidence and trust, whilst the third and third last psalms (17, 22) are psalms of lament, and the fourth and fourth last psalms (18, 20–21 [taking these two battle psalms as a unity]) are royal psalms, with Ps. 19 at the heart of the collection being a celebration of the God of Creation and the God of Torah (Ps. 19a: vv. 1-6; Ps. 19b: vv. 7-14).[63] Speaking historically, it is also possible to discern a redactional process in the growth of this collection, with the royal psalms (18, 20–21) and the entrance liturgies (15, 24) originating from pre-exilic times, and the psalms of confidence (16, 23) being brought in to the collection in post-exilic times. Psalm 19 (on God as Creator and Giver of the Law, echoes in many ways the earlier theology of God as Creator and Judge in Ps. 24) and could well be the last psalm to be included in the heart of the collection.[64] Speaking with a more literary emphasis, Pss. 16 and 23 in this chiasmus may be seen as a pair: this offers some interesting interpretations of Ps. 23 when seen in comparison with its 'partner'.

Setting aside the themes of the king (Pss. 18, 20–21) and the law (Pss. 15, 19, 24) within this collection, Pss. 16 and 23, and Pss. 17 and 22 stand out in the collection as more personal prayers—the former pair being individual expressions of confidence and the latter pair, individual expressions of lament. One of the most interesting motifs linking Pss. 16 and 23 together is the expression 'my cup' (כּוֹסִי) in both psalms—the only times the term is used in the Psalter.[65] Psalm 16.5 states 'The Lord is my chosen

---

63. For one of the earliest works on this so-called collection, see P. Auffret, *La Sagesse a bâti sa maison: Études de structures littéraires dans l'Ancien Testament et spécialement dans les psaumes* (Göttingen: Vandenhoeck & Ruprecht, 1982), pp. 407-38. See also P.D. Miller, 'Kingship, Torah Obedience, and Prayer: The Theology of Psalms 15–24', in K. Seybold and E. Zenger (eds.), *Neue Wege der Psalmenforschung* (Freiburg: Herder, 1994), pp. 127-42.

64. See F.L. Hossfeld and E. Zenger, '"Wer darf hinaufziehen zum Berg YHWHS?" (Ps. 24.3). Zur Redaktionsgeschichte und Theologie der Psalmengruppe 15-24', in G. Braulik (ed.), *Lohfink Festshcrift* (Freiburg: Biblische Theologische und gesell-schaftlicher Wande, 1993), pp. 166-82.

65. See Miller, 'Kingship, Torah Obedience and Prayer', p. 135.

portion and my cup' and Ps. 23.5, 'my cup overflows'. There are other more general correspondences: the intimate expression of trust in 16.1 'Thou art my Lord' alongside Ps. 23.1 'The Lord is my Shepherd'; the well-being of body and soul in 16.9 ('my soul rejoices; my body also dwells secure') alongside the same sense of well-being in 23.2 ('he leads me beside still waters…he restores my soul'); the affirmation that God will deliver from the threat of death in the midst of life in 16.10 ('For thou dost not give me up to Sheol, or let thy godly one see the Pit') and in 23.4 ('Even though I walk through the valley of the shadow of death, I fear no evil'); the sense of being brought into the 'path of life' in 16.11 and 'the paths of righteousness' in 23.3; and the knowledge that with God there is life in abundance as long as the suppliant lives, in 16.11, 'in thy right hand are pleasures for evermore' and in 23.6, 'I shall dwell in the house of the Lord for ever'.[66]

It could be argued that such associations are overdone, because the Hebrew in the one psalm does not correspond in a formulaic way with the Hebrew of the other. But when we see the placing of Pss. 16 and 23 within the collection of Pss. 15–24 as a whole, their connection seems more convincing. For example, Ps. 16, a psalm of confidence, is followed by a psalm of lament (Ps. 17): the order is the opposite to what one would expect, although the language of these two psalms has much in common.[67] This combination works in the opposite way to Pss. 22 and 23, which, as we have seen, also have motifs in common: here the confidence follows the lament, and this moves naturally to the public liturgy, Ps. 24, as the finale of the collection. From a literary and thematic perspective, Pss. 15–24 constantly move between opposing tensions—between the public and the private, confidence and lament, and a piety focused on the king and a piety focused on the law.

How does such movement between opposites affect our interpretation of the Shepherd Motif in Ps. 23? It places this voice of trust within an ever-changing framework. It enables us to see that the affirmation of faith living in the protective presence of God (Pss. 16, 23) needs to be set against the darker backcloth of doubt living with the absence of God (Pss. 17, 22). And it also enables us to see personal piety expressed in all these four

---

66. In no sense is this list of comparisons intended to indicate any linguistic dependence on the part of the composers of each psalm; the point being made is that within the chiasmus of Pss. 15–24, these two psalms have more in common [in terms of expressions of trust] than with any other psalms in this collection.

67. See Miller, 'Kingship, Torah Obedience and Prayer', pp. 134-35.

psalms against the broader backcloth of community's theology as a whole
—a theology founded upon the royal promises to David and his house
(Pss. 18, 20–21), and established upon the teachings of the law (Pss. 15,
24 and 19).

Hence Ps. 23 becomes a smaller voice in a greater chorus. It may be that
it contains 'truths of peace and consolation…the nightingale of psalms
…small, of a homely feather, singing shyly out of obscurity…it has
charmed more griefs to rest than all the philosophy in the world'.[68] But
once a broader context is found for the psalm, it is to be read as more than
this. It was noted earlier that even of itself there are hints of some discord,
both in the medium and in the essence of the psalm.[69] This is confirmed
further by reading the psalm within the context of other less serene and
comforting psalms in the collection of 15–24; so Ps. 23 is more about the
discovery of resources for faith in the midst of the crises of life, rather than
a quiet contemplation of faith away from them.

*Looking at Psalm 23 in the Context of Psalms 1–41 (Book One): A Psalm
Sung for Temple Liturgy*
Psalm 23 is placed almost at the heart of Book I. Taking the psalm within
this larger anthology, it may be seen to have as many affiliations with the
psalms which follow it (not least, Ps. 27) as with those which precede it
(such as Ps. 16). Two key studies have looked in detail at the overall
structure of Book I.[70] Of these, the more recent article by Hossfeld and
Zenger is particularly important. This divides up Book I into smaller
groups of psalms. Taking aside Pss. 1–2, with their themes of the Torah
and the King, which is seen as a Prologue to the Psalter as a whole, Hossfeld and Zenger isolate four other sub-groups. Psalms 3–14 form a unit
with Ps. 8 at the heart, with Pss. 3–7 united under the theme of the oppres-
sive enemy and Pss. 9–10 and 11–14 linked together under the theme of

---

68. Quoted by Buttenweiser, *The Psalms*, p. 552, referring to words of an American preacher, H.W. Beecher.

69. See pp. 64-65.

70. See C. Barth, 'Concatenatio im ersten Buch des Psalters', in B. Benzing,
O. Bächer and G. Mayer (eds.), *Wort und Wirklihkeit: Studien zur afrikanistik und
orientalistik* (Festschrift E.L. Rapp; Hain: Meisenheim am Glan, 1976), pp. 30-40; and
F.-L. Hossfeld and E. Zenger, '"Selig, wer auf die Armen achtet" (Ps. 41,2): Beobachtungen zur Gottesvolk-Theologie des ersten Davidpsalters', *JBTh* 7 (1992), pp.
21-50.

God's protection of the poor.[71] Psalms 15–24 form another unit; this has been discussed previously. Psalms 25–34 create yet another unit, arranged in a chiasmus with Ps. 29 as the centre, with 25 and 34 being closely linked in their expressions of personal piety (e.g. 25.9, 16; 34.3, 7). Psalms 35–41 have Ps. 38 as the centre, with correspondences between 35 and 41 linked as prayers for help in times of need, and the collection as a whole concerned with the protection of 'the poor'.[72]

What are the implications here for our reading of Ps. 23? The psalm should be read not only in terms of the similar expressions of trust found in Ps. 16, but also in terms of its general associations with Ps. 27. Psalm 27.1 begins 'The Lord is my Light', which in its more personal expression of trust echoes Ps. 23.1 'The Lord is my Shepherd'. In Ps. 27.11, 'Teach me thy way, O Lord' has an affinity with Ps. 23.3 'He leads me in the paths of righteousness'. In Ps. 27.4, the phrase 'that I may dwell in the house of the Lord all the days of my life' (שבתי בבית־יהוה כל־ימי חיי) is particularly close to Ps. 23.6 'and I shall dwell in the house of the Lord for ever' (ושבתי בבית־יהוה לארך ימים). Finally, Ps. 27.6 'And now my head shall be lifted up above my enemies round about me' is expressed in a similar way to Ps. 23.5 'Thou preparest a table before me in the presence of my enemies'.[73] But the most important theme which links together each psalm—made more explicit in Ps. 27 than in Ps. 23—is that of being secure and protected when in the temple. Two such references are found in Ps. 27.4 ('house of the Lord': בבית־יהוה , and 'to inquire in his temple': ולבקר בהיכלו), and another in Ps. 27.5 (under the cover of his tent': בסתר אהלו), whilst Ps. 23.6 has one ('house of the Lord': בבית־יהוה).

Setting Ps. 23 in the overall context of Book I, this theme of the house of the Lord (or Temple, or holy place, or sanctuary) offering protection to the psalmist is found in other places. Most notably, it occurs in the two psalms on either side of Ps. 27: Ps. 26.8 reads 'O Lord, I love the habitation of thy house' and Ps. 28.2 has 'I lift up my hands toward thy most holy sanctuary'. The theme of God's glory in the Temple is also the climax of Ps. 29 (see v. 9: 'and in his Temple all cry, "Glory!"'). After this, the explicit references to the Temple recede towards the end of Book

71. See Hossfeld and Zenger, 'Selig, wer auf die Armen achtet', pp. 34-46 (Pss. 3–7, 11–14) and pp. 46-49 (Pss. 9–10).

72. See Hossfeld and Zenger, 'Selig, wer auf die Armen achtet', pp. 23-34.

73. See Smith, 'Setting and Rhetoric', pp. 61-62; also Gunkel, *Die Psalmen übersetzt und erklärt*, pp. 100-101; Freedman, 'The Twenty-Third Psalm', pp. 162-63; and Barré and Kselman, 'New Exodus', p. 115.

I, where the theme moves on more generally to that of the oppression of
the poor and prayer for God's help. It was noted earlier that Ps. 24 may be
read as a liturgy for entrance to the Temple. Thus Pss. 22–29 (with an
interesting exception in Ps. 25, at the heart of this unit) form an interesting
nucleus within Book I as a whole: they are a group of psalms which highlight the resources that are to be found in the 'house of God'.

Within this broader literary context, Ps. 23 is to be read not as a general
cult-free spiritual song—with a faith in God founded upon the realities of
life but independent of the liturgical traditions of the people—but as a
psalm embedded in liturgy, advocating the importance of finding God in
his 'house'. If the psalm is to be read as having a liturgical orientation, the
reference to 'God as Shepherd' may thus be interpreted as the one who
tends his flock not only in the midst of life but who also brings his sheep
safely home to their dwelling place: the Temple, like the sheepfold, is the
place of safety and security provided by God himself, out of his steadfast
mercy for his people.

Book I (the first 'Davidic Psalter') is characterized by its superscriptions
ascribing the psalms in honour of David. Only three psalms do not have a
Davidic heading in this collection (Pss. 8, 10 and 33, of which Ps. 10 may
be excluded as a continuous part of Ps. 9). Given the associations of David
with the founding of the Temple (developed, for example, by the Chroni-
cler) the Davidic heading could be seen to create not so much a biographical
reading, linking the psalm back to the best-known king of Israel, but a more
liturgical one, linking the psalm back to the king who 'founded' the Temple.
This Temple theme, implicit in the Davidic headings, is brought to the fore
in psalms that form the heart of Book I (Pss. 22–29). When Ps. 23 was
placed in the setting of Pss. 15–24, the psalm was given a broader perspective of faith in all its variety; by contrast, when the psalm is placed within
Book I as a whole this gives the expression of faith a more liturgical focus.

*Looking at Psalm 23 in the Context of the Psalter as a Whole: A Daring
Expression of Personal Faith*
The only other reference to God as Shepherd in the Psalter is found in Ps.
80.1: 'Give ear, O Shepherd of Israel, thou who leadest Joseph like a flock!'
Setting aside whether this may be a psalm with northern associations, and
hence whether the designation of God as Shepherd of his people may be of
northern origins, the important point for our purposes is that this is a corporate designation of the title 'shepherd of Israel' (רעה ישׂראל). This is
confirmed by other references in the Psalter (three of which are found in
Book III) to the people as God's flock, or as God's sheep: for example, Ps.

74.1 'O God, why dost thou cast us off for ever? Why does thy anger smoke against the sheep of thy pasture?' (בצאן מרעיתך); Ps. 78.52 'Then he led forth his people like sheep (כצאן) and guided them in the wilderness like a flock' (כעדר); Ps. 79.13 'Then we are thy people, the flock of thy pasture' (וצאן מרעיתך). Within Book IV, there are two examples: Ps. 95.7 reads 'For he is our God, and we are the people of his pasture, and the sheep of his hand' (ואנחנו עם מרעיתו וצאן) and Ps. 100.3 reads 'Know that the Lord is God! It is he that made us, and we are his [*or,* and not we ourselves]; we are his people, and the sheep of his pasture' (עמו וצאן מרעיתו). Two of these examples (74 and 79) are part of the communal lament form, and two (95, 100) are found in hymns, indicating further the communal liturgical setting for this designation and understanding of God. Their occurrence in Books III and IV, where the emphasis on communal psalmody is more noticeable, is also significant.

Psalm 78, a historical psalm, could be seen as a commentary on Psalm 23, not only in its designation of God as shepherd (v. 52), but also in its transference of the title to David as king (vv. 70-71: 'He chose David his servant...to be the shepherd of Jacob his people'). We noted earlier how Ps. 78 combines together the imagery of God as Shepherd with the Exodus themes of the escape through the sea and the Wilderness theme of provision and leading (using the verb נחל) in the journey through the desert, two themes which are also found in Ps. 23.[74] Its linking of this theme to the importance of David at the end of the psalm (Ps. 78.70-71) links it further to Ps. 23, with its Davidic superscription.

Thus our reading of the Shepherd Motif in Ps. 23 could take one of two directions. Either we could give the psalm a communal interpretation, alongside all the other psalms that use the same theme and are more clearly communal in orientation (noting that what adds to this in Ps. 23 is the reference to David in the superscription, giving the psalm the same royal/national concerns as Ps. 78). Or we could see that Ps. 23 applies these corporate traditions in a new individualized sense: 'the Lord is *my* Shepherd'. Hence rather than Ps. 78 being seen as a commentary on Ps. 23, the reverse becomes the case, with the traditions of the people and the king being democratized and used as resources for personal faith. This would place Ps. 23 much closer to the personal prayers of the Songs of Ascents, with its similar pilgrimage theme; it was never included into that collection because by the time of compilation it had a part already in the collec-

---

74. See Milne, 'Psalm 23', pp. 240 and 242; also Freedman, 'The Twenty-Third Psalm', pp. 148-49.

tion of Pss. 15–24 instead. Yet even in the particular collection where it is found, the argument for it being a personal rather than communal prayer is strong: Ps. 16, the partner to Ps. 23 in the collection, is undoubtedly personal in its emphasis.

In this way of reading Ps. 23 within the Psalter as a whole, it becomes a striking example of a *deconstruction* of the Shepherd Motif found elsewhere: instead of the traditional corporate meaning, Ps. 23 offers a daring personal appropriation of the term.[75]

Looking at Psalm 23 within the Hebrew Bible as a Whole: Looking Towards the Future Hope of Israel

One of the significant developments in the shepherding imagery outside the Psalter is the way the phrases 'Shepherd of Israel' (referring to God) and 'shepherd(s) of Israel' (referring to the community's leaders) are both used from exilic times onwards in the context of some future hope. In terms of God as Shepherd, the imagery is found in Jer. 23.3 ('Then I will gather the remnant of my flock out of all the countries where I have driven them') and Jer. 31.10 ('He who scattered Israel will gather him, and will keep him as a shepherd keeps his flock'). It is also found in Ezek. 34.9-11, in the context of the people falling foul of 'false shepherds', so that God becomes the true shepherd of his flock: 'Behold I, I myself will search for my sheep, and will seek them out.' It is used similarly to describe God's returning the exiles to their land in Isa. 40.1-11 ('He will feed his flock like a shepherd, he will gather the lambs in his arms…') and in Isa. 49.8-10 ('they shall feed along the ways, on all bare heights shall be their pasture;…for he who has pity on them shall lead them…'). In restoration times, the future orientation of the term applied to God still persists: see, for example, Zech. 10.2, 3 ('Therefore my people wander like sheep; they are afflicted for want of a shepherd…for the Lord of hosts cares for his flock, the house of Judah, and will make them like his proud steed in battle…').

In these examples the future hoped for is to take place within a this-worldly context—the restoration of the people to the land. In later tradi-

---

75. In this reading, the Davidic heading serves to confirm the more individual and biographical bias of the psalm, rather than the liturgical one, noted earlier. The close affiliation of רעה 'to pasture the flock' with רעה 'to be a friend' should also be noted in this context: רעי ('my friend') is close in sound to רעי ('my shepherd'). See 1 Kgs 4.5, where Zabud, Nathan's son, is described as רעה המלך (LXX: ἑταῖρος τοῦ βασιλέως)—the king's friend.

tion, the references to God as Shepherd begin to take on an other-worldly meaning. The gradual transference can be seen in passages such as Sir. 18.13, 14, where God is described as the universal shepherd, teaching the whole of mankind, and 2 Esd. 2.34, where the picture takes on a more other-worldly and eschatological dimension: 'Await your shepherd: he will give you everlasting rest, because he who will come at the end of the age is close at hand.'

Another example of this more future-orientated image, also found in literature from this later intertestamental period, is not so much of God as the coming Shepherd but rather of another Davidic king as the coming Shepherd of his flock. *Psalms of Solomon* 17.21-46 is an interesting example, where the picture focuses mainly on a more this-worldly figure. For example, the prayer in vv. 21-22, 46: 'Behold, O Lord, and raise up for them their king, the son of David...and purify Jerusalem of the nations which trample her down in destruction...shepherding the flock of the Lord faithfully and righteously.'

In later tradition, as the images of God as Shepherd and another Davidic king as Shepherd were directed increasingly towards the future, Ps. 23 itself could have been read within this more corporate and eschatological context. The psalm is indeed about hope, perhaps originally about the more personal and individual hope within the life of the psalmist; but the hope could also be seen as concerning the community of faith and their corporate restoration.[76]

Thus Ps. 23 begins to take on an eschatological tone in context of the theme of Shepherd in the Hebrew Bible as a whole. We may see again how this deconstructs earlier readings. For example, references to the 'future life' could now be interpreted not with a this-worldly meaning, but in other-worldly terms instead. Expressions such as 'the valley of the shadow of death' and 'dwelling in the house of the Lord for ever' could now refer to a future hope beyond death; the descriptions of being fed and watered could be seen as references to the heavenly banquet of the faithful departed; and the staff of protection could be read as the Torah, the means of preparing the community for life forever with God.[77]

---

76. This is the way in which Jewish commentators have often read the psalm: see Braude, *Midrash on the Psalms*, pp. 332-33, and Cohen, תהלים, p. 67.

77. Ps. 23 was of course not the only psalm to be read in this way. But it serves as an example of the ways in which liturgical texts began to take on an eschatological reading. That this was the practice at Qumran is evident in the tradition of David as having the divine gift of prophecy as in 11Q5 xxvii.2-11: the psalms are thus texts

Looking at Psalm 23 within the Christian Bible: The Fulfilment of Prophecy
The Christian interpretation of the psalms was initially influenced by the
Jewish interpretations referred to above, with their more eschatological
and other-worldly bias. But rather than looking ahead to a distant future or
a time beyond death when the words of 'psalmic prophecy' might be fulfilled, the Christian reading of psalmody turns this process on its head.
These are prophetic words, and they have begun to be fulfilled in the life
of Christ here and now and they are continuing to be fulfilled in the life of
the Christian community.[78]

This means that as far as Ps. 23 is concerned, the words which were
once read as a prayer in the life of an individual or the community now
take on a emphasis as 'realized eschatology'. The image of God as Shepherd was undoubtedly an influence in this respect. The early Christian
tradition, with its understanding of Christ as the Good Shepherd (taken in
the main from Jn 10.1-18) used this psalm extensively as a commentary on
the person and work of Christ and the ways in which he had fulfilled the
hopes expressed by the psalmist.[79] This was the Good Shepherd who laid
down his life for his sheep (Jn 10.11), the one who knows his own and
whose own know him (Jn 10.14).[80]

which give the community a hope in a new and different future. Although Ps. 23 is not
explicitly used as part of the *pesher* method of exegesis by the community, this form of
prophetic and eschatological interpretation has been found to have been used for other
psalms (e.g. 37, 45, 57, 68 and 127) and this further illustrates that a future-orientated
reading of the psalms was a common practice by the time of Qumran. See, for example, P.W. Flint, *The Dead Sea Scrolls and the Book of Psalms* (Leiden: E.J. Brill,
1997), pp. 218-19.

78.   It is no surprise to read that, like Qumran, the New Testament portrays 'David'
not only as the 'author' of the psalms, but also as a 'prophet' whose words are now
being fulfilled: see, for example, Acts 2.29-33, with the writers of the New Testament
exercising a similar *pesher* approach to the psalms as that used in Qumran. See, for
example, W.L. Holladay, *The Psalms through Three Thousand Years* (Minneapolis:
Fortress Press, 1993), pp. 115-30.

79.   Shepherding imagery occurs frequently in the Synoptic Gospels as well as in
John. Mk. 6.34 speaks of Christ pitying the crowd, seeing them as sheep without a
shepherd; Mt. 15.24 refers to Christ who has come to the lost sheep of the house of
Israel; Lk. 15.3-6 relates the parable of the lost sheep, found by the faithful shepherd.

80.   Ps. 23 is not the only sub-text here. We may refer back to Ezek. 34.11-16 and
23–24, and to the suffering shepherd in Zech. 9–13 (see especially Zech. 13.7). Some
of the very earliest representations of Christ on engravings in the catacombs of second-
century Rome are of Christ as the Good Shepherd, and some two centuries later,
statues from post-Constantinian Rome depict Christ in the same way: the Shepherd

From an understanding of Christ as the Good Shepherd of Ps. 23, a number of variant readings of other motifs in the psalm became possible. The references to anointing (v. 5) were seen to be direct references to Christ's, the anointed one, who carried the cup of suffering (v. 5) in the presence of God's enemies (v. 5) for others. The waters of rest and refreshment (v. 2) were seen to be references to the cleansing and renewing waters of Baptism, and the motif of feasting at God's table (v. 5) was understood as an allusion to participation in the Eucharist. The confidence in dwelling in God's presence 'for ever' (v. 6), thus conquering the dark shades of the valley of death (v. 4), allowed the psalm to be read in the light of the Christian belief in the resurrection from the dead—a belief which is as much about a present experience as about future hope. And the psalmist's affirmation of being secure in the house of the Lord (v. 6) was now seen not as a reference to the physical Temple but to living in the fellowship of God's people, the church, not only now, but 'forever' into eternity.

The key characteristic of this prophetic interpretation of Ps. 23 is that it seeks to apply as many motifs as possible 'Christwards'. This is quite different from earlier readings. The focus is no longer on the appropriation of the language of prayer in a typical and repeatable way; what was once a liturgical text with a universal application about the life of faith and doubt is now a prophetic text with a particular focus on the life of Christ and his church.[81]

Some Final Observations

We have noted some dramatic shifts of meaning in the ways in which the psalm would have been read within the Hebrew Bible as a whole, but it is when it is read within the context of the Old and New Testament overall that the greatest change in interpretation is to be found. This is because the historical focus and the literary boundaries are applied in an entirely different way. From a positive point of view, it could be argued that this is an

motif, found throughout the Hebrew Bible, abut perhaps most personally expressed in Ps. 23, becomes an important means of interpreting the person and work of Christ.

81. This mode of interpretation of psalmody survived for several centuries CE. One interesting example of it is that as late as the sixth century, Junilius Africanus places the Psalter with the Prophets in his canonical collection: see *Instituta regularia* I, 4, referred to in J.-M. Auwers, *La Composition Littéraire du Psautier: Un État de la Question* (Paris: J. Gabalda et Cie Éditeurs, 2000), pp. 173-74.

'opening up' of new vistas, and it is not as dramatic as it might first appear: much in the Christian prophetic reading has been prepared for by late Jewish modes of eschatological reading.

There is partial truth in this observation. But speaking more realistically, we have to accept that there is a world of difference between a text such as Ps. 23 being read from an anthropocentric perspective and then a Christocentric one. We have seen how a Christian reading of Gen. 2–3 took the attention away from Adam (who is seen as representing all people) and transferred this to Christ, creating a whole range of new meanings. So too a similar range of new meanings occur when a Christian reading of Ps. 23 takes the focus away from David (who like Adam in Genesis, becomes in liturgical use an archetypal figure), and transfers it to Christ. The psalm is no longer about David; it is about Christ.

This is not to undermine a Christian reading of Ps. 23. It is practice which has fed Christian faith for centuries. But, especially in the context of a plea for multivalency, greater honesty is required in recognizing how much deconstruction has taken place in the process of reading. A Christian reading, distinctive and important as it is, must be held alongside (rather than above) other valid interpretations: no one reading has a monopoly over all others.

Chapter 4

IN AND OUT OF THE LAWCOURTS:
MULTIVALENT READINGS IN AMOS

[5.1]Hear this word which I take up over you in lamentation, O house of Israel:
[2]'Fallen, no more to rise,
is the virgin Israel;
forsaken on her land,
with none to raise her up.'

[3]For thus says the LORD God:
'The city that went forth a thousand
shall have a hundred left,
and that which went forth a hundred
shall have ten left
to the house of Israel.'

[4]For thus says the LORD to the house of Israel:
'Seek me and live;
[5]but do not seek Bethel,
and do not enter into Gilgal
or cross over to Beer-sheba;
or Gilgal shall surely go into exile,
and Bethel shall come to nought.'

[6]Seek the LORD and live,
lest he break out like fire in the house of Joseph,
and it devour, with none to quench it for Bethel,
[7]O you who turn justice to wormwood,
and cast down righteousness to the earth!

[8]He who made the Plei'ades and Orion,
and turns deep darkness into the morning,
and darkens the day into night,
who calls for the waters of the sea,
and pours them out upon the surface of the earth,
the LORD is his name,
[9]who makes destruction flash forth against the strong,
so that destruction comes upon the fortress.

¹⁰They hate him who reproves in the gate,
and they abhor him who speaks the truth.
¹¹Therefore because you trample upon the poor
and take from him exactions of wheat,
you have built houses of hewn stone,
but you shall not dwell in them;
you have planted pleasant vineyards,
but you shall not drink their wine.
¹²For I know how many are your transgressions,
and how great are your sins —
you who afflict the righteous, who take a bribe,
and turn aside the needy in the gate.
¹³Therefore he who is prudent will keep silent in such a time;
for it is an evil time.

¹⁴Seek good, and not evil,
that you may live;
and so the LORD, the God of hosts, will be with you,
as you have said.
¹⁵Hate evil, and love good,
and establish justice in the gate;
it may be that the LORD, the God of hosts,
will be gracious to the remnant of Joseph.

¹⁶Therefore thus says the LORD, the God of hosts, the LORD:
'In all the squares there shall be wailing;
and in all the streets they shall say, "Alas! alas!"
They shall call the farmers to mourning
and to wailing those who are skilled in lamentation,
¹⁷and in all vineyards there shall be wailing,
for I will pass through the midst of you,' says the LORD.

¹⁸Woe to you who desire the day of the LORD!
Why would you have the day of the LORD?
It is darkness, and not light;
¹⁹as if a man fled from a lion,
and a bear met him;
or went into the house
and leaned with his hand against the wall, and a serpent bit him.
²⁰Is not the day of the LORD darkness, and not light,
and gloom with no brightness in it?

²¹I hate, I despise your feasts,
and I take no delight in your solemn assemblies.
²²Even though you offer me your burnt offerings and cereal offerings,
I will not accept them,

and the peace offerings of your fatted beasts
I will not look upon.
²³Take away from me the noise of your songs;
to the melody of your harps I will not listen.
²⁴But let justice roll down like waters,
and righteousness like an ever-flowing stream.
²⁵'Did you bring to me sacrifices and offerings the forty years in the wilderness, O house of Israel? ²⁶You shall take up Sakkuth your king, and Kaiwan your star-god, your images, which you made for yourselves; ²⁷therefore I will take you into exile beyond Damascus,' says the LORD, whose name is the God of hosts.

Compared with the archetypal stories in Gen. 1–11 and the liturgical prayers in the Psalter, prophetic texts are usually more specifically rooted within the social and religious life of ancient Israel, being part of a particular dialogue between a prophet and his audience. This difference raises some interesting questions about reading such texts in multivalent ways.

Amos 5.18-27, the text under consideration, provides a good example of multivalent readings within the prophetic literature. The section is an indictment against a people who are anticipating the 'day of the Lord' as a day of celebration (probably involving some military victory over their enemies), and the prophet's message is a clear reversal of that expectation, announcing that the day of the Lord will be 'darkness, not light': those who do not execute justice and righteousness within their own community have no right to expect justice and righteousness from their God. Such a message is clearly embedded in specific social and religious issues of the day, and we cannot fully understand its impact without asking questions about the identity of this people and the particular concerns of this speaker. There may be no clear answers to such historical questions, but this does not negate the fact that the text addresses a particular historical situation: universal concerns, evidenced so clearly in the Garden of Eden story and 'the Shepherd psalm', are secondary. In this way, reading a prophetic text with a *historical* lens is a vital part of understanding it—more so than is the case with non-prophetic texts such as Gen. 2–3 and Ps. 23.

This is not to say that we can know with any certainty which proposed historical setting may be the most convincing. A number of possible contexts for Amos 5.18-27 will be proposed, each of them illustrating the particularity of the message in multivalent ways.

Multivalency is evident not only in historical approaches to reading the text, but in literary approaches as well. By gradual movement of the outward limits of the text (in the same way as we have done with Gen. 2–3 and Ps. 23) the meaning changes subtly every time. Amos 5.18-27 offers one particular emphasis if it is read on its own, but if the whole of chapter 5 is included, another layer of meaning can be added; and if the boundaries include Amos 3–6, still another reading may be found. There would be yet others if the literary framework were the whole book of Amos, or the overall collection of the twelve prophets, or the Hebrew Bible. The most marked reconstruction of the text occurs when it was read within the literary framework of the New Testament and Old Testaments together.

Such multivalency, whether of a historical or a literary nature, requires a focal *Leitmotif*. Just as the motifs of knowledge and of shepherding were the foci for Gen. 2–3 and Ps. 23, there is also a dominant motif in Amos 5—that of 'justice and righteousness'. This is found explicitly in Amos 5.24, and is the climax of the indictment in the whole section. The verse runs as follows:

> But let justice (מִשְׁפָּט) roll down like waters,
> and righteousness (צְדָקָה) like an ever-flowing stream.

By employing 'justice and righteousness' (מִשְׁפָּט and צְדָקָה) as a *Leitmotif*, it is apparent that these terms offer a focus for multivalent readings, whether starting from a hypothetical historical or literary context. There is some continuity, but there are also constant changes in perception.

Historical Readings of Amos 5.18-27:
Where is 'Justice and Righteousness' to be Found?

Although the heart of the following analysis is to be found in vv. 21-24, with the *Leitmotif* as the climax to it, the preceding verses (vv. 18-20, with their woes against the people's complacency) have been included as well, for they provide some preparation for what is to come, and the following verses (vv. 25-27, with their focus on the ultimate threat of exile) have also been included in that they provide some explanation for the pericope before it. But the key passage is undoubtedly vv. 21-24, and the historical questions, working through several possible stages of development, will be mostly concerned with these verses as the central unit.[1]

---

1.   On the division of 5.18-27 into three units, with vv. 21-24 at the heart of them, see commentaries as diverse as F.I. Anderson and D.N. Freedman, *Amos: A New Translation with Introduction and Commentary* (AB, 24A; Garden City, NY: Doubleday,

Justice and Righteousness in the Eighth-Century Message of Amos the Prophet: Divine Judgment on Human Responsibility

A notable feature of scholarship since the mid-eighties has been the number of commentators who are confident that Amos 5.21-24 originates from Amos the eighth-century prophet.[2] They assume that the prophet's vision of the forthcoming destruction of Israel initially was of a cataclysmic natural disaster, and that the earthquake which occurred shortly after his departure from the northern kingdom would have ratified this message of judgment.[3] This relatively new confidence in the eighth-century context of this passage arises from an equal confidence (again, unusual in the light of earlier scholarship) that the heart of the book comprises elements of chapters 3–4 and 5–6, compiled from early traditions of Amos's preaching by later editors: this may be seen in the use of the introductions 'Hear this word…' before both sections, at 3.1 and 5.1.[4] Taken together, these four

1989), p. 523, and W.R. Harper, *A Critical and Exegetical Commentary on Amos and Hosea* (ICC; New York: Charles Scribner's Sons, 1905), pp. 129-41. Even if one takes the unit as vv. 21-27, as, for example, J.A. Soggin, *The Prophet Amos: A Translation and Commentary* (OTL; London: SCM Press, 1987), pp. 96-101, and H.W. Wolff, *Joel and Amos: A Commentary on the Books of the Prophets Joel and Amos* (Hermeneia; Philadelphia: Fortress Press, 1977), pp. 258-68, v. 24 is still the pivotal point, with vv. 21-23 and vv. 25-27 in different ways emphasizing the people's insufficiency. But to add on vv. 18-20 is critical, for it prepares the way for the point that judgment is inevitable, and no human effort can divert it.

2. For example, see J.H. Hayes, *Amos: The Eighth-Century Prophet. His Times and his Preaching* (Nashville: Abingdon Press, 1988); Anderson and Freedman, *Amos*; S.M. Paul, *Amos: A Commentary on the Book of Amos* (Hermeneia; Minneapolis: Fortress Press, 1991); M.E. Polley, *Amos and the Davidic Empire: A Socio-Historical Approach* (Oxford: Oxford University Press, 1989); S.N. Rosenbaum, *Amos of Israel: A New Interpretation* (Macon, GA: Mercer University Press, 1990).

3. See, for example, D.N. Freedman and A. Welch, 'Amos's Earthquake and Israelite Prophecy', in M.D. Coogan *et al.* (eds.), *Scripture and Other Artifacts: Essays in Honor of Philip J. King* (Louisville, KY: Westminster/John Knox Press, 1994), pp. 188-98.

4. Although 4.1 has a similar introduction ('Hear this word') both 3.1 and 5.1 are followed by a relative clause, whilst 4.1 has no such clause; it is more likely that chapters 3 and 4 form one pair, and 5 and 6, another pair. 3.1, although probably an original heading to the collection of chapters 3–4, has been expanded, introducing Yahweh as speaker ('Hear this word that the Lord has spoken against you') and addressing the whole people as sons (בני) of Israel (3.1, 12; see also 4.5). (5.1 by contrast introduces the prophet as speaker ['Hear this word which I take up over you'] and 5.4, 25 and 6.1, 14 by contrast address the northern kingdom with the term 'house' (בית) of Israel). See J. Jeremias, 'Amos 3–6: From the Oral Word to the Text', in G.M.

chapters focus on the reasons for the coming disaster, laying the blame for the corruption of justice on all levels of society, particularly the sanctuaries at Bethel (4.4-5; 5.4-5; see also 7.10-17) and Samaria (3.9-4.3 and 6.1-11).[5]

Some commentators, believing that the visions in Amos 7 must have happened before these oracles, argue that the judgment threatened in Amos 3–4 and 5–6 is the result of an earlier stage after the prophet's initial longing for the people to repent (7.1-3, 4-6) at a time when he gradually saw the judgment as inevitable (7.7-9). This gives the tenor of the indictment in chapters 3–4 and 5–6 even more force.[6]

It is possible to use another chronological approach in the book, whereby chapters 1.1–7.9 are seen as a collection of oracles delivered before the encounter of Amos and Amaziah at Bethel (7.10-17) whereas chapters 8 and 9, with more allusions to God's favour of Judah, have been added some time after this encounter.[7] This would result in seeing chapters 5–6 as less bleak than, say, chapter 8, for they would be more of a *threat* of judgment than an *announcement* of it. Another adaptation of the message would be to interpret the favourable view of Judah in the book as part of Amos's own bias, present from the beginning of his message, not a

Tucker, D.L. Petersen and R.R. Wilson (eds.), *Canon, Theology and Old Testament Interpretation: Essays in Honor of Brevard S. Childs* (Philadelphia: Fortress Press, 1988), pp. 217-29, especially pp. 223-25.

5.   If indeed the more localized, personal indictments are earlier, and only later are connected together to broaden the judgment on individual sanctuaries to include larger representative groups of people, then this would again suggest that these oracles are more likely to be from Amos's own preaching.

6.   See Anderson and Freedman, *Amos*, pp. 5-8, who argue that Amos's ministry actually begins with the two visions in 7.1-6, where the prophet still sees repentance as possible. Chapters 5–6, with the three woe sections, thus belong to this early phase where Israel is still under call to repent. The third and fourth visions pertain to a later stage, where punishment is unavoidable (7.8, 8.2): chs. 1–2, with its reversal theme of judgment against Israel, and chs. 3–4, which develops further this theme of doom, belong to this period.

7.   The first collection would thus comprise judgment on nations (1, 2), the 'Hear this word' prophecies (3, 4, 5.1-6), the three 'woe to' denunciations (5.7, 5.18, 6.1) and the three visions (7.1, 4, 7). The second collection, following a turning point in Amos's attitude to Israel after the hostile encounter with Amaziah, would emphasize utter judgment on Israel *but* hope for the survival of his own people, Judah (9.11-12). See, for example, R. Gordis, 'The Composition and Structure of Amos', in *idem*, *Poets, Prophets and Sages: Essays in Biblical Interpretation* (Bloomington: Indiana University Press, 1971), pp. 217-29, especially pp. 223-25.

result of it. This would mean that the judgment speeches are intended more for Israel alone, and their negative content is thus heightened.[8] A more extreme position, still assuming much of Amos 5 to be an essential part of Amos's own message, is the proposal that almost all the speeches were given on one single occasion, during an autumnal festival, near the end of the reign of Jeroboam II.[9] In this case the judgment is intensive and unremitting—Israel has broken her relationship with God and will suffer for it.

In spite of the variations in views about chronology, the general agreement throughout all these more recent commentators is that chapter 5 forms an intrinsic part of Amos's own message, and that it belongs to an early stage of it. This has several implications for an understanding of the motif of 'justice and righteousness' in 5.24. Three interrelated interpretations may be proposed.

'Justice and Righteousness' as Initiated by God. This can be understood in two ways—either as a means of explaining the forthcoming judgment on the people, or a last-resort offer of salvation.

Divine Justice as Judgment: A Case for Theodicy. If one sees this as essentially about judgment, with the prophet inveighing against the religious and social evils of the northern kingdom, threatening the people with some violent end if they do not mend their ways by reforming their cultic life, the appeal to 'justice and righteousness' is a means of explaining that this coming disaster is not arbitrary or accidental, but emanates from the just and righteous purpose of God. Amos 5.24 is an important verse in this interpretation. One could translate the Hebrew verb וְיִגַּל (meaning 'roll down', and used once to refer to both nouns) by way of a jussive: '*Let* justice roll down like waters...*let* righteousness roll down like an everflowing stream.' This puts more emphasis on the responsibility of the people. But וְיִגַּל could also be translated as an imperfect, using the tense of the verb as if it were an action not yet completed: in this way the

8. See, for example, Polley, *Amos and the Davidic Empire*, pp. 107-111, who argues that Amos is pleading for the righteous remnant in the north to join with the Davidic dynasty in Judah—thus seeing the polemic as pro-southern rather than anti-northern *per se*.

9. See Hayes, *Amos: The Eighth-Century Prophet*, p. 47 and pp. 178-79; the basic theme of the reversal of the hopes of the coming day of the Lord at such a festival would be the loss of fertility as a result of abuse of prosperity, and the loss of territory in war with Assyria as a result of the abuse of the gift of the land.

verse would read 'Justice *will* roll down like waters… Righteousness *will* roll down like an everflowing stream.' In this reading, the implication is that this is to be brought about as an act of God: the people can do little to avert God's act of judgment.[10]

This latter meaning is highly plausible. It is clear that Amos foresees a natural disaster is about to take place (see Amos 4.6-12, which compares God's judgment with the plagues against the Egyptians, and Amos 5.16-17, which describes its effects on the land and its fertility). The God who controls the cycles of nature must be within this act (see Amos 4.6-11: the 'I' form that emphasizes God is the subject of all this) and because this God loves justice (Amos 5.15), the crisis about to happen must be due to his righteous judgment.[11] The wealthy have abused their right to possess land by their corruption of justice, so God must hold them accountable by removing his own presence from the land as a whole and hence allowing natural disaster to engulf them.[12] An example of Amos's disdain for the pretence of the people, whose lives are tainting the cult through their injustice towards their neighbour, is seen in the force of the human and divine contrasts in 5.21-23—'*your* feasts…*your* solemn assemblies…*your* burnt offerings' and '*I* hate…*I* despise…*I* take no delight in…'

If this more theologically-orientated approach to justice is indeed part of Amos's own message, it marks the beginnings of a 'theodicy', where the actions of God in inflicting suffering on his chosen people are defended as 'just' and 'right'.

Divine Justice as Salvation: A Conditional Promise. It may be that within this unit, the preaching of Amos has not yet reached the final point of announcement of crisis; here there are only the threats of it. In this case, the appeal to 'justice and righteousness' still concerns the action of God, rather than an appeal for action from the people; but it is about God

10. See J.L. Berquist, 'Dangerous Waters of Justice and Righteousness: Amos 5.18-27', *BTB* 23 (1993), pp. 54-63, especially p. 56.

11. See S.E. Gillingham, ' "Who Makes the Morning Darkness": God and Creation in the Book of Amos', *SJT* 45 (1992), pp. 165-84, especially pp. 174-77.

12. This resembles the Yahwist's account of the punishment on Adam and Eve, and later on Cain, in Gen. 2–3 and 4—the land will produce 'thorns and thistles' (Gen. 3.16). Cain is 'cursed from the ground' which will 'no longer yield to you its strength' (4.11-12). See also W. Schottroff, 'The Prophet Amos: A Socio-Historical Assessment of His Ministry', in W. Schottroff and W. Stegemann (eds.), *God of the Lowly: Socio-Historical Interpretations of the Bible* (trans. M.J. O'Connell; Maryknoll, NY: Orbis Books, 1984), pp. 27-46, especially p. 40.

offering the possibility of an alternative future.[13] He is giver of life and the promoter of order in the community; his mercy is greater than his anger. Thus the offer of the divine qualities of justice and righteousness to the people (how it will come about is not made clear from this verse) is a means of enabling the people to escape chaos and death.[14] Elsewhere 'righteousness' (צדקה) is often paired with 'salvation' (ישׁועה) and the two together could be translated as 'saving acts'.[15] Amos 5.21-24 could thus be read as pleading with the people to stop their preoccupation with excessive cultic activity, which is an attempt on their part to placate and control God, and instead advocating that they turn to Yahweh in all humility and dependence, so that he can send his deliverance and salvation to them. This then will result in justice and righteousness flowing out through the land for the right ordering of society. This interpretation thus sees 5.24 as a conditional promise of salvation.[16]

'Justice and Righteousness' as Initiated by the People. This reading emphasizes instead the jussive form of the verb יגל reading it as 'let (justice) roll down...let (righteousness) roll down...', and hence focuses on what humans can and should do, rather than what God will do. It presumes again that the timing of the passage is from an earlier stage in Amos's preaching, when the prophet hoped that the people might yet change their ways. It is thus to be read as a *threat* of judgment, rather than an *announcement* of it. There are again two ways in which this might be read.

Justice and Righteousness as the Responsibility of the Courts of Law. This presumes a plea for specific acts of justice—acts which the people would

13. See Gordis, 'The Composition and Structure of Amos'. See also J. Jeremias, *The Book of Amos* (trans. D.W. Stott; OTL; Louisville, KY: Westminster/John Knox Press, 1998), pp. 103-104.

14. This view on the establishment of justice as a gift which only God can bring about is argued by S.S. Schwarzschild, 'Justice', in *Encyclopedia Judaica*, X (Jerusalem: Keter Publishing House, 4th edn, 1978), pp. 476-77, using passages such as Gen. 18.25 and Deut. 13.5.

15. On צדקה alone as 'deliverance' or as 'saving acts', see, for example, Isa. 41.2 and Judg. 5.11 and Mic. 6.11 (where the term is often translated as 'triumph' or 'victory', particularly when the plural form is used). On the pairing of צדקה and ישׁעה, see, for example, Isa. 51.5-8, where the pairing occurs three times; משׁפט and ישׁעה can also be paired together—for example in Deut. 33.21.

16. On this view, see J.P. Hyatt, 'The Translation and Meaning of Amos 5.23-24', *ZAW* 68 (1956), pp. 17-24, especially p. 24.

be informed about, for they would have been taught them by cultic officials at local sanctuaries and witnessed their execution (or the abuses of it)
in the local courts of law held by the city gates (Amos 5.15).[17] Even
though the people may not have known the Covenant Code in Exod.
20.22–23.33 in the form we now have it, it is clear from references to the
oppression of the poor in Amos 2.7 and 4.1 (corresponding with Exod.
21.2-7), and from specific cases such as the keeping of garments taken in
pledge in Amos 2.8 (see Exod. 22.26-27), the perversion of justice by way
of taking bribes in Amos 5.10, 12 (see Exod. 23.6-8) and the exacting of
interest from the poor in Amos 5.11, 8.4 (see Exod. 22.25) that recognizable acts of injustice are being cited. The point at issue is the way that
cultic officials and judges alike abuse their power by conspiring with the
rich and exploiting the poor who have no right of redress; the same theme
runs throughout the relevant passages in Amos 2.6-8, 5.10-12 and 8.4-6.
And ultimately the accountability goes beyond those in the courts of law
to those in absolute power—in this case, to Jeroboam II, whose responsibility as king is to uphold justice in the courts of law, and to the priest
Amaziah, who represented the king within the state cult at Bethel.[18] When
Amos is indicting particular practices in 5.21-23, this is because he sees
the failure of particular sanctuaries as a small part of a much larger problem—the failure of those in power to uphold 'justice and righteousness'
throughout the land.[19]

17. See Berquist, 'Dangerous Waters', pp. 55-56; Hyatt, 'Amos 5.23-24', pp. 17-
24, and J.L. Mays, *Amos: A Commentary* (OTL; Philadelphia: Westminster Press,
1969) both argue for Amos 5.20-24 being a plea for ethical action, not least through the
courts (see Mays, *Amos*, pp. 108-109).

18. This reading makes sense of the encounter between Amos and Amaziah in
Amos 7 which was provoked by the prophet's words that Jeroboam would die a violent
death (7.9; 7.11). That the idea of justice being an indictment not just of the judges but
more particularly of the king is inherent in the traditions regarding Davidic kingship:
see 2 Sam. 8.15 (concerning David), 1 Kgs 9.9 (concerning Solomon), Jer. 22.5
(concerning Josiah) and Ps. 72.1-4 (the ideal king as portrayed in this psalm). Cf.
M. Weinfeld, ' "Justice and Righteousness" in Ancient Israel against the Background
of "Social Reforms" in the Ancient Near East', in H.-J. Nissen and J. Renger (eds.),
Mesopotamien und seine Nachbarn (Berlin: Dietrich Reimer, 1982), pp. 491-519.

19. This point is made most forcibly by I. Jaruzelska's sociological study of the
background to the prophet's message. Using archaeological and epigraphic data,
Jaruleska concludes that the problem outlined by Amos is not against individuals, but
rather against the entire institution. See I. Jaruzelska, *Amos and the Officialdom in the
Kingdom of Israel: The Socio-Economic Position of the Officials in the Light of the*

Justice and Righteousness as a Common Consensus about Appropriate Behaviour. A second variation of this interpretation, which also places the responsibility on the people rather than on God, is to see that Amos is appealing not so much to the leaders as to the ordinary people—particularly the wealthy—who carry out the acts of injustice against their neighbours.[20] In this scenario, Amos could be using 'justice and righteousness' as a reference to a well-known universal standard of what was right and wrong, which the ordinary Israelites would surely recognize from their folklore. This is in effect an appeal to 'natural justice', and refers to those standards of acceptable behaviour which the prophet expects even foreign nations to know about (as evident in the oracles against the six foreign nations in Amos 1–2). The key point is that just as the people expect other nations to recognize some international standard of behaviour appropriate in war, so Israel too should be able to apply this standard to herself—and in her case, an appropriate form of behaviour not in relation to her enemies but for the sake of order and justice in her own community.[21]

This more natural and 'common-sense' appeal to justice is employed in the wisdom literature and at the time of Amos would probably have been part of a familiar tradition of popular folk-wisdom.[22] That justice seems to have been thought of in this way elsewhere in Amos is evident in two

Biblical, the Epigraphic and Archaeological Evidence (Seria Socjologia, 25; Poznan: Wydawnictwo Naukowe Uniwersytetu im. Adama Mickiewicza, 1998).

20. See, for example, Hayes, *Amos: The Eighth-Century Prophet*, pp. 162-63, who argues that Amos's use of the term 'justice in the gate' in 5.1-15 is not so much about justice through the courts as about a more general dialogue about the meaning of justice as debated by the wealthy and well-informed at the city gates. In this way Amos's audience is not so much the judges and cultic officials and the king, as any one capable of knowing the meaning of justice in such a way that they could have demonstrated it to their neighbour.

21. See J. Barton, *Amos's Oracles against the Nations* (Cambridge: Cambridge University Press, 1980); also J. Barton, 'Natural Law and Poetic Justice in the Old Testament', *JTS* NS 30 (1979), pp. 1-14.

22. Although works on popular wisdom evident in Amos have more recently been questioned, due to the ambiguities within the wisdom tradition itself, the significant contributions include H.H. Schmid, 'Amos. Zur Frage nach der "geistige Heimat" des Propheten', *WuD*, NF X (1969), pp. 85-103; S. Terrien, 'Amos and Wisdom', in B.W. Anderson and W. Harrelson (eds.), *Israel's Prophetic Heritage: Essays in Honor of James Muilenburg* (London: SCM Press, 1962), pp. 108-115; J.L. Crenshaw, 'The Influence of the Wise upon Amos', *ZAW* 79 (1967), pp. 42-52; and H.W. Wolff, *Amos the Prophet: The Man and his Background* (trans. S.D. McBride *et al.*; Philadelphia: Fortress Press, 1977), pp. 44-53.

other passages which use the terms 'justice and righteousness' together. Amos 5.7 reads:

> O you who turn justice to wormwood,
> and cast down righteousness to the earth!

and Amos 6.12, introduced by rhetorical questions which are typical of the style of wisdom, reads:

> Do horses run upon rocks?
> Does one plough the sea with oxen?
> But you have turned justice into poison
> and the fruit of righteousness into wormwood…

Both these passages presume the teaching about natural justice which is prevalent in the wisdom tradition: the people's behaviour transgresses the boundaries of what is normally acceptable. Hence if the term 'justice and righteousness' is used with the same implications in Amos 5.24, this implies that Amos is advocating a *different* and more universal standard of justice than that taught by the cult, whose representatives have failed miserably in their promotion of it. He is appealing rather to what might be termed a 'common-sensical' approach to justice which can be known and practised apart from the cultic officials and religious leaders. He is by implication criticizing and condemning these leaders as well, by advocating the importance of natural order within the community as a whole.

'Justice and Righteousness' as the Vindication of Judah. This reading presumes that alongside the prophet's concern for judgment on the northern kingdom, the well-being of his own people, Judah, was an equal concern.[23] The execution of God's 'justice and righteousness' on the people of the north would result in the start of a new period of restoration for Judah. During the long reign of Jeroboam II, much of the land of the south had been taken by the north, so that the latter's borders extended to those which had traditionally been ascribed to David and Solomon. The expression in Amos 'from Dan to Beersheba' (Amos 8.14) and 'from Hamath to Arabah' (Amos 6.14; see also 2 Kgs 14.25) gives some evidence of this.

---

23. See Gordis, 'The Composition and Structure of Amos', pp. 223-25, and Polley, *Amos and the Davidic Empire*, pp. 107-11. This reading assumes Amos was originally from Tekoa in the south, that when Amos 1.2 speaks of the Lord roaring from Zion, it measures Zion favourably against Samaria, and that message moves increasingly towards hope for the restoration of Judah by the last two chapters of the book.

Hence any devastation upon Israel in the north would result in the opportunity for Judah to gain back its old territories. What looked like 'injustice' for one kingdom was in effect 'justice' for the other.

Furthermore, any devastation upon the sanctuaries and royal court in the north would have had positive ramifications for the renewal of life in the Temple and Davidic king in the south. Hence when Amos appeals for the establishment of 'justice in the gate', rather than this being an appeal to the reinstitution of the laws of the courts, or an appeal to a natural sense of justice, his ideal may instead be based upon the traditions of justice he knew best from his homeland, Judah. Believing the northern kingdom to be beyond redemption, his hope may well have been founded upon an alternative form of justice and righteousness through those in power in the Temple and royal court in the south.[24]

The constant thread through these three historical readings of the prophet Amos's appeal 'justice and righteousness' is his need to explain the reasons for the coming judgment. Whether the pair of terms is used literally to describe the inadequate performance of justice in the cult and courts in the north; or whether it advocates an alternative form of justice, either through a different form of teaching upheld by the wise, or through a different social setting, namely in the cult and court in the south; or whether it is used metaphorically as a theological term, either defending the just judgment about to be executed by God, or offering one last conditional promise—this appeal to 'justice and righteousness' is undoubtedly an inventive way of explaining the social and religious implications of such a damning message of judgment. One might even suggest that the term was chosen precisely because of its many levels of meaning.

Justice and Righteousness in the Eighth-Century Message of Amos's Disciples: Explaining God's Judgment on the North
Even if the term 'justice and righteousness' is an intrinsic part of Amos's own message, disciples of the prophet who had a role in compiling independent units of sayings into larger collections (and not least, chapters

24. This view is particularly represented by Polley, *Amos and the Davidic Empire*. To establish 'justice in the gate', according to Polley, was to encourage northerners to seek God in Jerusalem (p. 154). By the north and south together seeking to rebuild Zion in justice, 'the ideal Davidic king would establish a proper judicial system to ensure that justice rolls on like waters and righteousness as a never-ceasing stream' (pp. 174-75).

3–4 and 5–6) must have interpreted the words of the prophet for their own time.[25]

The very earliest time that such a re-working of the prophet's message could have taken place is after the prophet's expulsion from Bethel. If indeed some two years later an earthquake did occur (as noted in Amos 1.1) it would have been seen by the prophet's followers as a portent of worse to come, and would have had some impetus for their preservation of his message. And in the period of violence which followed Jeroboam's death (when three kings ruled in the space of a single year, and the Jehu dynasty came to an end, as recorded in 2 Kgs 15.8-16) the memory of Amos's words against the king would have had a certain resonance, and motivated his followers further to preserve them. Then as Assyrian power increased under the reign of Tiglath-Pileser III, with attacks on northern territory and threats to local sanctuaries, the words of Amos would have been recalled once more. In remembering these events, disciples of the prophet would apply Amos's more localized and short-term prophecies against Israel from within a broader perspective; perhaps at this stage his oracles about natural disaster were expanded by further details about a coming military threat.

A momentous point would have been the fall of Samaria in 722/721. How any of the northern traditions were preserved and taken to Judah will never be known; but parts of the book do seem to bear the mark of this early adaptation of Amos's prophecies. Words against local groups were now read as if against the whole people (the 'house of Israel' in Amos 5.1 is likely to be such an addition by disciples) and oracles referring to natural disaster were adapted and included a military crisis as well (as in Amos 3.11 and 6.14).[26]

---

25. See Jeremias, 'Amos 3–6', pp. 217-18, on the way the prophet's message is broadened and generalized to include a larger circle of addressees. See also R.B. Coote, *Amos among the Prophets: Composition and Theology* (Philadelphia: Fortress Press, 1981), who marks out Stage A 'The Prophet Amos's from Stage B 'Justice and the Scribe', noting the continuity and the change in the Amos tradition of justice at this stage (pp. 103-109). For Coote, the 'justice and righteousness' theme is one which Amos himself inherited; hence the line of continuity is there from at least the eighth century, if not before: 'The issue at stake, therefore, is not that Amos 5.21-24 might or might not simply go back to Amos but that, whether it was Amos who adapted it or someone else, it goes back even further…' (p. 106).

26. A good illustration of this is in Amos 7. The visions of 7.1-3, 4-6 and 7-8 could be seen as the earliest stage of the prophet's message of judgment, with their focus on the imminent end of the people, and the prophet's attempts to prevent it. Although the

Hence by the end of the eighth century, an interesting development would have taken place in the message of Amos. If the prophet's own message occurred some time between 760 and 750 BCE, some recognition of the validity of his words could have been brought about by events soon after 745 BCE, and a substantial development of the message itself could have taken place after the actual fall of the north in 722/721 BCE. Against this background, the reference to 'justice and righteousness' as in Amos 5.24 would have had some interesting connotations. The terms would explain the devastation of the northern people as a just and righteous act, brought about by God himself.[27] Following from this the terms would also imply God's preferential treatment of Judah.[28] If the judgment executed in 722/721 confirmed that God was displeased with every aspect of the cultic life of the people of the north (vv. 21-23)—their festivals, sacrifices, hymns and prayers—then it followed that the cultic life and royal dynasty in the south, which had not received such punishment, was now the only valid centre of worship.[29] A purging fire had devoured the north, as the prophet had foreseen (5.6—'Seek the Lord and live, lest he break out like fire in the house of Jacob') and this was all because they had turned

details are not clear, all we know is the imminent occurrence of some awful natural disaster, symbolized in ordinary terms first by a plague of locusts, and then in primordial terms by a fire devouring the waters of the deep (7.4). A development of this early message can be seen in 7.9 ('I will rise against the house of Jeroboam with the sword') which speaks explicitly of the end of the *dynasty* of Jeroboam, and not just of the king himself, as seems to have been the message of the prophet, as in 7.11 ('Jeroboam shall die by the sword'). Another development may be seen in the references to the destruction of a large number of sanctuaries, not only in the northern part of Israel but also in the southern territory as well: the 'high places of Isaac' which will be made desolate (7.9), alongside the sanctuaries of Israel, refer more particularly to Beersheba in the south. Altogether these expansions in Amos 7 suggest the message of later disciples in the light of events following the end of the Jehu dynasty and the rise of Tiglath-Pileser III. See R.E. Clements, 'Amos and the Politics of Israel', in D. Garron and F. Israel (eds.), *Storia e tradizioni di Israeli: Scritti in onore di J Alberto Soggin* (Brescia: Paedeia, 1991), pp. 49-64, especially pp. 60-63.

27. See pp. 83-84 previously. This reading plays up the enmity between the northern and southern kingdoms from Amos onwards.

28. See pp. 90-91 previously.

29. Amos 5.25-26 may be additions from this period, for this makes clear the perpetual inadequacy of the cult in the northern kingdom: from wilderness days until now they had compromised their faith, and the worship of Assyrian astral deities such as Sakkuth and Kaiwan was confirmation of it. The sins of the north have hence been expanded to include not only the corruption of justice but also syncretism and idolatry.

'justice to wormwood, and cast down righteousness to the earth' (5.7). Only Zion was left as the legitimate place of worship, where (in their view) the continuation of festivals, sacrifices and prayer reinforced God's pleasure with his people.[30]

In this way, Amos 5.21-24, ending with its climatic appeal 'let justice roll down like waters' has become a way of *ratifying* (from a southern point of view) God's judgment on the north, rather than a means of *defending* it, as had been the case in Amos's day.

Justice and Righteousness in the Seventh-Century Amos Tradition: Further Support for the Inviolability of Zion

There is inevitably some continuity between the Judahite interpreters of the prophet's message in the eighth century and the Judahite reading of it in the seventh. For between these centuries, little had changed in terms of Judah's continued survival. Sennacherib's siege of Jerusalem in 701, threatening a similar fate to the south as to Samaria in the north, had been and gone, thus encouraging further the traditions of the inviolability of Zion; the Assyrian threat had lifted, with that nation absorbed with affairs to the north (Urartu), the south (Egypt) and the east (Babylon). Hence a century or more later, it would seem that Amos's message as received by the southern kingdom from the period after 722/721 was vindicated: judgment upon Israel had indeed resulted in justice for Judah.[31]

One possible area of editing and interpretation at this stage could have been the way that an exhortation such as 'let justice roll down like waters' could become a means of polarizing further the sanctuaries at Bethel and Jerusalem. 'Seek me and live; but do not seek Bethel... Seek the Lord and live, lest he break out like fire in the house of Joseph, and it devour, with none to quench it for Bethel' (Amos 5.4, 5, 6) may well have been part of

30. The appearance and the reality were of course very different. This was the period in the south when Ahaz, and then Hezekiah, had to place Assyrian deities in the temple and pay tribute to Assyria out of Temple tax, as narrated in 2 Kgs 16 (Ahaz) and 18 (Hezekiah). Isaiah had to face a battle for integrity and false pride, both with Ahaz (see Isa. 3.16-26) and Hezekiah (see Isa. 28.14-22). But the fact that Isaiah has to address these issues shows clearly that such a reading of presumption in security by those in the south was in fact accepted by most.

31. If Josiah's reforms are to be believed, they did little to deflate optimism in the inviolability of the southern kingdom. They may have begun with a certain flagellation, on what had not been done in terms of the law (see 2 Kgs 22.11-13, 16-17) but the account of the reforms ends clearly with praise for what had been achieved (2 Kgs 22.19-20; 23.24-25).

Amos's own tirade against Bethel, but the intervening period would have given this message a new impetus. Bethel encapsulated all that had been rotten in the northern kingdom: for those appropriating Amos's message in the south, they would understand that just as injustice was the hallmark of Bethel, so justice was the hallmark of Jerusalem.[32] This was what seems to have been intended by Josiah's final destruction of Bethel in his efforts to centralize the cult in Jerusalem (2 Kgs 23.15-20), and it also marked the beginning of Deuteronomistic theology, safeguarding Jerusalem as the centre of orthodoxy. The reappropriation of the message of Amos, the prophet who took on the injustices at Bethel, would have played a part in establishing this.

We see here how a curious change of audience and speaker has taken place. In the northern context of eighth-century Amos, the audience accused of injustice and corruption was especially the wealthy—the religious and political élite. Now the interpreters of the Amos tradition were themselves part of that religious and political élite—for they were after all writers, scribes, within a particular intellectual tradition—but in Judah, not in Israel. The religious and political classes who were originally the recipients of the message of judgment had now become the preachers of it. This change of audience brings about a critical problem—that of the *institutionalization* of justice.[33] It was important to *justify* the lifestyle of the social élite, in order to safeguard the concerns of Jerusalem and its personnel, rather than attack them, as Amos had done with Bethel.

Within this context, the terms 'justice and righteousness' in Amos 5.21-24 would have been most important. At the time of Amos, these words would have been part of the various indictments against the northern sanctuaries because of their excesses in liturgy, their lack of integrity in worship, their attempts to placate and control God through festivals, sacrifices and prayer. How one interprets the beginning of 5.24 is important in this respect. '*But* let justice roll down like waters' could be read from the Hebrew (וְיִגַּל, with its initial *vav*) as 'therefore'—reading the *vav* as a causal connection between vv. 21-23 and v. 24. An alternative reading could be 'but now…'—reading the *vav* as an adversive, contrasting what has gone before with what is about to happen now, and so making a stark contrast between a corrupt cult and social morality.[34] It is hard to see that a

---

32. See Coote, *Amos among the Prophets*, pp. 95-96.

33. Amos was of course 'independent' of any institutionalization, by profession (a shepherd) and by origin (from Tekoa in the south).

34. This use of the 'adversive *vav*' is defended by R.S. Cripps, *A Critical and*

prophet with as much knowledge of cultic practices as Amos would propose a choice between *either* cultic worship *or* social justice; but he nevertheless seems to have placed social justice—with all its variant meanings—as primary, seeing that appropriate cultic worship arose out of it. But by the seventh century, Jerusalem and its temple were now the obvious point of reference for any indictment against the cult; the choice had to be less stark. So the appeal to justice and righteousness in Amos 5.21-24 would be read not as absolute indictment upon cultic liturgy but as a *warning* lest such worship lost its way as it had in the north.[35] Worship was seen to be just as important as social justice: both went hand in hand, integrated together. The conflict between the two, if such there had been at the time of Amos, had now to be muted. And anyway, what Amos had been referring to was Bethel, not Jerusalem.

Hence by the end of the seventh century, 'justice and righteousness' would have been seen primarily in terms of warning the community in Jerusalem of the need to combine liturgy with social action. The impact of this pair of terms is thus far more pragmatic. There was no need to read it in terms of justifying the justice of God in acting against the northern kingdom—the people of the south (at least those who followed a certain Deuteronomistic theology) did not need to have such an explanation, for they fully commended the judgment of God on the people of the north. What they needed to have clear was how they could further the cause of justice themselves, and so avoid the same fate of the north; and for them the justice was achieved *within* the cult, rather than outside it. Hence we may see a clear shift in the use of the appeal to 'justice and righteousness' over one and a half centuries—from an indictment of the cult in the north, to some support of it in the south.[36]

Justice and Righteousness amongst the Sixth-Century Exiles: An Explanation of God's Judgment on the South

To read the message of Amos from a sixth-century viewpoint would be to recognize that the seventh-century Judahite interpreters had got it wrong.

Exegetical Commentary on the Book of Amos (London: SPCK, 1929), pp. 26-27, and Mays, *Amos*, pp. 108-109, and Anderson and Freedman, *Amos*, pp. 539-42. See also Berquist, 'Dangerous Waters', p. 56.

35. The same integrated reading of the cult might be seen in the so-called prophetic liturgies, Pss. 50 and 81, for in spite of all their purported anti-cultic polemic, they are as psalms firmly rooted within the cult.

36. See also W.J. Doorly, *Prophet of Justice: Understanding the Book of Amos* (Mahwah, NJ: Paulist Press, 1989), pp. 78-81.

The events of 597 and 587 were a dreadful echo of the events of 722/721. Jerusalem having suffered the same fate as Samaria, the 'house of Israel' (5.1) were not the only recipients of the judgment of God; the recipients are now the entire 'people of Israel...the whole family which I brought up out of the land of Egypt' (3.1).[37]

Just as the passage in Amos 7.7-20 may well reveal the way in which the message of Amos was understood in 722/721, the doxologies (especially 4.13 and 5.8-9) may well indicate how the message was interpreted after the exile. Each unit is in praise of Yahweh's just rule, and this indicates that the judgment is to be seen as the righteous hand of God.[38] It may well be that the doxologies were used, along with the surrounding text in Amos, as part of an atonement liturgy by the exiles.[39]

Amos 4.13 reads:

> For lo, he who forms the mountains, and creates the wind,
> and declares to man what is his thought;
> who makes the morning darkness,
> and treads on the heights of the earth—
> the LORD, the God of hosts, is his name!

If Amos 4.6-13 as a whole was read as some liturgy of penitence by the exiles, it shows how at long last there has been some recognition by the people of their complicity in their fate.[40] The whole passage reads rather

37. Because the superscription in 5.1 addresses the northern kingdom specifically, it is likely to be closer to the time of prophet, whilst the superscription in 3.1 is applied to the whole people and not just the north, and is likely to be a later expansion of the message. On the debate about these two superscriptions, see pp. 83-84 and n. 10 previously.

38. Of course, the doxologies may well have been composed and added by the time of 722/721; in which case, the praise of God's just rule is appropriate then, too, for it fits with the view of those in Judah that the judgment of God was indeed just and right—for Israel was at an end, and they had escaped. But even if this is the case, the doxologies would have still been read in a different way by the time of the exile—for the judgment of God had now encompassed those reading it, rather than by-passing them. This was no longer a time for self-righteousness, but for penitence and confession of guilt.

39. See S.B. Frost, 'Asservation of Thanksgiving', *VT* 7 (1958), pp. 380-90; J.L. Crenshaw, *Hymnic Affirmation of Divine Justice: The Doxologies of Amos and Related Texts in the Old Testament* (Missoula: Scholars Press, 1975); Gillingham, '"Who Makes the Morning Darkness"', pp. 171-73.

40. See J. Jeremias, 'The Doxologies in the Book of Amos', in *idem*, *The Book of Amos: A Commentary* (trans. D.W. Stott; Louisville, KY: Westminster/John Knox

like the recital of the people's history in terms of their inability to respond either to the mercy or the judgment of God, and corresponds with similar exilic texts—for example Ezek. 16 and 20, Ps. 106, and perhaps also Lam. 5. 'Yet you did not return to me' (4.6, 7, 9, 10, 11) is an important refrain in this respect, for it indicates that what was once a message of judgment directed originally against the sanctuaries in the north is now applied to a people suffering the final devastation upon Jerusalem.[41]

Moving closer in to Amos 5.18-20, the doxology in 5.8-9 reads:

> He who made the Plei'ades and Orion,
> and turns deep darkness into the morning,
> and darkens the day into night,
> who calls for the waters of the sea,
> and pours them out upon the surface of the earth,
> the LORD is his name,
> who makes destruction flash forth against the strong,
> so that destruction comes upon the fortress.

This follows an indictment of the people for their lack of justice (5.7), and is more likely to be from Amos the prophet. The inclusion of this doxology here makes it clear that just as the people have reversed the values of justice and righteousness ('O you who turn justice to worm-wood') so too God will reverse his values, and fail to do what the people expected of him: their day will become night (anticipating the 'day of the Lord' as darkness in 5.20) and waters will be poured out in judgment and destruction against them (anticipating 'let justice roll down like waters' in 5.24).[42] The whole passage from 5.1-17 forms an interesting chiasmus with its beginning and ending formed as funeral laments (5.1-3, 16-17) and the parts before and after the doxology being clear expressions of guilt (5.7, 10-12). Hence rather like 4.6-13, Amos 5.1-17 could be read as a collection of earlier oracles now organized around the theme of guilt and

---

Press, 1998), pp. 76-80; Jeremias argues that 4.6-13 has been compiled as the result of exilic penitential worship; the hymns in 1.2 and 9.5-6 similarly reflect this type of worship forming a framework to the whole, with the doxologies in 4.13 and 5.8-9, in the heart of the book, illustrating it further.

41. Noting in Amos 4.5 the phrase בני ישראל—'people of Israel'—implying here the entire people, as in 3.1.

42. The word ויגל translated as 'roll down' in 5.24 suggests the 'pouring down' of waters as in a flash flood. Certainly כנחל איתן in the same verse could mean a 'mighty stream'; given the associations of flood waters with judgment in the people's tradition, from Noah onwards, this is a possible interpretation of 5.24.

penitence. It thus anticipates the penitential way in which Amos 5.18-20 might have been read.

Furthermore, other passages in Amos (some of which have an affinity with the Deuteronomistic theology of the need for repentance) bring out the same sense of guilt: passages which speak of the hardness of the people's hearts throughout their history (2.4, 10; 3.1) and passages which affirm the value of the prophetic word in speaking out about inevitable judgment (2.11-12; 3.7; 8.11-13) may also be part of this editing process.[43] Given that now God's judgment had come upon Jerusalem in the same way as it had on Samaria, passages which speak explicitly of the guilt of Zion may also be part of this process. Amos 2.4-5, again with recognizable affinities with Deuteronomistic theology, and Amos 6.1, which places the guilt of Zion alongside that of Samaria, are good examples. It is quite likely that the third doxology in Amos 9.5-6 once formed the end of the exilic book of Amos; the book would then suitably begin and end with the language of the earthquake (1.1; 9.5-6). This doxology undoubtedly meets the situation of those in exile, and gives this edition of Amos a more penitential feel, for its key element is to ascribe to God the honour that is his due. ('The Lord, God of hosts, he who touches the earth and it melts... who calls for the waters of the sea...the Lord is his name.')

In this way the people saw themselves as the whole 'people of Israel', addressed through the trajectory of time in the words of Amos to Israel in the north through to the exiles beyond Judah. Relating this directly to an understanding of Amos 5.21-24 at this time, this means that the earliest audience of Amos and the audience of those in exile would have had very similar concerns. The Judahites who had seen themselves as just and righteous, deserving the protection of God from the time of Amos to the end of the seventh century, and hence distancing themselves from the indictment in this text, had to reverse their perception from the standpoint of exile, and had now to see themselves as in need of justice and mercy from God. Amos's words which had failed to take root in the north might at last succeed with a later community of faith: 'justice and righteousness' was now understood as something which God alone could offer, rather than a means of escape which the community could achieve for itself.

---

43. See W.H. Schmidt, 'Die Deuteronomistische Redaktion des Amosbuches', *ZAW* 77 (1965), pp. 168-93, who argues that the most likely Deuteronomistic passages are those which defend prophetic activity, those which look back darkly on the people's history and those which reiterate the guilt and punishment rightly due for the people: these include 2.4-5, 2.11-12 and 5.25-27.

Hence 'justice and righteousness' at the time of the exile was seen primarily in terms of judgment and destruction which reminded the people of their dependency on God. At this stage the emphasis on human initiative was less important; but a reversal of this reading would again have taken place once the promise of restoration was apparent.

Justice and Righteousness in Fifth-Century Judah: A Hope of Restoration
Most commentators would agree that Amos 9.7-10, 11-15 belongs to the post-exilic period of restoration. Many see this as the most critical period in the growth of the book, arguing that the most fundamental compilation and redaction, giving form to the book in the way we have it today, took place at this time.[44] Clearly Amos 9.11-12, 13-15 stands out from the rest of book in its hope for restoration—in specific terms, concerning the reinstitution of the Davidic dynasty, and in general terms, concerning the repossession of the land—and the echo here of other exilic and post-exilic passages, for example from Isa. 40–66, is most marked.[45] However, because no other passage in the book resembles this sort of theology, the argument that this has been the formative influence on the book is not convincing; it reads more as an appendix to it.

Nevertheless, it may well be that a few other passages were reinterpreted during the restoration period because of this renewed hope that God's justice ultimately meant salvation for his people. In order to keep consistency with the doom-laden picture in the rest of the book, a compromise idea of a *remnant* may well have come about at this time. The remnant was thus the 'just and righteous few' whom God could trust to build up the new community in 'justice and righteousness'. The 'remnant of Joseph' to whom the Lord *may* be gracious (Amos 5.15) is one such reference; and another may be the promise in Amos 9.8 not utterly to destroy the house of Jacob (לא השמיד אשמיד את בית יעקב).[46] The idea of a believing remnant emerging from the devastation of the exile is consonant with the theology of the exilic prophets Jeremiah, Ezekiel and Isa. 40–55, so an exilic date for Amos 9 is not impossible. Certainly in reading

---

44. See, for example, Wolff, *Joel and Amos*, p. 325; also D. Rottzoll, *Studien zur Redaktion und Komposition des Amosbuches* (BZAW, 243; Berlin: W. de Gruyter, 1996), pp. 285-90.

45. See, for example, Isa. 32.1-2, 16-20; 35.1-2, 6-7; 41.17-20; 49.8-13.

46. The reference to the community in exile as 'Jacob' is certainly an exilic term, as is clear from the use of it, usually in parallelism with 'Israel', in Isa. 40–48 (e.g. 41.14; 42.23; 43.1; 44.1)

Amos 9.11-12 and 13-15, the impression here is that the recipients of this new period of promise are the remaining few of the 'house of Jacob' referred to in Amos 9.8.

This has again interesting ramifications for the way the terms 'justice and righteousness' in 5.24 might have been read. In an eighth-century context, this would have implied both the lack of justice and righteousness on the part of the people and also the need for the God of Israel to bring about justice and righteousness instead, through purging judgment. A century or so later, they would have been used by the survivors in Judah for their own self-justification. By the time of the exile, they would have been part of penitential expressions of faith by the displaced Judeans, in their tension between faith and experience, trying to preserve the idea of a just and righteous God. Against this background, the restoration period would be the first time that this passage in 5.20-24 could have spelt out genuine hope. A reading of Haggai shows how this was a time for the renewal of the cult and an opportunity to combine justice with ritual. The issues of establishing social justice were at this time all important, as shown in the readings of third Isaiah (for example 58.6-7; 59.1-4) and the actions of Nehemiah (as in his action to release people from debt in Neh. 5).[47] Hence by restoration times, a passage such as Amos 5.24 would no longer be read negatively as a threat, or as a motive for penitence; rather it is understood positively, as an ideal to follow. The liturgy of the second Temple cultus was to stand for morality as a vital part of its liturgy in a way that the northern sanctuaries, and even the Jerusalem Temple itself, had failed to do. The great reforming figures of this period, including Haggai, Zechariah, Malachi, Nehemiah and Ezra undoubtedly followed this goal.

Hence at this time, 'justice and righteousness' had a new meaning for the sixth-century community of Yehud. In the light of their reading of the conclusion to the book, it indicated a hope in restoration—albeit more an idealized situation than a real one. Hence with regard to Amos 5.21-24, it implied the importance of a purified cult upholding mercy as justice in its own affairs. As the goal of a purified cult failed to materialize, the text, like many prophetic texts, would have taken on an increasingly future orientation: justice and righteousness would be the hallmarks of the purified cult in the age to come, when God returned in the fulness of time to his Temple. Hence during this period the passage would have been read in an

---

47. Note here the specific references to the desire for the restoration of 'justice and righteousness' in Isa. 59.9 and 59.14—an echo of the term used in the promises of God for the people in the passages such as Isa. 33.16, 17.

entirely different way from its original audience: on the one hand, it offered positively an ideal for the present, but on the other, it also offered the fulfilment of this ideal some time in the future.

This 'broad spectrum' of interpretation of the motif of 'justice and right-eousness' in Amos 5.21-24 shows both the strengths and weakness of the historical approach. It offers a wide range of intriguing meanings, but not one of them is certain and thus 'correct': this is just as imaginative and reconstructive as the literary approach, to which we now turn.

Literary Approaches to Amos 5.18-17: The Search for Justice and Right-eousness Continued
Because the historical approach is so dependent upon imaginative recon-struction, illustrated by the number of different permutations possible in reading the same text, other approaches are needed, for they throw new light on the text and show the historical method for what it is—just another mode of reading.[48] Because the literary approach openly acknowl-edges that subjectivity is an essential part of understanding a text , and so layers of interpretation can be freely added to it, multivalency is inevita-ble. The only determining factor is where one starts and ends.[49]

Amos 5.21-24 as a Self-Contained Unit: Practical Justice Alone can Save
The variant readings of Amos 5.21-24 are contingent upon whether one sees vv. 21-23 (against the cult) set against v. 24 (for social justice) and hence as two polarized ideas of the cult or social justice,[50] or whether vv. 21-23 are seen as leading up to v. 24, with the ideal being that of 'justice through the cult'.[51]

48. See, for example, G.M. Tucker, 'The Futile Quest for the Historical Prophet', in E.E. Carpenter (ed.), *A Biblical Itinerary: In Search of Method, Form and Content. Essays in Honor of George W. Coats* (JSOTSup, 240; Sheffield: Sheffield Academic Press, 1997), p. 144-52, especially p. 152.
49. With regard to Amos 5.21-24, and our interpretation of v. 24 from a literary point of view, we note A.G. Auld's observation: 'The delimiting of the unit can shift the interpretation of v. 24, since the boundaries of the unit associate different materials with it' (*Amos* [OTG; Sheffield: JSOT Press, 1986], p. 66).
50. For example, see Harper, *Amos and Hosea*, p. 136; also Mays, *Amos*, pp. 108-109; also Hayes, *Amos: The Eighth-Century Prophet*, p. 172.
51. Much depends again on the interpretation of the 'and' and the form of the verb יִגַּל in v. 24—whether it implies 'and [therefore] justice will roll down' or '*but* let justice roll down'. On these possibilities, see n. 34 earlier.

J. Limburg points out that this unit reflects what he calls 'the number seven + one' formula found elsewhere in the book.[52] The first list is of seven things God does not like—feasts, solemn assemblies, burnt offerings, cereal offering, peace offerings, noise of songs, melody of harps. Verse 24 lists the one thing God does desire: 'justice and righteousness'. Setting aside whether Limburg's 'one thing' should really be two, this nevertheless shows that the text has echoes with the style of the rest of the book, but that this text has an internal completeness of itself. Such a reading results in seeing the unit in contrasts—that of the cult (seven things where God is not pleased) over and against justice (one thing which can please God).

If this were a historical reading, one might qualify this by arguing that the passage is not about a negation of the cult *per se* but the abuses of the cult at a particular time and place. But here we are only interested in the text; and a reading of vv. 21-24 as one unit does seem to indicate that the contrast is a stark one: *not* the cult (with its human institutions which displease God) *but* justice and righteousness (which God loves because they are expressions of his character). There is thus some conflict here between liturgy and morality; social justice *on its own* is seen as the only hope of regaining God's pleasure.

Amos 5.21-24 in the Context of Ch. 5.1–6.14: Seek Justice whilst there is Still Time
That chapters 5–6 form an important unit distinct from chapters 3–4 has also been recognized in historical approaches to the text. Our literary assessment will work progressively outwards from the core of the text, first looking at the unit as it is set within chapter 5, then within chapters 5–6 together.

Amos 5.1-17 and 18-27. Within vv. 18-27, it is clear that v. 24 is pivotal. Not only does it form a climax to vv. 21-23, but vv. 18-20 is a prologue to vv. 21-23, with v. 24 as the climax, in its general announcement of the day of the Lord as darkness, not light, and vv. 25-27 is an expansion of vv. 21-24 describing the punishment in detail.

---

52. See J. Limburg, 'Sevenfold Structures in the Book of Amos', *JBL* 106 (1987), pp. 217-22, here p. 220. Other examples include 3.3-7, 8; 4.6-11, 12; 6.4-6b, 6c; 9.9.1-4b, 4c. On the general background of 7+1 as a pattern in the ancient Near East and the Bible, see Paul, *Amos: A Commentary*, pp. 22-24.

The patterning of 5.1-17 is more intricate and distinct because of its chiastic structure.[53] The words of lamentation in 5.1-3 (the prophet's lament) and 5.16-17 (the people's lament) make this clear; the other five matching parts in vv. 7-13 make, not surprisingly, a chiasmus of seven parts in all. Verses 4-6a are a call to repentance (noting again the seven imperatives—come, transgress, multiply, bring, offer, proclaim, publish) as also are vv. 14-15 (also with seven verbs—seek, live, be, hate, love, maintain, be gracious); vv. 6b-7 form a warning and condemnation, with the theme of the lack of justice, and vv. 10-13 similarly offer warning and condemnation, on the theme of judgment. The hymn of Yahweh's power at the heart of this unit in vv. 8-9 speaks of his ability to create and destroy —again seven verbs may be noted (makes, turns, darkens, calls, pours, causes to flash, comes). The whole unit thus could be read as follows:

a.	**5.1-3**	the prophet's lament
b.	**5.4-6a**	call to repentance
c.	**5.6b-7**	warning and condemnation
d.	**5.8-9**	hymn of praise
c¹.	**5.10-13**	warning and condemnation
b¹.	**5.14-15**	call to repentance
a¹.	**5.16-17**	the people's lament

The passage as a whole works progressively towards judgment, which can only be staved off by genuine repentance: when combined with vv. 18-27, it is possible to see the same theme repeated. Taking Amos 5 as a whole (vv. 1-17 and vv. 18-27) it is possible to read in v. 24 'let justice roll down...' another appeal to the people to avert the disaster, still within the context of the possibility of repentance, but all the time within the growing threat of inevitable death and destruction. Hence v. 24, when taken in the broader context of Amos 5 with its two other calls of repentance, can be read in a less doom-laden way than when read as a unit (vv. 21-24) on its own: the polarization between cult and justice is less to the fore, and the people still have the option of changing their fate. In this

53. See, for example, J. de Waard, 'The Chiastic Structure of Amos V 1-17', *VT* 27 (1977), pp. 170-77; N.J. Tromp, 'Amos V 1-17: Towards a Stylistic and Rhetorical Analysis', *OTS* 23 (1984), pp. 56-85; D.A. Dorsey, 'Literary Architecture and Aural Structuring Techniques in Amos', *Bib* 73 (1992), pp. 305-30; H.N. Rösel, 'Kleine Studien zur Entwicklung des Amosbuches', *VT* 43 (1993), pp. 88-101; and Jeremias, *The Book of Amos*, pp. 81-97.

broader context, with the two calls to repentance amidst the threats of doom being only a few verses away, one might read this as 'seek justice while yet there is time!'[54]

Amos 5.18-27 and 6.1-14. Limburg takes Amos 5–6 as a unit because they contain another seven formulae—'thus says the word of Lord'—which occurs in 5.3, 4, 16, 17, 27 and 6.8 and 14.[55] However, this seems to be somewhat forced, as not all the formulae are identical, and some occur at the end or in the middle of verses (5.17, 27; 6.8, 14).

There is another way in which 5.18–6.7 may be seen to be a unit alongside the unit of 5.1-17. This is in the threefold use of the 'woe to you/woe to those who...' sayings (5.18, 6.1, 6.4). In 5.18, the woe saying ('Woe to you who desire the day of the Lord!') follows the words of lamentation in 5.16-17; in 6.1-4, the saying ('Woe to those who are at ease in Zion...') follows the harsh words about exile in 5.27; and in 6.4-7, the reasons for the indictment against Zion are made more explicit: 'Woe to those who lie upon beds of ivory...' (with a further six crimes added in the following verses, again making seven in all).

The most convincing explanation for the unity of chapters 5–6 as a whole, however, is the proposal for another chiasmus.[56] This too has seven units. 5.18-20 and 6.11-14 begin and end the unit, on the reversal of fortunes (5.18-20 on natural disaster and 6.11-14 on military disaster); 5.21-25 and 6.8-10 are concerned with Yahweh's displeasure (noting the occurrence of what Yahweh hates [√שׂנא] and rejects [√מאס] in 5.21, and what Yahweh hates [√שׂנא] and detests [√תאב] in 6.8; 5.26-27 and 6.6-7 are both about the threat of the exile (in each case, using √גלה as in 5.27 and 6.7); and the middle of the chiasmus, 6.1-6, has the seven + one formula—seven verbs describing what the people do which displeases God (lie, stretch, eat, sing, invent, drink, anoint) and one thing they do not do which would please God (grieve him). The chiasmus thus could be read as follows:

54. This of course accords with some of the purportedly early historical readings of Amos.

55. See Limburg, 'Sevenfold Structures', p. 218; also C.C. Coulot, 'Propositions pour une structuration du livre d'Amos au niveau rédactionnel', *RevScRel* 51 (1977), pp. 169-86, especially pp. 179-81.

56. See Anderson and Freedman, *Amos*, pp. 519-608; also Dorsey, 'Literary Architecture', pp. 315-17.

a.	**5.18-20**	the reversal of fortunes (natural disaster)
b.	**5.21-25**	Yahweh's displeasure
c.	**5.26-27**	the threat of exile
d.	**6.1-6**	what pleases and displeases God (7+1 formula)
c^1.	**6.6-7**	the threat of exile
b^1.	**6.8-10**	Yahweh's displeasure
a^1.	**6.11-14**	the reversal of fortunes (military disaster)

This places our unit in a different context, for 5.21-24 now is seen as an actual part of the chiasmus, rather than as the consequence of the earlier one in 5.1-17. What one now has to balance together is Yahweh's displeasure at cultic sins in 5.21-23, and the prophet's displeasure at social sins in the woe passage of 6.1-6. This puts the plea for social justice in a very different context: this is not just about an attack on the *cult* in its plea for social justice, but it is as much an attack on *society* in its plea for social justice. The blame on the cult is only one part of a much larger whole—and this includes not only other social sins, but the much more insidious and internalized sin of pride (6.6-8). Hence 5.24 is not just about shaming the cult—the shame lies throughout the entire society. Furthermore, within this unit as a whole, the plea for justice is, in each case, followed by the threat of exile (5.26-27, 6.6-7). This reading thus puts less emphasis on the possibility of repentance, which was one interpretation when looking at 5.24 in the literary context of 5.18-27 and 5.1-17, and places more on the inevitability of judgment, which arises when one looks at 5.24 more in the context of what follows it.

Amos 5.21-24 in the Context of Chapters 3-4, 5-6: An Attack on the Heart of the Establishment

A rhetorical reading of these chapters as a unit is different from the redactional reading of them, which was considered earlier, where the essential issue is 'who added what, and when, and why'. Here it is important to take the text as a final unit, and to ask questions about the patterns that occur throughout, and then to ascertain what implications this might have for the theme of justice and righteousness (5.24) within this unit.

As discussed previously, chapters 3–4 and 5–6 divide into two sub-units of roughly equal length, each introduced by a similar heading: 'Hear this word that the Lord has spoken against you…' (3.1) and 'Hear this word which I take up over you…' (5.1). Together they all return to a central theme—that some cataclysmic ending will come upon the people, and that the reasons for it need to be given.

One way of viewing these four chapters would be to see five sections (what S. Dempster refers to as 'discourse units')[57] comprising 3.1-15, 4.1-13, 5.1-17, 5.18-27 and 6.1-14. The first three units could be separated on account of the introduction 'Hear this word!' (שמעו את הדבר הזה, with the particle את omitted in 4.1) and the latter two sections similarly by 'Woe' (הוי). However this does not work, for it does not take account of a third woe saying at 6.4, and it does not emphasize sufficiently the clear distinction between the more developed formulae in 3.1 and 5.1 and the more brief expression in 4.1.

A more interesting approach would be—yet again—to see some sort of chiasmus within chapters 3–6 as a whole.[58] This would work as follows. Amos 3.1-2 starts with the announcement of God's punishment on Israel's over-confidence; 3.3-8 forms a series of didactic questions undermining this self-assurance; and 3.9-15 speaks about Israel's forthcoming devastation, which will involve destruction of both strongholds (vv. 10-11) and houses (v. 15). Amos 6.13-14 ends with an announcement of God's punishment on Israel's self-confidence; 6.12 is a didactic question undermining her self-assurance; and 6.8-11 refers to Israel's forthcoming devastation, against the houses (v. 11) and against the strongholds (v. 8). Hence the overall structure would appear as follows:

a.	**3.1-2**		God's punishment on Israel's *hubris*
b.		**3.3-8**	Questions undermining self-assurance
c.			**3.9-15** Forthcoming devastation (strongholds and houses)
d.			Chapters 4–5 (also chiasmus) Oracles against cultic abuses
c[1].			**6.8-11** Forthcoming devastation (strongholds and houses)
b[1].		**6.12**	A question undermining self-assurance
a[1].	**6.13-14**		God's punishment on Israel's *hubris*

This then is the outer circle of these four chapters. Moving inwards, we may see 4.1-3 directed explicitly against Samaria, with 4.4-5 leading on to

57. See S. Dempster, 'The Lord is His Name: A Study of the Distribution of the Names and Titles of God in the Book of Amos', *RB* 98 (1991), pp. 170-89; here, p. 175.

58. See, for example, P.R. Noble, 'The Literary Structure of Amos: A Thematic Analysis', *JBL* 114 (1995), pp. 209-226, especially pp. 210-17 ; also J. Lust, 'Remarks on the Redaction of Amos V 4-6, 14-15', in A.S. von der Woude (ed.), *Remembering All the Way: A Collection of Old Testament Studies Published on the Occasion of the Fortieth Anniversary of the Oudtestamentisch Werkgezelschep in Nederland* (OTS, 21; Leiden: E.J. Brill, 1981), pp. 129-54; and Rottzoll, *Studien zur Redaktion und Komposition*, pp. 3-10.

an oracle against the excessive practices of the cult, and 4.6-13 being an oracle (with an element of the fear and bewilderment of the people recurring within it) concerning the natural disaster from Yahweh about to strike the land. At the other side, we may see 6.1-7 as an oracle directed again against Samaria; 5.21-27 is an oracle against the excessive practices of the cult, and 5.18-20 is an oracle concerning the dark day of Yahweh about to strike the land (again noting the themes of fear and bewilderment in this passage). Hence the chiasmus in chapters 4–5 may be demonstrated as follows:

a.	**4.1-5**	Oracle against Samaria
b.	**4.4-5**	Excesses of the cult
c.	**4.6-13**	Natural disaster to come on the land
d.	**5.1-17**	A further chiasmus: 'seek the LORD'
c^1.	**5.18-20**	Day of Yahweh to come on the land
b^1.	**5.21-27**	Excesses of the cult
c^1.	**6.1-7**	Oracle against Samaria

The inner ring—Amos 5.1-17—is the sevenfold chiasmus which has already been illustrated, beginning and ending with lamentations (vv. 1-3, 16-17), with the next concentric circle (vv. 4-6, 14-15) serving as pleas to seek Yahweh, with the next part being the corruption of justice (vv. 7, 10-13) and with the doxology of praise to Yahweh's destructive power at the heart (vv. 8-9). Thus the four chapters fall together as three complex and interrelated patterns—Amos 3 and 6 forming one, Amos 4 and 5.18-27 forming another, with 5.1-17 at the very heart. Whether this was in any way the intentions of those who compiled the text will never be known; there are several places where sections are far longer and more diffuse than their counterparts, which may suggest this is more a case of eisegesis than exegesis.[59] But nevertheless, overall, it works, and does not deny the earlier connections we have proposed between the smaller units.

The question remains as to how this affects our reading of 'justice and righteousness' in Amos 5.24. In this unit we can see how 5.21-24 (along with 25-27) mirror 4.4-5, as oracles against the excessive practices of the cult. One interesting observation is that Bethel and Gilgal are the places of worship attacked in 4.4-5, so if 5.21-24 is intended to be a corre-

---

59. One illustration of possible eisegesis is whether or not to give the hymns in 4.13 and 5.8-9 a central place. The reading of 5.1-17 does so with regard to 5.8-9; but the way we have read Amos 4 fails to do so with 4.13.

sponding unit, this may also be a specific attack on Bethel and Gilgal; if
so, it explains more about the antagonistic encounter between Amos and
Amaziah in 7.10-17, where Amos is warned 'never again prophesy at
Bethel, for it is the king's sanctuary, and it is a temple of the kingdom'
(7.13). If Bethel is indeed one of the sanctuaries at issue, then it would
suggest that the references to cultic malpractices in 5.21-23 and to 'justice and righteousness' in 5.24 included the failure of all those at Bethel
(king and priests alike) to keep the basic tenets of order in the community. 'Justice and righteousness' are terms used to undermine the heart of
the establishment, by demonstrating how little regard those in power had
for the right order of things.

Amos 5.21-24 in the Context of the Book of Amos: There may yet be Hope
Within the framework of the chiastic structure of Amos 3–6, it is relatively
easy to place the chapters 1–2 (the oracles against foreign nations which
place Israel's judgment in a more universal context) and 7.1-8.2 (the
encounter of Amos and Amaziah at Bethel, with the four visions) as the
outer circles, then to add on 8.3–9.10 (another judgment oracle, with many
links with chapters 3–6); the final part is then the book's conclusion (9.11–
15), with its radically different picture of hope. The most important collections, coming immediately before and after chapters 3–6, are the foreign
nation oracles in chapters 1–2, evoking a vision of justice far beyond that
upheld by Israel, and the encounter between Amos and Amaziah, in chapter 7, eliciting a distinctive vision of justice in specific Israelite terms.

But we could take a different approach and see chapters 1–7 as one
overall unit, with oracles of judgment leading up to the conflict at Bethel
as an inevitable climax, and then chapters 8–9 as additional oracles reflecting the result of this encounter.[60] Another view would be to see chapters
1–6 as a complete unit, and 7–9 as another.[61] A different, more poetic way

60. For example, see Gordis, 'The Composition and Structure of Amos', pp. 220-
21.

61. See A. van der Wal, 'The Structure of Amos', *JSOT* 26 (1983), pp. 107-113. In
his view, Amos 1–6 progresses inexorably towards the announcement of disaster in
6.7-12. The break is at chapter 7. A slightly different reading would be to see the whole
book united in its 'theophanic' view of God, with the first half describing God's anger
and Israel's refusal to listen (chapters 1–6) and the second half (chapters 7–9) describing the inevitable judgment, using the various types of figurative language to describe
death: see R.F. Melugin, 'Amos', in E.E. Carpenter and W. McCown (eds.), *Ashbury
Bible Commentary* (Grand Rapids, MI: Zondervan, 1992), pp. 735-49.

of looking at the book would be to see chapters 1–6 as (in essence) God speaking, 7.1-8.3 as the prophet speaking, but only to be silenced, and 8.4–9.10 as God being silenced and the consequences of that silence being explained for the people.[62]

There are many different ways in which the book may be seen to cohere as a unity. Limburg's numerical organization would be on a sevenfold numerical basis—the '2 × 7' divine speech formulae in chapters 1.3–2.16, the seven similar formulae in chapters 3, 4, 5–6, and 7.1–8.3, and finally in 8.4–9.15.[63] Dempster, by contrast, would divide the book up according to the distribution of divine names—most obviously in chapters 1–2, 3–6 and 9.7-15.[64] On the other hand, Noble, whilst noting the importance of 'divine speech formulae' in the opening and closing sections, sees the structure as more open-ended and divides the book up into only three sections, 1.2–3.8, 3.9–6.11-14, 7.1–9.15, whilst noting the ways in which parallel structures and thematic correspondences divide the book into similar sections.[65] Rottzoll, by contrast, sees the axiomatic points as the beginning (1.2) and first ending (9.5-6) of the book, with their language of earthquake and destruction, and argues that the book revolves around these two focal points.[66]

62. See F. Landy, 'Vision and Poetic Speech in Amos', *HAR* 11 (1987), pp. 223-46. In this reading, 5.21-24 would thus be found in the passages before both the prophet and God become silent. Hence one could argue that there is still the possibility of a new start, and the appeal to justice is an appeal to what the people might be able to do to put things right.

63. Limburg notes the smaller divisions into seven—for example, the oracles against seven nations in Amos 1.3-2.5, followed by Israel's seven transgressions in 2.6-16, the seven questions in 3.3-8, the seven plagues of 4.6-11, the seven verbs describing God's judgment in 5.8-9, the seven things God does not like in the call for justice in 5.21-24, the seven acts of punishment by God in 9.1-4 and the seven acts of restoration in 9.11-15.

64. See Dempster, 'The Lord is His Name', pp. 184-85.

65. See Noble, 'The Literary Structure of Amos', pp. 225-26. For a similar but more complex and chiastic division of the book into three sections, see W.A. Smalley, 'Recursion Patterns and the Sectioning of Amos', *BT* 30 (1979), pp. 118-27.

66. See Rottzoll, *Studien zur Redaktion und Komposition*, p. 3: both Amos 1.2 and 9.5-6 have hymnic forms, and together these create a 'hymnic framework' to the entire book; Amos 1.3–2.16 and 7.1–9.4 have different material, concerning oracles against the nations (chs. 1–2) and the visions of the prophet (chs. 7–9). But Amos 3.1–6.14 forms a clear chiastic structure: this fits in with the different chiasmi illustrated with respect to chs. 3–6 above. In this, the central section is 5.1-17, with 4.6-13/5.18-20 (as

Dorsey's analysis is perhaps the most useful for our purposes. Taking Limburg's idea of the number seven, he applies it to the whole book.[67] He notes seven major units, the first four of which correspond closely to Limburg's outline: (i) chapters 1–2, the oracles against foreign nations (with their common introduction 'for three transgressions…even for four…'); (ii) chapter 3, on the theme of the validity of prophecy, also with its seven rhetorical questions; (iii) chapter 4, again with seven stanzas on the theme 'yet you did not return to me'; (iv) 5.1-17, 'seek good that you may live', with its internal sevenfold chiasmus; (v) 5.18–6.14 'woe to you who desire the day of the Lord', also with an internal sevenfold ring composition; (vi) 7.1–8.3, concerning the prophet at Bethel (again we may note the number seven—four vision reports and a three-part narrative of Amaziah and Amos); and (vii) 8.4–9.15, with its eventual promise to restore the Davidic dynasty, again with an internal sevenfold chiasmus.

Dorsey then views this chiasmus within the larger whole by giving special attention to the first and last sections of Amos. This concerns Israel's place among the other nations (chapters 1–2, 8.4–9.15). These are the only places where God's dealings with Syria, Philistia and Edom are noted (1.3-8, 11-12; also 9.7-12); furthermore, these sections are the only places where the seven sins of the wealthy are listed (2.6-8; also 8.4-6); both sections cohere in stressing the inescapability of God's judgment (2.14-16; also 9.1-4); the references to coming out of Egypt (2.10 and 9.7), on Aram being brought from Kir (1.5 and 9.7), and on God's presence on Carmel (1.2 and 9.3) occur only here and nowhere else in the book. The next inner sections concern the role of the prophet and the coming destruction on Bethel (chapters 3 and 7.11–8.3). Moving further inwards, the next correspondences concern judgment on self-confidence with the resultant punishment being exile (chapters 3 and 5.18–6.4). Hence at the heart of this is the section on lament and the call to repentance (5.1-17), with the hymn in praise of God's righteous judgment at the heart of this (5.8-9). This places 5.21-24 in yet another framework, as seen in the table below:

judgment oracles) being the next outer layers, and 4.4-5/5.21-27 (oracles of judgment against the cult) as the next outer layers. This again interprets our verses, Amos 5.21-24, with a more particular judgment emphasis.

67. See Dorsey, 'Literary Architecture', pp. 303-30.

a. **1.1–2.16**		Israel among the nations (e.g. Syria, Philistia, Edom); Israel brought out of Egypt (2.10)
b.	**3.1-15**	The validity of prophecy in seven rhetorical questions; the fate of Bethel
c.		**4.1-13** 'Yet you did not return to me': a sevenfold aggrievance
d.		**5.1-17** 'Seek good that you may live': a sevenfold appeal for repentance
c¹.	**5.18–6.14**	'Woe to you who desire the Day of the LORD': a seven-fold aggrievance
b¹. **7.1–8.3**		The validity of prophecy, in seven parts; the fate of Bethel
a¹. **8.4–9.15**		Israel among the nations (e.g. Syria, Philistia, Edom); Israel brought out of Egypt (9.7)

When looking at 5.24 and its themes of 'justice and righteousness' within the context of the whole, four interrelated readings are possible. One reading is that even within the book as a whole, chapters 3 and 5.18–6.4 (both concerning the inevitable judgment against empty cultic activity) mirror each other, thus underlining the way in which, within the book as a whole, 5.24 could be read within the debate about the inadequacy of the cult and the need instead for social justice. A second reading is that these chapters frame 5.1-17, which still suggests that the judgment is not irrevocable (hence the calls to repentance), and this implies that the pleas for justice in 5.24 might in fact still offer some hope overall for the people's response. A third reading is that just as the hymn in 5.8-9 praises God for bringing about justice through things good and bad, so the same reference to divine rather than human justice may be proposed for the plea for justice to come about in 5.24. A fourth approach is that just as the two sections set Israel in the context of the foreign nations in a type of closure at the beginning and ending to the book, so too the plea for justice in 5.24 could also be seen in the light of a more universal and broad appeal to social morality.

In this way, by looking at the book as a whole, we may read 5.24 in negative terms, against the cult, or in positive terms, hoping for a response from the people, or more ambiguously, in broader theological terms, in the context of a more universal understanding of morality.[68]

68. We may note again how each of these readings has correspondences with the historical readings; but here one arrives at a similar destination by a very different route.

Amos 5.21-24 in the Context of the Scroll of the Twelve Prophets: Justice will Come in God's Own Time

Given that this wider canonical reading of Amos is very much dependent upon the books which come before and after it, our first problem is in knowing which collection to use as normative—if this is the LXX, then the books would be Hosea and Micah (Amos being second in this collection), and if it is the MT, then the books are Joel and Obadiah (Amos being third, with Hosea still at the beginning of the collection).

If we take the Hebrew collection, then several observations may be made. Joel 3 (Hebrew Joel 4), with its judgment on the foreign nations, runs naturally into the judgment on the nations in Amos 1–2. The link is made more explicit by Joel 3.16 (Hebrew 4.16) which is almost identical to Amos 2.2 ('And the Lord roars from Zion, and utters his voice from Jerusalem'). The reading of Amos as a sequel to Joel thus gives the book future connotations, concerning God's purposes for the future of Zion, and the city's place in the context of other nations: this gives a very different perspective on the passages about the northern kingdom Israel, and about Israel's place *alongside* other nations.

The link between Amos and Obadiah is equally interesting. The references to the destruction of Edom come at the beginning and end of Amos (1.11-12, 9.12). The ending of Amos adds that Israel will 'possess the remnant of Edom' once again: the explicit reference to just this one territory is odd in the light of the more general nature of the promises in Amos 9.13-15, but fits well with the anti-Edom oracle of Obadiah; Obad. 20 speaks in similar tones about the exiles 'possessing' (the verb √ יָרֵשׁ for 'possess' is the same in Amos 9.12 and Obad. 20) the cities of the Negeb. This again shows how Amos was seen, rather like its connection with Joel, in the context of ultimate salvation over the foreign nations.[69] As for the 'justice and righteousness' theme, within this overall framework a text such as Amos 5.21-24 would probably have been read in terms of justice being a gift from God, ultimately vindicating his people and giving them new hope. Both Joel and Obadiah have a future-orientated hope, concerned with the vindication of God's people over typical enemies (Obadiah,

---

69. The same theme is found in Jonah, which develops how the justice and righteousness of God relates to other nations. See Coote, *Amos among the Prophets*, pp. 129-34, who calls this a 'midsrashic interplay' whereby the author of Jonah implicitly used the traditions of Jonah's purported contemporary, Amos. The same might be said for the ways in which the book of Amos might now be read in the light of the later traditions of Obadiah.

with the enemy as Edom) resulting in the restoration of Zion (Joel); to place Amos between these two scrolls can only mean it had to be read eschatologically—from the end (the promises of restoration in Amos 9.11-15) backwards—and thus it would be most appropriate to read a text such as Amos 5.24 in this hopeful, Zion-centred and God-centred way.

But it is also important to place Amos within the larger context of the entire scroll of the twelve prophets. P.R. House offers some interesting insights here. Focusing on the Hebrew collection, House sees Hosea, Joel, Amos, Obadiah, Jonah and Micah as books each describing the predicament of the people in terms of their abuse of their covenant relationship with God, whilst Nahum, Habakkuk and Zephaniah spell out the consequences in terms of the punishment soon to take place; and Haggai, Zechariah and Malachi start to create a picture of a new age of restoration.[70] According to House, Amos is very much the darker side of the picture, analysing the situation before it has come about.[71] This results in a more negative reading of 'justice and righteousness': Amos's preaching on the subject had more to do with the whole nation's culpability than it had to do with the offer of a new start from God. This comes in the message of the restoration prophets.

In the Septuagint tradition, where Amos is placed between Hosea and Micah, yet another reading of 5.24 may be brought out. For within the minor prophets, only Hosea and Micah echo the teachings of Amos regarding morality and the cult. Hosea 6.4-6 is an important passage which sets 'steadfast love' (חסד) over sacrifice, and 'knowledge of God' (דעת אלהים) over burnt offerings. There is no obvious reference to justice and righteousness, but the teaching on integrity of worship in the latter part of Hos. 6.4-6, and on practical morality in the first half, does seem to be an echo of Amos 5.21-24. Micah 6.6-8 offers a similar observation about morality and liturgy: justice (משפט), loving kindness (חסד) and a humble dependence upon God (הצנע לכת עם אלהיך) are more pleasing

---

70. See P.R. House, *The Unity of the Twelve* (JSOTSup, 97; Sheffield: Sheffield Academic Press, 1990), p. 72.

71. An obvious weakness in this interpretation is the way in which Amos is read in terms of the announcement of punishment rather than the threat of it. To argue that the fortunes of Israel 'begin to plunge downward in Hosea and Joel, fall even further in Amos-Micah, reach their nadir in Habakkuk, begin to inch upward towards the end of Zephaniah, climb sharply in Haggai and Zechariah, and complete their ascent in Malachi' (House, *Unity of the Twelve*, p. 123) would seem to be allowing the picture of the whole to over-dominate the details of the smaller parts.

than a multitude of sacrifices ('thousands of rams, ten thousand rivers of oil'). So, although the theme of justice and cultic practice is dealt with in different ways in all three prophets, the desire to purify the cult through morality (whether in terms of steadfast love or justice is immaterial here) is a distinctive theme which unites all three prophets and distinguishes them from the other nine prophets in the scroll. In this way, focusing on Amos 5.21-24, we may conclude that the reading here, when taking all three prophets within a continuum together, would be of justice and righteousness in a pragmatic way—one which has more to do with practical behaviour than with any gift from God.

Hence a reading of Amos 5.21-24 within the context of the scroll of the twelve minor prophets could have at least two variations. In the case of the Hebrew collection, the text offers a more eschatological orientation, with hints of a new age (with Zion set over the other nations) picked up from Joel in particular. So 5.24 would read 'and justice *will* roll down like waters...' in terms of a God-given hope for the future, within a purged cult. But in the case of Amos's position in the Greek collection, the text is placed within a more didactic context, and picks up the similar themes of warning and judgment from Hosea and Micah. So 5.24 in this case would read 'and *let* justice roll down like waters...' This would thus encourage an appropriate 'Torah-piety' based upon the integration of cultic practice and social justice.[72]

Amos 5.21-24 within the Hebrew Bible: God's Justice is Coming Soon
If we read Amos in the broader context of the Law, the Prophets and the Writings, a different perspective on Amos 5.21-24 begins to emerge. Firstly in the Torah, the premiss is of the complementary nature of cultic practice and social justice, with no indication that festivals and sacrifices are anything but a means of the people drawing close to God. Despite the different views of the value of cultic practice (expressed, for example, in the ritual decalogue in Exod. 34.11-26, compared with the cultic laws of Deut. 16.1-21, and the priestly laws throughout Leviticus) there is no suggestion that these practices are in any way abhorrent to God. Furthermore, nowhere in the Torah is there any suggestion that the orderly practices legislated in the cult should not be mirrored in the community: order in liturgy and order in society are two sides of the same coin. For example,

---

72. By the later restoration period this combination of cultic practice with social morality seems to be the hallmark of the heroes of faith: examples include Job 1.1-5 and Dan. 6.10.

the laws concerning festivals in Deut. 16 are set between the laws about social justice in Deut. 15 (the year of release) and the justice to be executed by the judges and king in Deut. 17. And the priestly laws in Leviticus are similarly interspersed with corresponding laws about social justice: the law of the sabbatical year and jubilee in Lev. 25 is a good example of this. The Torah provides an essential corrective against interpreting Amos 5.21-24 as an absolute polarization of the two ideals of liturgy and morality.

Furthermore, the Torah makes it abundantly clear that punishment is always followed by mercy. This is best illustrated in Gen. 1–11. Adam and Eve do not die, but are allowed to live outside Eden; Cain does not die, but is allowed to live in the land of Nod; Noah survives the flood, and God promises never to flood the whole earth again; and after the tower of Babel come the call and blessing of Abraham. This repetitive strand of mercy outdoing judgment runs throughout the entire Torah into the Former Prophets, making it impossible to read Amos 5 in an isolationist way, as God's emphatic 'No' to his people.[73] Instead, the larger narrative framework makes the reader see the passage beyond its specificity and particularity: if 'justice and righteousness' is as much about God's nature and God's initiative, than it explains that God's judgment is about mercy as well as punishment, about the day of the Lord as light as well as about darkness, about God as Creator as well as God as Destroyer.

The references to 'justice and righteousness' in the Writings offer another corrective view. Usually here the premiss is that the justice of God works ultimately for the right ordering of the world. This is most clearly expressed in the enthronement psalms: God will not forsake his creation, for justice and righteousness must prevail (Ps. 94.14-15); 'righteousness and justice are the foundation of his throne' (Ps. 97.2). In Ps. 89.14, in the part of the psalm which also celebrates the kingship of God, a similar phrase is found, with an additional comment: 'Righteousness and justice are the foundation of thy throne; steadfast love and faithfulness go before thee': God's justice and righteousness are as much about mercy and love as about judgment. Looking further at the Writings, the same theme is found in the book of Job. Job is inclined to doubt that there is any justice and order in the world: 'Does God pervert justice? Or does the Almighty pervert the right?' (Job 8.3), but when he speaks of wearing justice and righteousness 'like a robe and a turban'

73. See B.A. Asen, 'No, Yes and Perhaps in Amos and the Yahwist', *VT* 43 (1993), pp. 433-41; also G.P. Pfeifer, 'Das ja des Amos', *VT* 39 (1989), pp. 497-503.

(Job 29.14), this is an affirmation of his ultimate belief in his right before God. God's final appearance to Job out of the whirlwind vindicates this: God does indeed act in justice and righteousness, evidence of which may be found through the created order (Job 40.8).

Thus if Amos 5.24 is read against the background of the Torah and the Writings, the ultimate meaning of 'justice and righteousness' must be that God works from judgment to mercy, or from chaos to order; hence Amos 5.24 must be read ultimately in the light of God's justice as mercy, not as judgment.

One other relevant text with insights into the use of 'justice and righteousness' is in the prophetic canon. Within the book of Isaiah, this pair of terms recurs frequently. At the very beginning of the book, which in many ways summarizes the whole message, we find a passage strikingly similar to Amos in terms of its rejection of present cultic practices and its plea for social justice (1.12-17). Yet the passage is followed (1.21-26) by a description of God's purging act of judgment against Zion:

> Zion will be redeemed by justice,
> and those in her who repent, by righteousness (1.27).

In Isa. 5.1-7, the parable of the vineyard makes a plea for justice and righteousness in terms as stark and negative as in Amos, but in Isaiah this is set alongside another theme which does not occur explicitly throughout Amos—that justice executed through judgment will result ultimately in justice executed through salvation. Isaiah 11.1-5 makes this clear: a coming deliverer will bring in salvation by means of executing 'justice and righteousness'. He will 'judge in righteousness' (v. 4: בצדק ושפט) 'and righteousness (צדק) shall be the girdle of his waist' (v. 5). The same picture is evident in Isa. 16.5, which speaks of a coming king who will seek justice and be swift to do righteousness . A similar picture is found in Isa. 32.1, where again the figures are royal ('Behold, a king will reign in righteousness, and princes will rule in justice'). This theme is found again in Isa. 42.1-4, where the justice brought in by the coming figure appears to affect nations beyond Israel ('He will not fail or be discouraged till he has established justice in the earth'). In conclusion, 'justice and righteousness' within the Isaiah scroll offer us a vision of justice as an ideal to be sought after and as a gift from God, thus giving the broader context of Amos 5.21-24 the same connotation as in the Law and Writings. The terms are as much about cultic worship as about personal and social morality, as much about a vision for the future as about a quality to be attained fully in the here and now, and as much about mercy and faithfulness as about judgment. In looking beyond Amos, we are therefore able to read the terms in Amos in a more positive and less polarized way.

Amos 5.21-24 within the Christian Bible: Divine Justice has Come, Human Endeavour is Over

The New Testament explicitly cites Amos only twice, and although neither citation is from Amos 5.21-24, one example, using 5.25-27, throws some light on this passage.[74] This citation has to be seen from the debate about the authoritative status of the Jewish cultus by second and third generation Christians (a status which the fall of Jerusalem in 70 CE did little to help) as to whether festivals, sacrifices and Jewish prayers were less important than a moral life led with integrity before God. In negating the value of the Jewish cultus, some made an appeal to prophets such as Amos: it appeared to some that he anticipated the teaching of Christ in the Sermon on the Mount—that order and justice in society, accompanied by an inner attitude of dependency upon God, were more important than the ritual offerings of the Temple cult. To some, it appeared that the tradition of Jesus' cleansing of the Temple, which by its act indicated a new interpretation of the Temple cult, was an illustration of this.[75]

Against this background, the quotation of Amos 5.25-27 in Stephen's speech is informative. That the source used for Amos would have been the Greek version, and that it is in the LXX collection that the setting of Amos between Hosea and Micah shows up the more anti-cultic bias, is perhaps no coincidence. By using this text and this translation, Amos 5.25-27, according to Acts, encouraged a bias against Jewish cultic practice.[76] And the references to 'justice and righteousness' in the previous verses of Amos, interpreted here as an alternative way of life more pleasing to God, simply added fuel to this conflict. The anti-cultic reading of this Amos text

74. Amos 5.25-27 is quoted in Stephen's speech in Acts 7.42-53, which is to demonstrate the guilt (and idolatry) of the people ever since the days of Moses. Amos 9.11 is used in Acts 15.16, at the time of the Council of Jerusalem, and quoting the LXX, to illustrate that the new Davidic kingdom, under Christ, could include Gentiles who called on the name of Israel's God.

75. The Johannine commentary on this act, in Jn. 2.13-22, would indicate that this is the case: 'Destroy this Temple, and in three days I will raise it up' (Jn 2.19); 'he spoke of the temple as his body' (Jn 2.21).

76. There are some ironies here, regarding the similar way in which Judah looked at Israelite cultic practices, within their context of the supremacy of the Temple cult. By Acts the debate about the value of the cult no longer concerns Israel and Judah, but rather Jew and Christian.

within a New Testament framework makes an interesting contrast to the earlier more complementary 'justice and the cult' readings when the text is read within the confines of the Hebrew Bible.

Another reading arises out of this anti-cultic emphasis. If cultic worship was indeed seen as inadequate, and the appeal to justice and righteousness is about God's activity rather than about renewed liturgy, then the teaching in Pauline Christianity about grace and the law gives a new cutting edge to Amos 5.21-24. Working on a typology that justice and righteousness = God's grace, and the law = the Jewish cult, then God's justice and righteousness are what he offers as an act of grace to render ineffective the Jewish cult. Insofar as much New Testament teaching is concerned with the way that God both brings about judgment on sin, yet also provides a means of escape from it, passages such as Amos 5.21-24 offer a most pertinent example of the way that the grace of God (seen through his 'justice and righteousness') overcomes the insufficiency of human action (seen through the inadequacy of the cult).[77]

This reading of Amos from the point of view of the New Testament writings has turned the earlier readings on their head, in a way similar to my previous readings of Gen. 2–3 and Ps. 23. No longer is Amos 5.21-24 about the importance of social justice working *through* the cult; the reading of this text within a New Testament framework is of Amos as an iconoclast against the Jewish cult. No longer is Amos 5.21-24 to be read in terms of how human endeavour might be able to cooperate with divine initiative; the reading of the text within a New Testament framework is of divine justice working over and against human endeavour: God had to do what humans were incapable of doing for themselves. No longer is Amos 5.21-24 to be read with a glance over the shoulder to the past, explaining how and why the people are where they are now—rather, the New Testament reading uses this passage as an illustration of a vision for the future inauguration of justice. And most important of all, no longer is the text to be read in the context of some hope for God's coming age of justice and righteousness: that age has now dawned, and now judges the hopes and fears of the earlier prophetic texts such as Amos 5 in that light.

---

77. This point is made by D.A. Hubbard, *Joel and Amos* (TOTC; Leicester: Inter-Varsity Press, 1989), pp. 117-18: justice and righteousness are by New Testament time something God does for us rather than something we do in order to bring about our own salvation.

Some Final Observations

Writing on the problem of reconstruction in the prophet books, both historical and literary, R.F. Melugin speaks of how both the historical and the literary interpretations go far beyond the available evidence.[78] In terms of the historical approach, Melugin argues that this is more likely to be a picture painted by the historian than a reproduction of the past as it really was. He speaks of the poetic language of the prophet Amos creating its own world, which prevents any clear-cut reconstruction taking place:

> Any proposed historical reconstruction is in no small degree the *historian's* story. Whenever we inquire concerning the intent of a text's author or how a text was originally used, it is *we* who *imagine* what the author intended or how a text was employed. *We* decide what questions to ask; we decide which aspects of the 'record' are important...[79] (his italics)

Nevertheless, Melugin concludes that providing any portrayal of historical development is recognized as a construct designed for interpretative conventions, the reader must nevertheless continue to ask historical questions. The same applies to the use of literary approaches: literary questions about the meanings of the text within its many contours are equally critical. But this will inevitably mean that the text offers as many different readings as there are questions, with each reading being dependent upon our own historical and/or literary reconstruction.

An article on Amos by D.J.A. Clines illustrates well the way in which my interpretation of the text is as much dependent upon the questions asked of it as upon one obvious meaning 'out there'.[80] Clines's concern is to strip away the ideological assumptions of commentators who are anxious to defend the views of the prophet and to criticize those the prophet attacked. Clines observes that this creates a problem of integrity of reading. This is particularly evident with respect to the teaching on 'justice and

---

78. See R.F. Melugin, 'Prophetic Books and the Problem of Historical Reconstruction', in S.B. Reid (ed.), *Prophets and Paradigms: Essays in Honor of Gene M. Tucker* (JSOTSup, 229; Sheffield: Sheffield Academic Press, 1996), pp. 63-78.

79. See Melugin, 'Prophetic Books', p. 64, in the context of a criticism of H.W. Wolff's six-stage reconstruction of the stages of growth of the book of Amos. See also S. Fish, *Is There a Text in This Class? The Authority of Interpretative Communities* (Cambridge, MA: Harvard University Press, 1980), pp. 15-17, 167-73.

80. See D.J.A. Clines, 'Metacommentating Amos', in H.A. McKay and D.J.A. Clines (eds.), *Of Prophets' Visions and the Wisdom of Sages: Essays in Honour of R. Norman Whybray on his Seventieth Birthday* (JSOTSup, 163; Sheffield: Sheffield Academic Press, 1993), pp. 142-60.

righteousness' in Amos. If a central part of the prophet's message is his belief in a God of justice, and his consequent demand for justice in the community, it is hard to see either divine or social justice being brought about by the threats of famine, fire and exile. Although these are directed against the leaders, such threats involve the whole community, and those who would suffer most would be the poor and weak—the very individuals who most need 'justice and righteousness' to work on their side. So when we seek to discover the assumptions behind a text such as Amos 5.21-24 one possible answer might be of an avenging God, intent upon the break-up of a society struggling, through good and bad times, for survival. Clines points out that at this stage we need to extract ourselves from the ideology of those who have given us the text and pronounce a moral judgment on them.[81]

For theological reasons, rather than ideological ones, this is perhaps what the New Testament writers are trying to do. By extricating themselves from the theology of the early writers they pronounce a moral judgment on them, thus deconstructing previous interpretations. For when a text such as Amos is read within a canonical context of the Old and New Testaments together, the meaning changes dramatically: the approach is different in kind, rather than degree. This leaves us with an intriguing double question: should we still maintain a thoroughgoing pluralistic approach, whereby we see that multivalent readings offer no fixed or final answers, or should we uphold instead that the New Testament reading is distinctive and even unique in the way it adds such a radically different meaning to the Old Testament texts? Or conversely, can we affirm the view that the final New Testament reading is distinctive (for example, with Amos, the notion that divine justice has overcome human endeavour) but equally affirm that such a reading allows us more freedom of interpretation rather than any constraint? And having deconstructed the New Testament readings in the same way that the New Testament writers deconstruct the Old Testament texts, where, if anywhere, do we then draw the limits?

81. See Clines, 'Metacommentating Amos', pp. 158-59. In this way the *newer* meaning could be said to deconstruct the older ones, for it asks whether the earlier interpretations have really understood aright the theological concerns in the text. This in turn raises further questions about the 'newer' interpretation of Gen. 2–3 in terms of original sin, for this undoubtedly deconstructs many earlier readings. Perhaps what makes Clines's proposal for a different reading of Amos 5 work is that its focus is still on 'justice' as a key theme in the text, and what makes new and distinctive readings of Gen. 2–3 not work is that they do not focus on the key theological theme—that of 'knowledge'.

Chapter 5

CONCLUSION

The search for meaning in biblical texts is a little like the search for
Flaubert's Parrot.[1] A clever parody of the nature of both historical and
literary criticism, the book is a description of the search of a retired
doctor, Geoffrey Braithwaite, for the stuffed parrot which once belonged
to Gustav Flaubert and apparently influenced Flaubert's writings. In the
final chapter Braithwaite arrives at the Museum of Natural History at
Croisset, where the search culminates in the discovery of not one stuffed
parrot, but three out of some fifty or more.

> Everywhere I looked there were birds. Shelf after shelf of birds, each one
> covered in a sprinkling of white pesticide. I was directed to the third aisle. I
> pushed carefully between the shelves and then looked up at a slight angle.
> There, standing in line, were the Amazonian parrots. Of the original fifty
> only three remained. Any gaudiness in their colouring had been dimmed by
> the dusting of pesticide which lay over them. They gazed at me like three
> quizzical, sharp-eyed, dandruff-ridden, dishonourable old men. They did
> look—I had to admit it—a little cranky. I stared at them for a minute or so,
> and then dodged away. Perhaps it was one of them.

Whether our own search has taken a more historically-orientated bias or a
more literary-orientated one, it should have become clear that there is not
one meaning—not even three—but some 'fifty or more'.

The case studies of Genesis, Psalms and Amos may not have offered as
many readings as fifty, but they have suggested that there are certainly
more than three. It is surprising to find just how subjective an enterprise
reading the Bible can be. There is no problem with subjectivity in reading
when it comes to more general literary works; but given that the reading of
biblical texts has traditionally been steeped in 'the authority of the Church
as the interpreter of the Bible' or 'the authority of the Bible as the Word of

---

1.   Julian Barnes, *Flaubert's Parrot* (London: Picador, Jonathan Cape Ltd, 1985),
p. 190.

God', standing over and against the individual, the primary role of the reader comes more as a surprise and is one which needs emphasizing. Further, given the claims of historical criticism that it is a more objective enterprise (partly in reaction to this confessional position), the centrality of the reader in this process needs stating all the more.

My reading of Gen. 2–3 provided a good illustration of the primary role of the reader in interpreting the text. It showed that every answer depends upon the choice of question the reader asks of the text. For example, if one asks questions that presume the text is part of the Christian canon of biblical writings, one ends up with Christian-shaped answers: in this reading, Gen. 2–3 is about original sin and hence foreshadows the need for the redemptive act of Christ on the cross. But neither these questions nor these answers are the only valid ones: questions posed from, say, a pre-Christian Jewish tradition, or a post-Christian Jewish tradition, would offer a very different range of answers. The answers that are given echo the questions that have been imposed onto the text.

Following from this, another issue that these case studies highlighted is the contingent nature of the methods used. This is the case whether one uses a more historically-orientated approach, such as tradition-criticism, or a more literary-orientated one, such as rhetorical-criticism. Few today would deny that historical criticism has an element of contingency, given that over time it has been seen to offer limited insights about the actual context of a text. And the view that the more recent literary approaches are equally imaginative and reconstructive has always been freely acknowledged by those who read the Bible in a literary-critical way. So an observation about the contingent nature of both methods offers few surprises. But an important implication follows from this: the text itself is a resource for a vast array of different theological insights.

My reading of Amos was a good example of theological diversity. Historically speaking, it was impossible to ascertain when the first use of the term 'justice and righteousness' originated, whether at the time of Amos or a century or more later, and so any reading of the different theological emphases in those terms, at different periods of time, has to be arbitrary and hypothetical. And similarly from a literary point of view the theological interpretation of these terms shifted and changed depending upon reading it within (for example) the literary framework of the Hebrew Bible or the Old and New Testaments taken together, where in the latter collection 'justice and righteousness' took on a more theocentric and redemptive meaning than the more anthropocentric and practical one found in earlier pre-New Testament readings.

A third issue arising from the case studies is that each chapter high-lighted the interdependency of the historical and literary approaches to the text. For example, a typical tradition-critical question would be 'What difference does a historical context make to the formation of a particular tradition in a text, and how does this shape the theological concerns within that text?' A typical rhetorical-critical question would be almost identical: 'What difference does a literary context make to the formation of a par-ticular *Leitmotif* in a text, and how does this shape the theological concerns within that text?' The biblical text, as an ancient text accruing layers of meaning through the history of its reception, requires historically-orien-tated questions; and, given that there are layers of meaning, the reader requires literary skills as well in order to determine from the text as it stands, as well as from the history of the text, which meanings make sense.

An illustration of this is Ps. 23, where the metaphorical nature of the poetry as well as the anonymity of the author result in literary and histori-cal uncertainties. But, here, historically-shaped answers to historical ques-tions can offer some insights on the literary ambiguities by showing how the metaphorical imagery of 'shepherding' and the consequent imagery of 'feeding' and 'resting' could be read differently depending upon a monar-chic, exilic or restoration context. Conversely, literary-shaped answers to literary questions offer insights on the historical ambiguities: for example, by looking at the motif of 'feeding' and 'resting' in Ps. 23 from the con-text of the Psalter as a whole, or from the Hebrew Bible as a whole, the reception history of the psalm can be seen from a wider perspective.

This leads on to a more contentious issue. This is the way in which a particular interpretation of the biblical text—whether historical or literary —offers a different set of problems when the text is read from a specifi-cally New Testament perspective. In each of the three chapters, we saw that the Christian reading, which interpreted the text within the body of tradition of the Old and New Testaments taken together, often turned earlier readings on their head. It would not be too simplistic to state that a reading within the historical and literary confines of the Old Testament is mainly anthropocentric in its concerns: human experience is at the heart of the matter. Genesis 2–3 speaks of the failure of the first humans, Ps. 23 speaks of the vulnerabilities of being human, and Amos 5 speaks of the way humans fail to live out justice and righteousness in their society. By contrast, a reading within the historical and literary boundaries of the Old and New Testaments taken together is primarily theocentric, in that it starts with the assumption that there has been some specific divine intervention in Christ—an intervention that redeems what is lacking in human experience. Hence Gen. 2–3 is read as if Christ is restoring what Adam once lost; Ps. 23 is read as a prophecy, the content of which has been realized in the life of Christ who is the Good Shepherd for all time; and Amos 5 is read as if Christ is the one who brings in the justice and righteousness that humans seem unable to achieve on their own.

This raises the question: does this more overtly theocentric reading negate or fulfil the earlier ones? The answer taken from these case studies would appear to be mainly the former. Taking Ps. 23 as an example, a Christian reading certainly has some recognizable continuity with earlier tradition, especially in the way it picks up the more forward-looking hopeful reading of Ps. 23 in Jewish thinking: but, because it changes that hope into realization, by turning everything 'Christwards', it reads the text from the end point backwards, as it were. Hence ultimately one could argue that there is some continuity, but the essential mode of interpretation —exemplified by the use of the term 'New Testament'—is that it is discontinuous.

The discontinuity of tradition created by the New Testament reading of a text leads to another theological problem. If readings of the Hebrew Bible and readings of the Old and New Testaments taken together are a subjective process, coming at the text from a particular 'Blick' which creates a new and different interpretative tradition, with the only constraint being the text itself, then surely this way of reading ratifies other new and different readings of the text? Surely both sorts of reading—what we might term Jewish and Christian readings—actually challenge us to read the biblical texts in an increasingly open-ended way? This question was posed in the light of the ideological reading of Amos 5 by David Clines.[2] Certainly, a Christian mode of reading seems to give some grounds for the reader to question and reinterpret the New Testament readings in the same way that the New Testament readings have done with the Old; and a Jewish mode of reading, with its emphasis on *pesher* and *midrashic* interpretations of the Hebrew Bible from the late Second Temple period onwards, also seems to offer the same rationale.

If from within the Jewish and Christian traditions we are able to posit a reader-centred approach, with the possibilities of constantly open-ended readings of text, this has another important implication. Inherent within this tradition is an approach very close to that of postmodernism. It is not

2.   See pp. 120-21.

that Jewish and Christian readers have to imitate postmodernist ways of reading in order to appear relevant and contemporary; the *raison d'être* for this way of reading is already embedded within their own traditions. Pluralist, reader-centred, text-based ways of reading are nothing new: Jewish readers of texts have been practising them from the second century BCE onwards, and Christian readers of texts have been practising them from the first century CE onwards. For example, in the Christian tradition, it is clear that the reinterpretative element in the New Testament readings developed much further in the later Christian reception history of the biblical texts—from the period of the church fathers, to mediaeval exegesis, to readings of the texts in the Reformation and Enlightenment period, and so from modernism up to the present day—illustrating how much open-ended and pluralist readings have been an intrinsic part of the Christian tradition from New Testament times onwards.

But there is nevertheless one critical difference between Jewish and Christian ways of reading and reinterpreting and the postmodernist position. Each is embedded within a particular and recognizable 'tradition', and the reading and reinterpreting takes place within the context of this accepted body of interpretative tradition. Thus it could be argued that within the Judaic–Christian tradition there is an inherited practice of reading that is in dialogue both with something 'out there' (what in modernist terms would be called a 'metanarrative', but what we have termed here 'reception history') and as well as with something 'within' (what in postmodern terms would be the reader-centred approach). Hence both Jewish and Christian ways of reading are on the one hand receptive (reading the texts while plumbing the depths of a vast body of interpretative tradition that has gone before) and, on the other hand, proactive (reader-centred, subjectively orientated, concerned with a number of different readings on the *surface* of the texts).

This study has sought to demonstrate from the practice of reading that biblical studies is neither modernist nor postmodernist, but a complex blend of both, because the biblical text comprises both the historical elements that modernist studies have been interested in and the literary elements that postmodernists enjoy. Biblical studies, whether practised within the Jewish tradition focused on the Hebrew Bible, or the Christian tradition focused on the Old and New Testaments taken together, have been in danger of being polarized into a defensive 'pro-modernist' stance or a more contemporary 'pro-postmodernist' position. A new brief is required. Biblical students should be among the first to engage in ever-new ways of reading, being prepared to ask constantly new questions of the text without predetermining all the old answers, while recognizing that the old answers also have a part to play in the ongoing discourse.[3] The nature of the diverse and developing tradition of biblical interpretation, not only within the church and synagogue, but also within the academy, requires this of us.

3. A good example of the way of reading biblical texts from a reception-history point of view—with the similar emphasis on multivalency—is found in J.F.A. Sawyer, *The Fifth Gospel: Isaiah in the History of Christianity* (Cambridge: Cambridge University Press, 1996).

BIBLIOGRAPHY

Achtemeier, P.J. (ed.), *Society of Biblical Literature 1978 Seminar Papers* (Missoula: MT: University of Montana, 1978).

Albright, W.F., 'The Goddess of Life and Wisdom', *AJSL* 36 (1919), pp. 258-94.

Alexander, P.S., 'The Fall into Knowledge: The Garden of Eden/Paradise in Gnostic Literature', in Morris and Sawyer (eds.), *A Walk in the Garden*, pp. 91-104.

Allaway, R.H., 'Fall or Fall-Short?', *ExpTim* 97 (1986), pp. 108-110.

Alonso-Schökel, L., 'Sapiental and Covenant Themes in Genesis 2–3', in J.L. Crenshaw (ed.), *Studies in Ancient Israelite Wisdom* (New York: Ktav, 1976), pp. 456-68.

Alter, R., *The Art of Biblical Narrative* (London: Allen and Unwin, 1981).

Anderson, A.A., *The New Century Bible Commentary, Psalms 1–72* (Grand Rapids: Eerdmans; London: Marshall, Morgan and Scott, 1972).

Anderson, B.W., *Out of the Depths: The Psalms Speak for us Today* (Philadelphia: Westminster Press, 1983).

Anderson F.I., and D.N. Freedman, *Amos: A New Translation with Introduction and Commentary* (AB, 24A; Garden City, NY: Doubleday, 1989).

Anderson, G.A., *The Genesis of Perfection: Adam and Eve in Jewish and Christian Imagination* (Louisville, KY: Westminster/John Knox Press, 2001).

Asen, B.A., 'No, Yes and Perhaps in Amos and the Yahwist', *VT* 43 (1993), pp. 433-41.

Auffret, P., *La Sagesse a bâti sa maison: Études de structures littéraires dans l'Ancien Testament et spécialement dans les psaumes* (Göttingen: Vandenhoeck & Ruprecht, 1982).

Auld, A.G., *Amos* (OTG; Sheffield: JSOT Press, 1986).

Auwers, J.-M., *La Composition Littéraire du Psautier: Un État de la Question* (Paris: J. Gabalda et Cie Éditeurs, 2000).

Bachelard, G., *The Poetics of Space: The Classic Look at How we Experience Intimate Places* (trans. M. Jolas; Boston: Beacon Press, 1994 [1969]).

Baker, J., 'The Myth of Man's "Fall"—A Reappraisal', *ExpTim* 92 (1981), pp. 235-37.

Barker, M., *The Older Testament* (London: SPCK, 1987).

Barnes, J., *Flaubert's Parrot* (London: Picador, Jonathan Cape Ltd, 1985).

Barr, J., 'The Image of God in the Book of Genesis—A Study in Terminology', *BJRL* 51 (1968), pp. 11-26.

—*The Garden of Eden and the Hope of Immortality* (London: SCM Press, 1992).

Barré, M.L., and J.S. Kselman, 'New Exodus, Covenant and Restoration in Psalm 23', in C.L. Meyers and M. O'Connor (eds.), *The Word of the Lord Shall Go Forth: Essays in Honor of David Noel Freedman in Celebration of his Sixtieth Birthday* (AASOR Special Volume Series, 1; Winona Lake, IN: Eisenbrauns, 1983), pp. 97-127.

Barrett, C.K., *From First Adam to Last: A Study in Pauline Theology* (London: SPCK, 1962).

Barth, C., 'Concatenatio im ersten Buch des Psalters', in B. Benzing, O. Bächer and G. Mayer (eds.), *Wort und Wirklihkeit: Studien zur afrikanistik und orientalistik* (Festschrift E.L. Rapp; Hain: Meisenheim am Glan, 1976), pp. 30-40.

Barton, J., 'Natural Law and Poetic Justice in the Old Testament', *JTS* NS 30 (1979), pp. 1-14.

—*Amos's Oracles against the Nations* (Cambridge: Cambridge University Press, 1980).

—*Isaiah 1–39* (OTG; Sheffield: Sheffield Academic Press, 1995).

—'Historical-critical Approaches', in J. Barton (ed.), *Biblical Interpretation* (Cambridge: Cambridge University Press, 1998), pp. 9-20.

Bauks M., and G. Baumann, 'Im Anfang war…? Gen. 1,1ff und Prov. 8,22-31 im Vergleich', *BN* 71 (1994), pp. 24-52.

Bazak, Y., 'Psalm 23—A Pattern Poem', *Dor le Dor* 11 (1982–1983), pp. 71-76.

—'Numerical Devices in Biblical Poetry', VT 38 (1988), pp. 333-37.

Beattie, D.R.G., 'What is Genesis 2–3 About?', *ExpTim* 92 (1980), pp. 8-10.

Bechtel, L.M., 'Rethinking the Interpretation of Genesis 2.4b–3.24', in Brenner (ed.), *A Feminist Companion to Genesis*, pp. 77-117.

—'Genesis 2.4b–3.24: A Myth about Human Maturation', *JSOT* 67 (1995), pp. 3-26.

Bennett, J., and S. Mandelbrote (eds.), *The Garden, the Ark, the Tower, the Temple: Biblical Metaphors of Knowledge in Early-Modern Europe* (Oxford: Museum of the History of Science and Bodleian Library, 1998).

Bentzen, A., *Messias-Moses redivivus-Menschensohn* (ATANT; Zürich: Zwingli Verlag, 1948).

Berquist, J.L., 'Dangerous Waters of Justice and Righteousness: Amos 5.18-27', *BTB* 23 (1993), pp. 54-63.

Beyerlin, W., *Werden und Wesen des 107. Psalms* (BZAW, 153; Berlin: W. de Gruyter, 1979).

Bledstein, A.J., 'Are Women Cursed in Genesis 3.16?', in A. Brenner (ed.), *A Feminist Companion to Genesis* (Sheffield: Sheffield Academic Press, 1993), pp. 142-45.

Blenkinsopp, J., *The Pentateuch* (London: SCM Press, 1992).

—'P and J in Genesis 1.1–11.26: An Alternative Hypothesis', in A.B. Beck *et al.* (eds.), *Fortunate the Eyes that See: Essays in Honor of D.N. Freedman* (Grand Rapids, MI: Eerdmans, 1995), pp. 1-15.

Bloom, H., *The Book of J* (London: Faber and Faber, 1991).

Blum, E., *Studien zur Komposition des Pentateuch* (BZAW, 189; Berlin: W. de Gruyter, 1990).

Bonhoeffer, D., *Creation and Fall: A Theological Exposition of Genesis 1–3* (trans. J. Bowden; Dietrich Bonhoeffer Works, 3; Minneapolis: Fortress Press, 1996).

Boomershine, T.E., 'The Structure of Narrative Rhetoric in Genesis 2–3', *Semeia* 18 (1980), pp. 113-29.

Braude, W.G., *Midrash on the Psalms* (New Haven: Yale University Press, 1959), pp. 327-35.

Brenner, A. (ed.), *A Feminist Companion to Genesis* (Sheffield: Sheffield Academic Press, 1993).

Brett, M.G., *Genesis: Procreation and the Politics of Identity* (Old Testament Readings; London: Routledge, 2000).

Briggs, C.A., *A Critical and Exegetical Commentary on the Book of Psalms* (2 vols.; Edinburgh: T. & T. Clark, 1906).

Brueggemann, W., *The Message of the Psalms* (Minneapolis: Augsburg, 1984).

Buchanon, G.W., 'The Old Testament Meaning of the Knowledge of Good and Evil', *JBL* 75 (1956), pp. 114-20.

Burns, D.E., 'Dream Form in Genesis 2.4b—3.24: Asleep in the Garden', *JSOT* 37 (1987), pp. 3-14.

Buttenweiser, M., *The Psalms: Chronologically Arranged with a New Translation* (New York: Ktav, rev. edn, 1969 [1938]).
Carmichael, C.M., 'The Paradise Myth: Interpreting without Jewish and Christian Spectacles', in Morris and Sawyer (eds.), *A Walk in the Garden*, pp. 47-63.
Carr, D., 'The Politics of Textual Subversion: A Diachronic Perspective on the Garden of Eden Story', *JBL* 112 (1993), pp. 577-95.
Clark, W.M., 'A Legal Background to the Yahwist's Use of "Good and Evil" in Genesis 2–3', *JBL* 88 (1969), pp. 266-78.
Clements, R.E., 'Amos and the Politics of Israel', in D. Garron and F. Israel (eds.), *Storia e tradizioni di Israeli: Scritti in onore di J Alberto Soggin* (Brescia: Paedeia, 1991), pp. 49-64.
Clines, D.J.A., 'The Tree of Knowledge and the Law of Yahweh', *VT* 24 (1974), pp. 8-14.
—*The Theme of the Pentateuch* (JSOTSup, 10; Sheffield: JSOT Press, 1978).
—'Prefatory Theme', in *idem, The Theme of the Pentateuch*, pp. 61-79.
—*What Does Eve Do to Help? and Other Readerly Questions to the Old Testament* (JSOTSup, 94; Sheffield: JSOT Press, 1990).
—'Metacommentating Amos', in H.A. McKay and D.J.A. Clines (eds.), *Of Prophets' Visions and the Wisdom of Sages: Essays in Honour of R. Norman Whybray on his Seventieth Birthday* (JSOTSup, 163; Sheffield: Sheffield Academic Press, 1993), pp. 142-60.
—'A World established on Water (Psalm 24): Reader-Response, Deconstruction and Bespoke Interpretation', in J.C. Exum and D.J.A. Clines (eds.), *The New Literary Criticism and the Hebrew Bible* (JSOTSup, 143: Sheffield: JSOT Press, 1993), pp. 79-90.
Cohen, A., תהלים: *The Psalms* (The Soncino Books of the Bible; New York: Soncino Press, 1992).
Coote, R.B., *Amos among the Prophets: Composition and Theology* (Philadelphia: Fortress Press, 1981).
Coppens, J., *La connaissance du bien et du mal et le péché du paradis* (ALBO, II/3; Gembloux: J. Duculot, 1948).
Corney, R.W., '"Rod and Staff" (Psalm 23.4): a Double Image?', in S.L. Cook and S.C. Winter (eds.), *On the Way to Nineveh* (Atlanta: Scholars Press, 1999), pp. 28-41.
Coulot, C.C., 'Propositions pour une structuration du livre d'Amos au niveau rédactionnel', *RevScRel* 51 (1977), pp. 169-86.
Craigie, P.C., *Psalms 1–50* (Waco, TX: Word Books, 1983).
Crenshaw, J.L., 'The Influence of the Wise upon Amos', *ZAW* 79 (1967), pp. 42-52.
—*Hymnic Affirmation of Divine Justice: The Doxologies of Amos and Related Texts in the Old Testament* (Missoula: Scholars Press, 1975).
Cripps, R.S., *A Critical and Exegetical Commentary on the Book of Amos* (London: SPCK, 1929).
Croft, S.J.L., *The Identity of the Individual in the Book of Psalms* (JSOTSup, 44; Sheffield: JSOT Press, 1987).
Davies, P.R., 'Women, Men, Gods, Sex and Power: The Birth of a Biblical Myth', in Brenner (ed.), *A Feminist Companion to Genesis*, pp. 194-201.
—'Making It: Creation and Contradiction in Genesis', in M.D. Carroll, D.J.A. Clines and P.R. Davies (eds.), *The Bible in Human Society: Essays in Honour of John Rogerson* (JSOTSup, 200; Sheffield: JSOT Press, 1995), pp. 249-56.
Delitzsch, F., *Biblical Commentary on the Psalms* (trans. F. Bolton; Grand Rapids, MI: Eerdmans, 1952).
Dempster, S., 'The Lord is His Name: A Study of the Distribution of the Names and Titles of God in the Book of Amos', *RB* 98 (1991), pp. 170-89.

Dhorme, E., *La Bible, L'Ancien Testament* (2 vols.; Paris: Gallimard, 1959).

Doorly, W.J., *Prophet of Justice: Understanding the Book of Amos* (Mahwah, NJ: Paulist Press, 1989).

Dorsey, D.A., 'Literary Architecture and Aural Structuring Techniques in Amos', *Bib* 73 (1992), pp. 305-30.

Dowell, S., and L. Hurcombe, *Dispossessed Daughters of Eve* (London: SCM Press, 1992).

Dragga, S., 'Genesis 2–3: A Story of Liberation', *JSOT* 55 (1992), pp. 3-13.

Duhm, B., *Die Psalmen* (KHAT, 14; Tübingen: J.C.B. Mohr, 2nd edn, 1922).

Dyck, E. (ed.), *The Act of Bible Reading* (Carlisle: Paternoster Press, 1997).

Eaton, J.H., *Psalms* (Torch Bible; London: SCM Press, 1967).

Eissfeldt, O., 'Bleiben im Hause Jahwes', in R. Altheim-Stehl and H.E. Stier (eds.), *Beiträge zur Alten Geschichte und deren Nachleben* (Festschrift F.I. Altheim; Berlin: W. de Gruyter, 1969), pp. 76-81.

Eliade, M., *Patterns in Comparative Religion* (trans. R. Sheed; New York: New American Library, 1963).

Engnell, I., '"Knowledge" and "Life" in the Creation Story', *VTS* 3 (1955), pp. 103-119.

Fish, S., *Is There a Text in This Class? The Authority of Interpretative Communities* (Cambridge, MA: Harvard University Press, 1980).

Flint, P.W., *The Dead Sea Scrolls and the Book of Psalms* (Leiden: E.J. Brill, 1997).

Freedman, D.N., 'The Twenty-Third Psalm', in C.I. Orlin (ed.), *Michigan Oriental Studies in Honor of George C. Cameron* (Michigan: Ann Arbor, 1976), pp. 139-66.

Freedman, D.N., and A. Welch, 'Amos's Earthquake and Israelite Prophecy', in M.D. Coogan *et al.* (eds.), *Scripture and Other Artifacts: Essays in Honor of Philip J. King* (Louisville, KY: Westminster/John Knox Press, 1994), pp. 188-98.

Fretheim, T., 'Is Genesis 3 a Fall Story?', *WW* 14 (1994), pp. 144-53.

Frost, S.B., 'Asservation of Thanksgiving', *VT* 7 (1958), pp. 380-90.

Gardner, A., 'Genesis 2.4b-3: A Mythological Paradigm of Sexuality or of the Religious History of Pre-exilic Israel?', *SJT* 43 (1990), pp. 1-18.

Gelander, S., *The Good Creator: Literature and Theology in Genesis 1–11* (Atlanta: Scholars Press, 1997).

Gillingham, S.E., '"Who Makes the Morning Darkness": God and Creation in the Book of Amos', *SJT* 45 (1992), pp. 165-84.

—*One Bible, Many Voices* (London: SPCK, 1998).

Girard, M., *Les Psaumes: Analyse structurelle et interprétation. 1–50* (Recherches Nouvelle Série, 2; Montreal: Editions Bellarmin; Paris: Cerf, 1984).

Gordis, R., 'The Knowledge of Good and Evil in the Old Testament and the Qumran Scrolls', *JBL* 76 (1957), pp. 123-38.

—'The Composition and Structure of Amos', in *idem, Poets, Prophets and Sages: Essays in Biblical Interpretation* (Bloomington: Indiana University Press, 1971), pp. 217-29.

Grenz, S.J., *A Primer on Postmodernism* (Grand Rapids, MI: Eerdmans, 1996).

Gunkel, H., *The Legends of Genesis* (Chicago: Open Court, 1901).

—*Die Psalmen übersetzt und erklärt* (Göttingen: GHAT, 1926).

Habel, N.C., 'Discovering Literary Sources', in *idem, Literary Criticism of the Old Testament* (Guides to Biblical Scholarship; Philadelphia: Fortress Press, 1971), pp. 18-42.

Harper, W.R., *A Critical and Exegetical Commentary on Amos and Hosea* (ICC; New York: Charles Scribner's Sons, 1905).

Hauser, A.J., 'Genesis 2–3: The Theme of Intimacy and Alienation', in D.J.A. Clines, D.M Gunn and A.J. Hauser (eds.), *Art and Meaning: Rhetoric in Biblical Literature* (JSOTSup, 19; Sheffield: JSOT Press, 1982), pp. 20-36.

Hayes, J.H., *Amos: The Eighth-Century Prophet. His Times and his Preaching* (Nashville: Abingdon Press, 1988).

Hayter, M., *The New Eve in Christ* (London: SPCK, 1987).

Heaton, E.W., *Solomon's New Men: The Emergence of Ancient Israel as a National State* (London: Thames & Hudson, 1974).

—*The School Tradition of the Old Testament* (Oxford: Oxford University Press, 1994).

Hermisson, H.-J., 'Observations on the Creation Theology in Wisdom', in J. Gammi (ed.), *Israelite Wisdom: Theological and Literary Essays in Honor of Samuel Terrien* (Missoula, MT: Scholars Press, 1978), pp. 43-57.

Hirsch, E., 'Predigtmeditation zu Psalm 23', *Die Spur* 17 (1977), pp. 145-49.

Holladay, W.L., *The Psalms through Three Thousand Years* (Minneapolis: Fortress Press, 1993).

Hossfeld, F.-L., and E. Zenger, ' "Selig, wer auf die Armen achtet" (Ps. 41,2): Beobachtungen zur Gottesvolk-Theologie des ersten Davidpsalters', *JBTh* 7 (1992), pp. 21-50.

—' "Wer darf hinaufziehen zum Berg YHWHS?" (Ps. 24.3). Zur Redaktionsgechichte und Theologie der Psalmengruppe 15-24', in G. Braulik (ed.), *Lohfink Festschrift* (Freiburg: Biblische Theologie und gesellschaftlicher Wandel, 1993), pp. 166-82.

House, P.R., *The Unity of the Twelve* (JSOTSup, 97; Sheffield: Sheffield Academic Press, 1990).

Hubbard, D.A., *Joel and Amos* (TOTC; Leicester: Inter-Varsity Press, 1989).

Hunter, A.G., *Psalms* (Old Testament Readings; London: Routledge, 1999).

Hutter, M., 'Adam als Gärtner und König (Gen. 2,8.15)', *BZ* 30 (1986), pp. 258-62.

Hyatt, J.P., 'The Translation and Meaning of Amos 5.23-24', *ZAW* 68 (1956), pp. 17-24.

James, E.O., *The Tree of Life* (Leiden: E.J. Brill, 1966).

Jaruzelska, I., *Amos and the Officialdom in the Kingdom of Israel: The Socio-Economic Position of the Officials in the Light of the Biblical, the Epigraphic and Archaeological Evidence* (Seria Socjologia, 25; Poznan: Wydawnictwo Naukowe Uniwersytetu im. Adama Mickiewicza, 1998).

Jeremias, J., 'Amos 3–6: From the Oral Word to the Text', in G.M. Tucker, D.L. Petersen and R.R. Wilson (eds.), *Canon, Theology and Old Testament Interpretation: Essays in Honor of Brevard S. Childs* (Philadelphia: Fortress Press, 1988), pp. 217-29.

—*The Book of Amos* (trans. D.W. Stott; OTL; Louisville, KY: Westminster/John Knox Press, 1998).

—'The Doxologies in the Book of Amos', in *idem*, *The Book of Amos: A Commentary* (trans. D.W. Stott; Louisville, KY: Westminster/John Knox Press, 1998), pp. 76-80.

Jobling, D., 'A Structural Analysis of Genesis 2.4b–3.24', in P.J Achtemeier (ed.), *Society of Biblical Literature 1978 Seminar Papers* (Missoula, MT: University of Montana, 1978), I, pp. 61-69.

—'The Myth Semantics of Genesis 2.4b–3.24', *Semeia* 18 (1980), pp. 41-49.

Johnson, A.R., 'Psalm 23 and the Household of Faith', in J.R. Durham and J.R. Porter (eds.), *Proclamation and Presence* (London: SCM Press, 1970), pp. 255-71.

Joines, K.R., *Serpent Symbolism in the Old Testament* (Hadenfield, NJ: Hadenfield House, 1974).

Kennedy, J.M., 'Peasants in Revolt: Political Allegory in Genesis 2–3', *JSOT* 47 (1990), pp. 3-14.

Köhler, L., 'Psalm 23', *ZAW* 68 (1956), pp. 227-34.

König, E., *Die Psalmen eingeleitet, übersetzt und erklärt* (KAT, 3; Gütersloh: C. Bertelsmann, 1927).

Kraemer, S.N., *From the Tablets of Sumer* (Colorado: Indian Hills, 1959).

Kraus, H.-J., *Psalms 1-59: A Commentary* (trans. H.C. Oswald; Minneapolis: Augsburg, 1988).

Lacocque, A., 'Cracks in the Wall', in A. Lacocque and P. Riceour (eds.), *Thinking Biblically: Exegetical and Hermeneutical Studies* (trans. D. Pellauer; Chicago: University of Chicago Press, 1998), pp. 3-29.

Laffey, A., *Wives, Harlots and Concubines: The Old Testament in Feminist Perspective* (London: SPCK, 1988).

Landy, F., 'Vision and Poetic Speech in Amos', *HAR* 11 (1987), pp. 223-46.

Lanser, S.S., '(Feminist) Criticism in the Garden: Inferring Genesis 2–3', in H.C. White (ed.), *Speech Act Theory and Biblical Criticism* (Semeia, 14; Decatur, GA: Scholars Press, 1988), pp. 67-84.

Limburg, J., 'Sevenfold Structures in the Book of Amos', *JBL* 106 (1987), pp. 217-22.

Lundbom, J., 'Psalm 23: Song of Passage', *Int* 40 (1986), pp. 5-16.

Lust, J., 'Remarks on the Redaction of Amos V 4-6, 14-15', in A.S. von der Woude (ed.), *Remembering All the Way: A Collection of Old Testament Studies Published on the Occasion of the Fortieth Anniversary of the Oudtestamentisch Werkgezelschep in Nederland* (OTS, 21; Leiden: E.J. Brill, 1981), pp. 129-54.

Magonet, J., 'The Themes of Genesis 2–3', in Morris and Sawyer (eds.), *A Walk in the Garden*, pp. 39-46.

—'Through Rabbinic Eyes: Psalm 23', in *idem, A Rabbi Reads the Psalms* (London: SCM Press, 1994), pp. 64-65.

May, H.G., 'The King in the Garden of Eden: A Study of Ezekiel 28.12-19', in B.W. Anderson and W. Harrelson (eds.), *Israel's Prophetic Heritage: Essays in Honor of James Muilenburg* (London: SCM Press, 1962), pp. 166-76.

Mays, J.L., *Amos: A Commentary* (OTL; Philadelphia: Westminster Press, 1969).

Mazor, Y., 'Psalm 23: The Lord is my Shepherd—Or is he my Host?', *ZAW* 100.3 (1988), pp. 416-20.

McKane, W., *Prophets and Wise Men* (London: SCM Press, 1965).

Melugin, R.F., 'Amos', in E.E. Carpenter and W. McCown (eds.), *Ashbury Bible Commentary* (Grand Rapids, MI: Zondervan, 1992), pp. 735-49.

—'Prophetic Books and the Problem of Historical Reconstruction', in S.B. Reid (ed.), *Prophets and Paradigms: Essays in Honor of Gene M. Tucker* (JSOTSup, 229; Sheffield: Sheffield Academic Press, 1996), pp. 63-78.

Mendenhall, G.E., 'The Shady Side of Wisdom: The Date and Purpose of Genesis 3', in H.N. Bream, R.D. Heim and C.A. Moore (eds.), *A Light unto my Path: Old Testament Studies in Honor of Jacob M. Myers* (Philadelphia: Temple University, 1974), pp. 319-34.

Merrill, A.L., 'Psalm XXIII and the Jerusalem Tradition', *VT* 15 (1965), pp. 354-60.

Meyers, C., *Discovering Eve: Ancient Israelite Women in Context* (Oxford: Oxford University Press, 1988).

—'Gender Roles and Genesis 3.16 Revisited', in Brenner (ed.), *A Feminist Companion to Genesis*, pp. 118-41.

Miller, P.D., *Genesis 1–11: Studies in Structure and Theme* (JSOTSup, 8; Sheffield: JSOT Press, 1978).

—'Kingship, Torah Obedience, and Prayer: The Theology of Psalms 15–24', in K. Seybold and E. Zenger (eds.), *Neue Wege der Psalmenforschung* (Freiburg: Herder, 1994), pp. 127-42.

Milliard, M., *Die Komposition des Psalters* (Tübingen: J.C.B. Mohr [Paul Siebeck], 1994).

Milne, P., 'The Patriarchal Stamp of Scripture: The Implications of Structural Analyses for Feminist Hermeneutics', in Brenner (ed.), *A Feminist Companion*, pp. 146-72.

Milne, P., 'Psalm 23: Echoes of the Exodus', *SR* 4 (1974–75), pp. 237-47.

Morgenstern, J., 'Psalm 23', *JBL* 65 (1946), pp. 13-24.

Morris, P., 'A Walk in the Garden: Images of Eden', in Morris and Sawyer (eds.), *A Walk in the Garden*, pp. 21-38.

—'Exiled from Eden: Jewish Interpretations of Genesis', in Morris and Sawyer (eds.), *A Walk in the Garden*, pp. 117-66.

Morris, P., and D. Sawyer (eds.), *A Walk in the Garden: Biblical, Iconographical and Literary Images of Eden* (JSOTSup, 136; Sheffield: Sheffield Academic Press, 1992).

Mowinckel, S., *The Psalms in Israel's Worship* (trans. D.R. Ap-Thomas; 2 vols.; Oxford: Basil Blackwell, 2nd edn, 1982).

Müller, H.-P., 'Eine neue babylonische Menschenschöpfungserzählung im Licht keils- schrifticher und biblischer Parallelen', in *idem, Mythos—Kerygma—Wahrheit: Gesammelte Aufsatze Zum Alten Testament in Seiner Umwelt und Zur Biblischen Theologie* (BZAW, 200; Berlin: W. de Gruyter, 1991), pp. 43-67.

—'Schöpfung, Zivilisation und Befreiung', in M.D. Carroll, D.J.A. Clines and P.R. Davies (eds.), *The Bible in Human Society: Essays in Honour of John Rogerson* (JSOTSup, 200; Sheffield: JSOT Press, 1995), pp. 355-65.

Newman, J.H., 'Praise to the Holiest in the Height', Hymn 185 in *Hymns Ancient and Modern Revised* (London: William Clowes and Sons Ltd, n.d.), pp. 246-47.

Nicholson, E.W., 'The Meaning of the Expression 'am ha'arez in the Old Testament', *JSS* 10 (1965), pp. 59-66.

—'The Pentateuch in Recent Research: A Time for Caution', in J.A. Emerton (ed.), *SVTP Congress Volume XLIII, Leuven 1989* (Leiden: E.J. Brill, 1991), pp. 10-21.

Niditch, S., 'Genesis 1–11: Five Themes', in *idem, Chaos to Cosmos: Studies in Biblical Patterns of Creation* (Chico, CA: Scholars Press, 1985), pp. 11-24.

—'Genesis', in C.A. Newsom and S.H. Ringe (eds.), *The Women's Bible Commentary* (London: SPCK, 1992), pp. 10-25.

Noble, P.R., 'The Literary Structure of Amos: A Thematic Analysis', *JBL* 114 (1995), pp. 209-226.

Oduyoye, M., *The Sons of God and the Daughters of Men: An Afro-Asiatic Interpretation of Genesis 1–11* (Maryknoll, NY: Orbis Books, 1984).

Olshausen, J., *Die Psalmen erklärt* (Kurzgefaßtes exegetisches Handbuch zum Alten Testamentum, 14; Leipzig, 1853).

O'Reilly, J., 'The Trees of Eden in Medieval Iconography', in Morris and Sawyer (eds.), *A Walk in the Garden*, pp. 167-204.

Pagels, E., *Adam, Eve and the Serpent* (New York: Random House, 1987).

Parker, K., 'Repetition as a Structuring Device in 1 Kings 1–11', *JSOT* 42 (1988), pp. 19-27.

Parker, K.I., 'Mirror, Mirror on the Wall, Must We Leave Eden, Once and for All? A Lacanian Pleasure Trip through the Garden', *JSOT* 83 (1999), pp. 19-29.

Patte, D., *Genesis 2 and 3: Kaleidoscopic Structural Readings* (Semeia, 18; Chico, CA: Scholars Press, 1980).

Patte, D., and J.F. Parker, 'A Structural Exegesis of Genesis 2 and 3', *Semeia* 18 (1980), pp. 55-75.

Paul, S.M., *Amos: A Commentary on the Book of Amos* (Hermeneia; Minneapolis: Fortress Press, 1991).

Pfeifer, G.P., 'Das ja des Amos', *VT* 39 (1989), pp. 497-503.

Phillips, A., *Lower than the Angels: Questions Raised by Genesis 1–11* (Rome, NY: Can- terbury Press, 1996).

Polley, M.E., *Amos and the Davidic Empire: A Socio-Historical Approach* (Oxford: Oxford University Press, 1989).

Power, E., 'The Shepherd's Two Rods in Modern Palestine and Some Passages of the Old Testament', *Bib* 9 (1928), pp. 434-42.

Reike, B., 'The Knowledge Hidden in the Tree of Paradise', *JSS* 1 (1956), pp. 193-201.

Rendtorff, R., *Das Uberlieferungsgeschichtliche Problem des Pentateuch* (BZAW, 147; Berlin: W. de Gruyter, 1977).

—'The Yahwist as Theologian? The Dilemma of Pentateuchal Criticism', *JSOT* 3 (1977), pp. 1-10.

—Directions in Pentateuchal Studies', *CRBS* 5 (1997), pp. 43-65.

Roberts, R., 'Sin, Saga and Gender: The Fall and Original Sin in Modern Theology', in Morris and Sawyer (eds.), *A Walk in the Garden*, pp. 244-60.

Rogerson, J., *Genesis 1–11* (OTG, 1; Sheffield: JSOT Press, 1991).

—'Genesis 1–11' , *CRBS* 5 (1997), pp. 67-90.

Rose, M., *Deuteronomist und Jahwist* (ATANT, 67; Zürich: Theologischer Verlag, 1981).

Rösel, H.N., 'Kleine Studien zur Entwicklung des Amosbuches', *VT* 43 (1993), pp. 88-101.

Rosenbaum, S.N., *Amos of Israel: A New Interpretation* (Macon, GA: Mercer University Press, 1990).

Rottzoll, D., *Studien zur Redaktion und Komposition des Amosbuches* (BZAW, 243; Berlin: W. de Gruyter, 1996).

Sandberger, J.V., 'Hermeneutische Aspekte der Psalmeninterpretation dargestellt an Psalm 23', in K. Seybold and E. Zenger (eds.), *Neue Wege der Psalmenforschung* (Herder Biblische Studien, 1; Freiburg: Herder, 1994), pp. 317-44.

Sawyer, D.F., 'The New Adam in the Theology of St Paul', in Morris and Sawyer (eds.), *A Walk in the Garden*, pp. 105-116.

—'Resurrecting Eve? Feminist Critique of the Garden of Eden', in Morris and Sawyer (eds.), *A Walk in the Garden*, pp. 273-89.

Sawyer, J.F.A., 'The Image of God, the Wisdom of Serpents and the Knowledge of Good and Evil', in Morris and Sawyer (eds.), *A Walk in the Garden*, pp. 64-73.

—*The Fifth Gospel: Isaiah in the History of Christianity* (Cambridge: Cambridge University Press, 1996).

Schmid, H.H., 'Amos. Zur Frage nach der "geistige Heimat" des Propheten', *WuD*, NF X (1969), pp. 85-103.

—*Der Sogenannte Jahwist: Beobachtungen und Fragen zur Pentateuchforschung* (Zürich: Theologischer Verlag, 1976).

Schmidt, W.H., 'Die Deuteronomistische Redaktion des Amosbuches', *ZAW* 77 (1965), pp. 168-93.

—'Ein Theologe in salomonischer Zeit? Plädoyer für den Jahwisten', *BZ* 25 (1981), pp. 82-102.

Schottroff, W., 'Psalm 23. Zur Methode sozialgechichtlicher Bibelauslegung', in W. Schottroff and W. Stegemann (eds.), *Traditionen der Befreiung*, I (Münich: Kaiser Verlag, 1980), pp. 78-113.

—'The Prophet Amos: A Socio-Historical Assessment of His Ministry', in W. Schottroff and W. Stegemann (eds.), *God of the Lowly: Socio-Historical Interpretations of the Bible* (trans. M.J. O'Connell; Maryknoll, NY: Orbis, 1984), pp. 27-46.

Schwarzschild, S.S., 'Justice', in *Encyclopedia Judaica*, X (Jerusalem: Keter Publishing House, 4th edn, 1978), pp. 476-77.

Seybold, K., *Die Psalmen* (HAT, 1/15; Tübingen: J.C.B. Mohr [Paul Siebeck], 1996), pp. 100-102.

Smalley, W.A., 'Recursion Patterns and the Sectioning of Amos', *BT* 30 (1979), pp. 118-27.
Smith, M.S., 'Setting and Rhetoric in Psalm 23', *JSOT* 41 (1988), pp. 61-66.
Soggin, J.A., 'The Fall of Man in the Third Chapter of Genesis', in *idem, Old Testament and Oriental Studies* (BibOr, 29; Rome: Pontifical Biblical Institute, 1975), pp. 88-111.
—*The Prophet Amos: A Translation and Commentary* (OTL; London: SCM Press, 1987).
Southwell, P., 'Genesis is a "Wisdom" Story?', *Texte und Untersuchungen* 126 (1982), pp. 467-69.
Stern, H.S., ' "The Knowledge of Good and Evil" ', *VT* 8 (1958), pp. 405-18.
Stordalen, T., 'Man, Soil, Garden: Basic Plot in Genesis 2–3 Reconsidered', *JSOT* 53 (1992), pp. 3-26.
—*Echoes of Eden: Genesis 2–3 and Symbolism of the Eden Garden in Biblical Hebrew Literature* (Leuven: Peeters, 2000).
Stratton, B.J., *Out of Eden: Reading, Rhetoric, and Ideology in Genesis 2–3* (JSOTSup, 208; Sheffield: Sheffield Academic Press, 1995).
Tappy, R., 'Psalm 23: Symbolism and Structure', *CBQ* 57 (1995), pp. 255-80.
Terrien, S., 'Amos and Wisdom', in B.W. Anderson and W. Harrelson (eds.), *Israel's Prophetic Heritage: Essays in Honor of James Muilenburg* (New York: Harper & Row; London: SCM Press, 1962), pp. 108-15.
Tournay, R., and R. Schwab, *Les Psaumes* (La Sainte Bible; Paris: Cerf, 1955).
Treves, M., *The Dates of the Psalms: History and Poetry in Ancient Israel* (Gennaio: Giardini Editori e Stampatori in Pisa, 1988).
Trible, P., 'A Love Story Gone Awry', in *idem, God and the Rhetoric of Sexuality* (Overtures in Biblical Theology, 2; Philadelphia: Fortress Press, 1978), pp. 72-143.
Tromp, N.J., 'Amos V 1-17: Towards a Stylistic and Rhetorical Analysis', *OTS* 23 (1984), pp. 56-85.
Tucker, G.M., 'The Futile Quest for the Historical Prophet', in E.E. Carpenter (ed.), *A Biblical Itinerary: In Search of Method, Form and Content. Essays in Honor of George W. Coats* (JSOTSup, 240; Sheffield: Sheffield Academic Press, 1997), pp. 144-52.
Van Seters, J., 'Confessional Reformulation in the Exilic Period', *VT* 22 (1972), pp. 448-59.
Vawter, B., *On Genesis: A New Reading* (Garden City, NY: Doubleday, 1977).
Vogt, E., 'The "Place in Life" of Ps. 23', *Bib* 34 (1953), pp. 195-211.
von Rad, G., *The Problem of the Hexateuch and Other Essays* (trans. E.W. Trueman Dicken; Edinburgh: Oliver & Boyd, 1966).
—*Old Testament Theology* (2 vols.; trans. D.M.G. Stalker; London: SCM Press, 1975).
Vorländer, H., *Die Entstehungszeit des jehowistischen Geschichtswerkes* (Frankfurt: Peter Lang, 1978).
Waard, J. de, 'The Chiastic Structure of Amos V 1-17', *VT* 27 (1977), pp. 170-77.
Wagner, N.E., 'Pentateuchal Criticism: No Clear Future', *CJT* 13 (1967), pp. 225-32.
Wal, A. van der, 'The Structure of Amos', *JSOT* 26 (1983), pp. 107-113.
Wallace, H.N., *The Eden Narrative* (HSM, 32; Atlanta, GA: Scholars Press, 1985).
—'Tree of Knowledge and Tree of Life', in D.N. Freedman (ed.), *Anchor Bible Dictionary*, VI (6 vols.; New York: Doubleday, 1992), pp. 656-60.
Walsh, J.T., 'Genesis 2.4b–3.24: A Synchronic Approach', *JBL* 94 (1977), pp. 161-77.
Ward, G., 'A Postmodern Version of Paradise', *JSOT* 65 (1995), pp. 3-12.
Watson, F., 'Strategies of Recovery and Resistance: Hermeneutical Reflections on Genesis 1–3 and its Pauline Reception', *JSNT* 45 (1992), pp. 79-103.
Weinfeld, M., ' "Justice and Righteousness" in Ancient Israel against the Background of "Social Reforms" in the Ancient Near East', in H.-J. Nissen and J. Renger (eds.), *Mesopotamien und seine Nachbarn* (Berlin: Dietrich Reimer, 1982), pp. 491-519.

Wellhausen, J., *Prolegomena to the History of Israel* (Edinburgh: Adam and Charles Black, 1885).

—'Notes on Psalm 23', in J. Haupt (ed.), *The Polychrome Bible* (trans. H.H. Furness; London: James Clark & Co, 1898), p. 174.

Wenham, G., 'Sanctuary Symbolism in the Garden of Eden Story', *PWCJS* 9 (1986), pp. 19-25.

—*Genesis 1–15* (WBC, 1; Waco, TX: Word Books, 1987).

Westermann, C., *Genesis 1–11* (Darmstadt: Wissenschaftliche Buchgesellschaft, 1976; trans. J. Scullion; London: SPCK, 1984).

—*Ausgewählte Psalmen* (Göttingen: Vandenhoeck & Ruprecht, 1984).

Whedbee, J., *Isaiah and Wisdom* (Nashville: Abingdon Press, 1971).

Whitelam, K.W, 'The Social World of the Bible', in J. Barton (ed.), *Biblical Interpretation* (Cambridge: Cambridge University Press, 1998), pp. 35-49.

Whybray, N., *The Making of the Pentateuch* (JSOTSup, 53; Sheffield: JSOT Press, 1987).

Widengren, G., *Hebrew and Accadian Psalms of Lamentations as Religious Documents* (Stockholm: Aktiebolaget Thule, 1937).

—*The King and the Tree of Life in Ancient Near Eastern Religion* (Uppsala: Lundequistska bokhandeln, 1951).

Wilkinson, L., 'Hermeneutics and the Postmodern Reaction Against "Truth"', in E. Dyck (ed.), *The Act of Bible Reading* (Carlisle: Paternoster Press, 1997), pp. 114-47.

Williams, R., *The Wound of Knowledge* (London: Darton, Longman & Todd, 1979).

Williamson, H.G.M., 'Isaiah and the Wise', in J. Day, R.P. Gordon and H.G.M. Williamson (eds.), *Wisdom in Ancient Israel* (Cambridge: Cambridge University Press, 1995), pp. 133-41.

Winnett, F.V., 'Re-examining the Foundations', *JBL* 84 (1965), pp. 1-19.

Wittenberg, G.H., *King Solomon and the Theologians* (Pietermaritzburg: University of Natal Press, 1988).

Wolde, E. van, *A Semiotic Analysis of Genesis 2–3: A Semiotic Theory and Method of Analysis Applied to the Story of the Garden of Eden* (Studia Semitica Neerlandica, 25; Assen: Van Gorcum, 1989).

—*Words Become Worlds: Semantic Studies of Genesis 1–11* (Leiden: E.J. Brill, 1994).

—*Stories of the Beginning: Genesis 1–1 and Other Creation Stories* (trans. J. Bowden; London: SCM Press, 1995).

—'Facing the Earth: Primeval History in a New Perspective', in P.R. Davies and D.J.A. Clines (eds.), *The World of Genesis: Persons, Places, Perspectives* (JSOTSup, 257; Sheffield: Sheffield Academic Press, 1998), pp. 22-47.

Wolff, H.W., 'The Kerygma of the Yahwist', in W. Brueggemann and H.W. Wolff (eds.), *The Vitality of Old Testament Traditions* (Atlanta: John Knox, 1975), pp. 41-66.

—*Amos the Prophet: The Man and his Background* (trans. S.D. McBride *et al.*; Philadelphia: Fortress Press, 1977).

—*Joel and Amos: A Commentary on the Books of the Prophets Joel and Amos* (Hermeneia; Philadelphia: Fortress Press, 1977).

INDEX

INDEX OF REFERENCES

OLD TESTAMENT

Genesis

1–11	7, 12, 29, 37, 38, 46, 81, 116
1–3	34-37, 46
1	7, 15, 26, 29, 30, 34-36
1.10	35
1.12	35
1.18	35
1.20	35
1.22	35
1.25	35
1.26	7
1.27	35
1.28-30	35
1.28	15, 35
2–3	5, 7-9, 13, 15, 18, 19, 21, 23-28, 31, 34-38, 43, 45, 46, 62, 78, 81, 82, 86, 119, 121, 123-25
2.4-9	35
2.4–3.24	31
2.5-6	15
2.7	15, 32, 35
2.8-9	13

2.9	14, 15, 29, 32, 33
2.10-14	19, 20
2.14	35
2.15-17	13
2.15-16	32, 35
2.15	19
2.16-17	26
2.16	29
2.17	14, 29, 33, 35
2.18-20	20
2.19	19
2.25	14
3	38
3.1-13	13
3.1-5	32
3.1	23, 26, 29
3.2	29
3.3	29, 32
3.4-5	26
3.5-6	39
3.5	23, 29, 33
3.6	23, 29
3.7	23
3.11	29
3.12	29
3.13	29
3.14-19	15, 26
3.14	29
3.15	27
3.16	27, 86
3.17-19	27

3.17	29
3.18	29
3.19	27, 29, 32
3.20	33
3.21	38
3.22-24	13, 26
3.22	29
4	37, 86
4.1	13
4.7	37
4.11-12	86
4.13-16	22
4.15	38
5	37
5.21-24	37
6	37
6.1-4	14, 24, 37
6.2	14, 24, 37
6.3	14
6.9	37
6.11-22	38
7.1-5	38
9.4	29
9.12-17	39
10	37
11	24, 37
11.1-9	24, 37
11.4	24
17.4-8	39

Exodus

6.5-9	39
15	55

15.13	55	3.1-28	19	2.11	60
19–24	40	3.3-9	20	3.5	60
20.22–23.33	88	4.5	74	6.10	60
21.2-7	88	8.15-21	21	7.13	60
22.25	88	9.9	88	8.3	116
22.26-27	88	9.24	16	10.21	60
23.6-8	88	10–11	21	10.22	60
28.3	23	11.1-13	25	12.22	60
31.3	23	11.1-8	16	15.11	60
31.6	23	12.25-33	16	16.2	60
32–34	40	15.34	16	16.16	60
34.11-26	115	16.31	16	21.2	60
		22.52	16	21.34	60
				24.17	60
Leviticus				28	35
25	116	*2 Kings*		28.3	60
		3.3	16	28.28	23
Numbers		11.29	16	29.14	117
20.13	55	13.2	16	29.25	60
		14.24	16	34.22	60
Deuteronomy		14.25	90	38–41	35
1.39	14	15.8-16	92	38.17	60
4.15-31	16	15.9	16	40.8	117
7.1-5	16	15.24	16	42.6	60
13.12-18	16	15.29	16	42.11	60
15	116	16	94		
16	116	17.7-41	16	*Psalms*	
16.1-21	115	17.21-23	21	1–2	70
16.21-22	16	18	94	1	39
17	116	22.11-13	94	1.2-3	40
17.14-20	21	22.16-17	94	2.6	52
17.14-17	21	22.19-20	94	3–42	8
17.18-20	21	23.4-14	18	3–14	70
30.17-18	16	23.15-20	95	3–7	70, 71
33.21	87	23.24-25	94	3–4	47
		23.26-27	30	3	48, 58
Judges				4	58
5.11	87	*Ezra*		5–6	47
		9.1	30	5	58
2 Samuel		10.2	30	7	58
7.13-16	20	10.11	30	8	36, 70, 72
8.15	88			9–10	70, 71
14.20	23	*Nehemiah*		9	72
15–19	48	5	101	10	72
17.27-29	48	10.20-31	30	11–14	70, 71
				11	58
1 Kings		*Job*		15–24	8, 68-72,
1.32-37	51	1–2	38		74
3–12	21	1.1-5	115		

Psalms (cont.)

15	68, 70	23.5-6	59, 63	50	96		
15.1	68	23.5	48, 50, 52, 54, 63, 64, 67, 69, 71, 77	57	58, 76		
16	68-71, 74			63	58		
16.5	68			68	76		
16.9	69	23.6	48, 56, 57, 59, 60, 63-67, 69, 71, 77	72.1-4	88		
16.10	69			72.1-2	19		
16.11	69			72.3	19		
17	58, 68, 69			72.4	19		
18	68, 70	24	8, 46, 52, 53, 66, 68-70, 72	72.6	19		
19	8, 36, 68, 70			74	73		
				74.1	73		
19.1-6	68	24.1-2	67	77	56		
19.7-14	68	24.3	68	77.20	54, 56		
19.8	39	24.6	66	78	47, 55, 56, 73		
19.10	39	25–34	71	78.19	55		
20–21	68, 70	25	71, 72	78.20-29	54		
22–29	72	25.9	71	78.52-73	54		
22	8, 46, 52, 53, 66-69	25.16	71	78.52-53	47		
		26	58	78.52	54, 56, 73		
22.1-21	66	26.8	71	78.70-72	47		
22.14	66	27	57-59, 70, 71	78.70-71	73		
22.22-31	66			79	73		
22.26	67	27.1	71	79.13	73		
22.30	66	27.4	57, 71	80.2	54		
23	5, 8, 9, 45, 46, 48, 49, 51-56, 58-62, 64-78, 81, 82, 119, 124, 125	27.5	71	81	96		
		27.6	71	81.7	55		
		27.11	71	88	36		
		28.2	71	89.14	116		
		29	71	89.27-37	20		
		29.9	71	94.14-15	116		
		32.4	66	95	73		
23.1-4	63	33	36, 72	95.7-11	54		
23.1-3	59, 64	34	71	95.7	54, 73		
23.1-2	47, 48, 63	34.3	71	95.10-11	55		
23.1	48, 59, 64, 69, 71	34.7	71	95.11	51		
		35–41	71	97.2	116		
23.2-3	55, 64	37	76	100	56, 73		
23.2	50, 55, 63-65, 67, 69, 77	38	36, 71	100.3	54, 56, 73		
		42–43	59	104	36		
		43.3	59	106	98		
23.3-4	48, 63	44	36	106.32	55		
23.3	51, 63-65, 69, 71	45	76	111.10	23		
		46.3	51	120–134	57		
23.4-5	64	46.4	20	127	76		
23.4	50, 52, 55, 56, 59, 64, 65, 69, 77	46.4 [EV]	20	132.8	51		
		48.1-2 [EV]	20	132.14	51		
		48.2	20				

Proverbs
1.7 — 23
2.5 — 21
2.6 — 21
3.1-2 — 21
3.5-7 — 21

Isaiah
3.16-26 — 94
5.1-7 — 117
7.13-15 — 14
10.12 — 23
10.13 — 23
10.15 — 26
11.1-5 — 117
11.4 — 117
11.5 — 117
16.5 — 117
28.9-10 — 26
28.14-22 — 94
28.14-18 — 23
29.13-14 — 23
29.15-16 — 23
29.22-24 — 23
32.1-2 — 100
32.1 — 117
32.16-20 — 100
33.16 — 101
33.17 — 101
35.1-2 — 100
35.6-7 — 100
40–66 — 100
40–55 — 100
40–48 — 100
40 — 56
40.1-11 — 74
40.11 — 54
41.2 — 87
41.14 — 100
41.17-20 — 100
42.1-4 — 117
42.23 — 100
43.1 — 100
44.1 — 100
44.28 — 47
49.8-13 — 100
49.8-10 — 74
51.5-8 — 87

58.6-7 — 101
59.1-4 — 101
59.9 — 101
59.14 — 101
63.11 — 55

Jeremiah
2.6 — 55
22.5 — 88
23.3 — 74
31.10 — 74

Lamentations
5 — 98

Ezekiel
8.7-15 — 18
16 — 22, 98
16.6-14 — 18
17 — 22
20 — 98
23 — 22
23.5-21 — 18
27–28 — 23
28 — 19, 20
28.2 — 19
28.3-4 — 19
28.6 — 19
28.9 — 19
28.13 — 19
28.16 — 19
34 — 56
34.9-11 — 74
34.11-16 — 54, 76
34.23-24 — 76
34.25-31 — 54
37.16 — 52
47.1-2 — 20
48.2 — 20

Daniel
6.10 — 115

Hosea
4.1 — 17
4.6 — 17
6.4-6 — 114
6.6 — 17

Joel
3 — 113
3.16 — 113

Amos
1–7 — 109
1–6 — 109, 110
1–2 — 84, 89, 109-11, 113
1 — 84
1.1–7.9 — 84
1.1 — 92, 99
1.2–3.8 — 110
1.2 — 90, 98, 110, 111
1.3–2.16 — 110
1.3–2.5 — 110
1.3-8 — 111
1.11-12 — 111, 113
1.12-17 — 117
1.21-26 — 117
2 — 84
2.2 — 113
2.4-5 — 99
2.4 — 99
2.6-16 — 110
2.6-8 — 88, 111
2.7 — 88
2.8 — 88
2.10 — 99, 111
2.11-12 — 99
2.14-16 — 111
3–6 — 8, 82, 107, 109, 110
3–4 — 83, 84, 92, 103, 106
3 — 83, 84, 108, 110-12
3.1–6.14 — 110
3.1-15 — 107
3.1-7 — 26
3.1-2 — 107
3.1 — 83, 97-99, 106, 107
3.3-8 — 107, 110
3.3-7 — 103

Amos (cont.)					
3.7	99	5.1-3	98, 104, 108	5.21-24	82, 83, 87, 92, 94-96, 99, 101-104, 106, 108, 110, 111, 113, 115-19, 121
3.8	103	5.1	83, 92, 97, 106, 107		
3.9–6.14	110	5.3	105		
3.9–4.3	84	5.4-6	104, 108		
3.9-15	107	5.4-5	84		
3.10-11	107	5.4	83, 94, 105		
3.11	92	5.5	94	5.21-23	83, 86, 88, 93, 95, 102, 103, 106, 109
3.12	83	5.6-7	104		
3.15	107	5.6	93, 94		
4–5	108	5.7-13	104	5.21	105
4	83, 84, 108, 110, 111	5.7	84, 90, 94, 98, 108	5.24	82, 85, 87, 90, 93, 95, 98, 101-104, 106, 108, 109, 112, 114, 115, 117
4.1-13	107	5.8-9	97, 98, 104, 108, 110-12		
4.1-3	107				
4.1	83, 88, 107				
4.4-5	84, 107, 108, 111	5.10-13	104, 108		
		5.10-12	88, 98		
4.5	83, 98	5.10	88	5.25-27	82, 83, 99, 103, 108, 118
4.6-13	97, 98, 108, 110	5.11	88		
		5.12	88		
4.6-12	86	5.14-15	104, 108	5.25-26	93
4.6-11	86, 103, 110	5.15	86, 88, 100	5.25	83
				5.26-27	105, 106
4.6	98	5.16-17	86, 98, 104, 105, 108	5.27	105
4.7	98			6	83, 108
4.9	98			6.1-14	107
4.10	98	5.16	105	6.1-11	84
4.11	98	5.17	105	6.1-7	108
4.12	103	5.18-6.14	111	6.1-6	105, 106
4.13	97, 98, 108	5.18-6.7	105	6.1-4	105
		5.18-6.4	111, 112	6.1	83, 84, 99, 105
5–6	83, 84, 92, 103, 105, 106, 110	5.18-27	81, 82, 103, 104, 106-108		
				6.4-7	105
				6.4-6	103
5	5, 8, 9, 82, 83, 85, 103, 104, 116, 119, 121, 124, 125	5.18-20	82, 83, 98, 99, 103, 105, 108, 110	6.4	105, 107
				6.6-8	106
				6.6-7	105, 106
		5.18	84, 105	6.6	103
		5.19-20	26	6.7-12	109
5.1-17	98, 104-108, 110-12	5.20-24	101	6.7	105
		5.20	98	6.8-11	107
		5.21-27	83, 108, 111	6.8-10	105
5.1-15	89			6.8	105, 107
5.1-6	84	5.21-25	105	6.11-14	105
				6.11	107

6.12	26, 90, 107	7.11	88, 93	9.11-15	100, 109, 110, 114
6.13-14	107	7.13	109	9.11-12	84, 100, 101
6.14	83, 90, 92, 105	8–9	109		
		8	84	9.11	118
7–9	109, 110	8.2	84	9.12	113
7	88, 92, 93, 109	8.3–9.10	109	9.13-15	100, 101, 113
		8.4–9.15	110, 111		
7.1–9.15	110	8.4–9.10	110	1.1	99
7.1–9.4	110	8.4-6	88, 111	5.25-27	118
7.1–8.3	110, 111	8.4	88		
7.1–8.2	109	8.11-13	99	*Obadiah*	
7.1-6	84	8.14	90	20	113
7.1-3	84, 92	9	84, 100		
7.1	84	9.1-4	103, 110, 111	*Micah*	
7.4-6	84, 92			6.6-8	114
7.4	84, 93	9.3	111	6.11	87
7.7-20	97	9.4	103		
7.7-9	84	9.5-6	98, 99, 110	*Zechariah*	
7.7-8	92			9–13	76
7.7	84	9.7-15	110	10	55
7.8	84	9.7-12	111	10.2	74
7.9	88, 93	9.7-10	100	10.3	74
7.10-17	84, 109	9.7	111	13.7	76
7.11–8.3	111	9.8	100, 101		

OTHER ANCIENT REFERENCES

Apocrypha		*John*		*1 Corinthians*	
2 Esdras		2.13-22	118	15.22	41
2.34	50, 75	2.19	118		
		2.21	118	*Galatians*	
Sirach (Ecclesiasticus)		10.1-18	76	3.23-24	40
18.13	75	10.11	76		
18.14	75	10.14	76	Pseudepigrapha	
				1 Enoch	
New Testament		*Acts*		6–11	24
Matthew		2.29-33	76	7	24
15.24	76	7.42-53	118		
		15.16	118	*2 Enoch*	
Mark				30	32
6.34	76	*Romans*			
		5.12-14	40	*2 Baruch*	
Luke		5.14-15	41	17.3	32
4.1-13	38	5.15-17	40		
15.3-6	76	5.18-21	40	*4 Ezra*	
				3.7	32

Psalms of Solomon		*1QSa*		*Zohar*	
17.21-46	50, 75	1.9-11	15	1.26	40
17.21-22	75			2.162	40
17.46	75	Midrash		3.113	40
17.67-72	50	*Genesis Rabbah*			
		8	32	Classical	
Qumran		19.7	40	Maimonides	
11Q5		24.5	40	*A Guide to the*	
xxvii.2-11	75	24.7	40	*Perplexed* 1.2	40

INDEX OF AUTHORS

Albright, W.F. 24
Alexander, P. 34
Allaway, R.H. 34, 43
Alonso-Schökel, L. 24
Anderson, A.A. 56, 63
Anderson, B.W. 47
Anderson, F.I. 82-84, 96, 105
Anderson, G.A. 42
Asen, B.A. 116
Auffret, P. 68
Auld, A.G. 102
Auwers, J.-M. 77

Bachelard, G. 9
Baker, J. 33, 43
Barker, M. 20, 26
Barnes, J. 122
Barr, J. 32, 34, 43
Barré, M.L. 54, 55, 71
Barrett, C.K. 41
Barth, C. 70
Barton, J. 1, 23, 89
Bauks, M. 36
Baumann, G. 36
Bazak, Y. 64
Beattie, D.G.R. 33
Bechtel, L.M. 14, 33
Beecher, H.W. 70
Bennett, J. 12
Bentzen, A. 53
Berquist, J.L. 86, 88, 96
Beyerlin, W. 58
Bledstein, A.J. 28
Blenkinsopp, J. 17, 18, 26
Bloom, H. 20, 28
Blum, E. 17
Boomershine, T.E. 15
Braude, W.G. 50, 75
Brett, M.G. 34

Briggs, C.A. 51
Brueggemann, W. 58
Buttenweiser, M. 60, 70

Carmichael, C.M. 24
Carr, D. 27
Childs, B.S. 7
Clark, W.M. 26
Clements, R.E. 93
Clines, D.J.A. 34, 38, 39, 67, 120, 121,
    125
Cohen, A. 50, 75
Coote, R.B. 92, 95, 113
Coppens, J. 14
Corney, R.W. 47
Coulot, C.C. 105
Craigie, P.C. 50, 63
Crenshaw, J.L. 89
Cripps, R.S. 95
Croft, S.J.L. 53

Davies, P.R. 34, 39
Delitzsch, F. 49, 61
Dempster, S. 107, 110
Dhorme, E. 57
Doorly, W.J. 96
Dorsey, D.A. 104, 105, 111
Dragga, S. 15, 33
Duhm, B. 61

Eaton, J.H. 53
Eissfeldt, O. 59
Engnell, I. 19

Fish, S. 120
Flint, P.W. 76
Freedman, D.N. 54, 55, 64, 71, 73, 82-84,
    96, 105

Fretheim, T. 34
Frost, S.B. 97

Gardner, A. 28
Gelander, S. 34
Gillingham, S.E. 4, 86, 97
Gordis, R. 15, 84, 87, 90, 109
Grenz, S.J. 2
Gunkel, H. 27, 59, 71

Habel, N.C. 15, 25
Harper, W.R. 83, 102
Hayes, J.H. 83, 85, 89, 102
Hayter, M. 33
Heaton, E.W. 23, 25
Hermisson, H.-J. 26
Hirsch, E. 57
Holladay, W.L. 76
Hossfeld, F.-L. 68, 70, 71
House, P.R. 114
Hubbard, D.A. 119
Hunter, A.G. 53, 67
Hutter, M. 19
Hyatt, J.P. 87, 88

James, E.O. 14
Jaruzelska, I. 88
Jeremias, J. 83, 87, 92, 97, 98, 104
Jobling, D. 31, 33
Johnson, A.R. 49, 53
Joines, K.R. 14

Kennedy, J.M. 29
Köhler, L. 63
Kraemer, S.N. 47
Kraus, H.-J. 50, 52, 57, 63
Kselman, J.S. 54, 55, 71

Lacocque, A. 24
Laffey, A. 28
Landy, F. 110
Lanser, S.S. 33
Limburg, J. 103, 105, 110, 111
Lundbom, J. 48, 49, 61
Lust, J. 107

Magonet, J. 18, 34, 65
Mandelbrote, S. 12
May, H.G. 19

Mays, J.L. 88, 96, 102
Mazor, Y. 47, 63
McKane, W. 23
Melugin, R.F. 109, 120
Mendenhall, G.E. 25
Merrill, A.L. 51-53, 63, 66
Meyers, C. 28, 29
Miller, P.D. 37, 68, 69
Millard, M. 67
Milne, P. 54-56, 64, 73
Morgenstern, J. 63
Morris, P. 13, 39, 40
Mowinckel, S. 52
Müller, H.-P. 19

Newman, J.H. 41
Nicholson, E.W. 17, 30
Niditch, S. 28, 33, 36
Noble, P.R. 107, 110

O'Reilly, J. 42
Oduyoye, M. 29
Olshausen, J. 61

Pagels, E. 24
Parker, K.I. 21, 34
Patte, D. 43
Paul, S.M. 83, 103
Pfeifer, G.P. 116
Polley, M.E. 83, 85, 90, 91
Power, E. 47

Reicke, B. 15, 24, 36
Rendtorff, R. 17
Roberts, R. 43
Rogerson, J. 12-14, 38
Rose, M. 17
Rösel, H.N. 104
Rosenbaum, S.N. 83
Rottzoll, D. 100, 107, 110

Sandberger, J.V. 46
Sawyer, D.F. 28, 33, 41
Sawyer, J.F.A. 36, 127
Schmid, H.H. 17, 89
Schmidt, W.H. 16, 99
Schottroff, W. 58, 86
Schwab, R. 54

Schwarzschild, S. 87
Seybold, K. 58
Smalley, W.A. 110
Smith, M. 58, 59, 64, 71
Soggin, J.A. 14, 83
Southwell, P. 25
Stern, H.S. 24, 36
Stordalen, T. 20, 31
Stratton, B.J. 24, 33, 44

Tappy, R. 64
Terrien, S. 89
Tournay, R. 54
Trèves, M. 61, 62
Trible, P. 28, 33
Tromp, N.J. 104
Tucker, G.M. 102

Van Seters. J. 17
Van Wolde, E. 33, 36
Vawter, B. 24, 43
Vogt, E. 57, 58
von Rad, G. 16, 25
Vorländer, H. 17

Waard, J. de 104
Wagner, N.E. 17
Wal, A. van der 109
Wallace, H.N. 14, 19, 20, 23, 25, 36
Walsh, J.T. 31
Ward, G. 15
Weinfeld, M. 88
Welch, A. 83
Wellhausen, J. 16, 17, 59
Wenham, G. 14, 20
Westermann, C. 27, 59, 60
Whedbee, J. 23
Whitelam, K.W. 5
Whybray, N. 38
Widengren, G. 19, 52, 53
Wilkinson, L. 3
Williams, R. 36
Williamson, H.G.M. 23
Winnett, F.V. 17
Wittenberg, G.H. 20
Wolff, H.W. 16, 83, 89, 100, 120

Zenger, E. 68, 70, 71

JOURNAL FOR THE STUDY OF THE OLD TESTAMENT
SUPPLEMENT SERIES

324 P.M. Michèle Daviau, John W. Wevers and Michael Weigl (eds.), *The World of the Aramaeans: Studies in Honour of Paul-Eugène Dion*, Volume 1

325 P.M. Michèle Daviau, John W. Wevers and Michael Weigl (eds.), *The World of the Aramaeans: Studies in Honour of Paul-Eugène Dion*, Volume 2

326 P.M. Michèle Daviau, John W. Wevers and Michael Weigl (eds.), *The World of the Aramaeans: Studies in Honour of Paul-Eugène Dion*, Volume 3

327 Gary D. Salyer, *Vain Rhetoric: Private Insight and Public Debate in Ecclesiastes*

328 James M. Trotter, *Reading Hosea in Achaemenid Yehud*

329 Wolfgang Bluedorn, *Yahweh Verus Baalism: A Theological Reading of the Gideon-Abimelech Narrative*

330 Lester L. Grabbe and Robert D. Haak (eds.), *'Every City shall be Forsaken': Urbanism and Prophecy in Ancient Israel and the Near East*

331 Amihai Mazar (ed.), with the assistance of Ginny Mathias, *Studies in the Archaeology of the Iron Age in Israel and Jordan*

332 Robert J.V. Hiebert, Claude E. Cox and Peter J. Gentry (eds.), *The Old Greek Psalter: Studies in Honour of Albert Pietersma*

333 Ada Rapoport-Albert and Gillian Greenberg (eds.), *Biblical Hebrew, Biblical Texts: Essays in Memory of Michael P. Weitzman*

334 Ken Stone (ed.), *Queer Commentary and the Hebrew Bible*

335 James K. Bruckner, *Implied Law in the Abrahamic Narrative: A Literary and Theological Analysis*

336 Stephen L. Cook, Corrine L. Patton and James W. Watts (eds.), *The Whirlwind: Essays on Job, Hermeneutics and Theology in Memory of Jane Morse*

337 Joyce Rilett Wood, *Amos in Song and Book Culture*

338 Alice A. Keefe, *Woman's Body and the Social Body in Hosea 1–2*

339 Sarah Nicholson, *Three Faces of Saul: An Intertextual Approach to Biblical Tragedy*

341 Mark W. Chavalas and K. Lawson Younger Jr (eds.), *Mesopotamia and the Bible*

343 J. Andrew Dearman and M. Patrick Graham (eds.), *The Land that I Will Show You: Essays on the History and Archaeology of the Ancient Near East in Honor of J. Maxwell Miller*

345 Jan-Wim Wesselius, *The Origin of the History of Israel: Herodotus' Histories as Blueprint for the First Books of the Bible*

346 Johanna Stiebert, *The Construction of Shame in the Hebrew Bible: The Prophetic Contribution*

347 Andrew G. Shead, *The Open Book and the Sealed Book: Jeremiah 32 in its Hebrew and Greek Recensions*

350 David Janzen, *Witch-hunts, Purity and Social Boundaries: The Expulsion of the Foreign Women in Ezra 9–10*

352 William John Lyons, *Canon and Exegesis: Canonical Praxis and the Sodom Narrative*